THE WINES
VINEYARDS AND
VIGNERONS
OF AUSTRALIA

ANDRÉ SIMON

The Wines Vineyards and Vignerons of Australia

PAUL HAMLYN · LONDON

Published 1967 by
PAUL HAMLYN LTD.
Drury House · Russell Street · London WC2
© 1966 Lansdowne Press Pty. Ltd.

Planned and designed in Australia
Set by Dudley E. King, Melbourne
Printed by Lee Fung Printing Company Ltd.
Hong Kong

TO VICTOR GIBSON
A FRIEND IN NEED AND A FRIEND INDEED
GRATEFULLY AND AFFECTIONATELY

ACKNOWLEDGEMENTS

Grateful acknowledgements are made to the many people in Australia who gave invaluable help in collecting material for this book. In particular, I wish to thank the members of Australian branches of the Wine and Food Society; the Director of the Australian Wine Research Institute, Mr J. C. M. Fornachon, and his staff; the Australian Wine Bureau; the *vignerons* and vintners of Australia, who not only gave me their complete co-operation but made me understand the meaning of Australian hospitality; the Principal Viticulturist of the New South Wales Department of Agriculture, Mr Graham Gregory, who compiled an informative Appendix on the varieties of wine-grapes grown in Australia; The La Trobe Library, Melbourne; Australian National Travel Association; and Mr A. J. Ludbrook, of Adelaide.

CONTENTS

		page
FOREWORD		xi
PART 1 THE VINEYARDS		1
PART 2 THE WINES		35
PART 3 THE VIGNERONS		53
APPENDIXES		
I.	Historical	129
II.	Australian Wine Grape Varieties . . .	152
III.	Characteristics To Look For In Australian Wines	161
IV.	A Wine-Lover Names His Favourites . .	165
V.	The Care And Service Of Wine . . .	169
VI.	Wine In The Kitchen	173
VII.	The Work Of The Australian Wine Institute .	181
A GLOSSARY OF WINE-TASTING TERMS .		185
BIBLIOGRAPHY		188
INDEX		191

ILLUSTRATIONS

COLOUR

Facing page

Gramp's Steingarten Vineyard 18
Underground galleries, Great Western 19
Old cellars, Auldana 34
Palomino grapes at Griffith 35
Ulliade grapes at Kalimna 66
New plantings at Seaview 67
Chateau Tahbilk Winery 82
Vat storage at Clare 83
Resealing a cask, Stanley Winery 98
Bottle storage, Yalumba 99
Cabernet Sauvignon grapes at Griffith . . . 114
Waikerie Co-operative Winery 115

MAPS

page

Key map of principal Australian vine-growing areas . 7
Hunter Valley. Muswellbrook. Mudgee. Rooty Hill . 14
Murrumbidgee Valley. Swan Hill 17
Robinvale. Murray Valley 25
Tahbilk. Shepparton. Rutherglen. Wahgunyah. Corowa . 33
Glenrowan. Milawa 33
Great Western. Drumborg. Coonawarra. Langhorne Creek 42
Nildottie. Southern Vales 50
Adelaide Metropolitan 61
Barossa Valley. Clare-Watervale 75
Swan Valley. Roma 89

MONOCHROME ILLUSTRATIONS

	page
Coonawarra Estate Vineyard .	1
Vine-dresser at work . . .	9
Training vines after pruning .	10
Mount Pleasant Vineyard . .	11
Irrigated vineyards, Hanwood .	12
Max Lake in his winery, Hunter Valley	13
Vintage time, Mount Pleasant .	15
Survivors of Phylloxera, Chateau Tahbilk	20
Lyndoch, gateway to the Barossa Valley	23
Barossa Valley near Tanunda .	24
St John's Church, Tanunda .	27
Eden Valley panorama . .	28
Sevenhill Vineyard . . .	29
View of McLaren Vale . .	31
Frost pots at Coonawarra .	34
Maturing Champagne, Great Western	35
Red wine ferment, Coonawarra .	39
White wine ferment, Clare .	40
Brandy maturing at Renmark .	41
Sweet wine storage, Rutherglen .	44
Brandy barrels, Horndale Distillery	45
A 5,000 gallon cask, Corowa .	47
Brother Hanlon, Sevenhill Winery	49
The craft of the cooper .	52
Drayton family at their Bellevue Winery	53
Fifth generation at work, Bleasdale	56
A grower delivers his grapes .	59
The Cave Cellar, Reynella .	62
Grapes arrive at Ewell Winery .	63
Grape-pickers at Kalimna Estate .	68
Rhine Riesling vines, Steingarten	69
Port maturing at Yalumba .	71

	page
Yalumba Winery . . .	73
Seppeltsfield Winery . . .	77
Maturing Sherry, Mildara . .	78
Underground cellars, Great Western	78
Grapes come in, McLaren Vale .	81
Ben Chaffey samples a red . .	84
Stonyfell, a vineyard in the suburbs	86
A Stonyfell scene . . .	87
Quelltaler Vineyard, Watervale .	91
Old lever press, Bleasdale .	94
Peter Weste, Stanley's wine-maker	97
Stacking sparkling wines, Magill .	103
The old tower, Chateau Tahbilk .	109
Cellar at Tahbilk . . .	110
Sterilizing bottles, Great Western	112
Maurice O'Shea, a great winemaker	116
All Saints Vineyard, Wahgunyah	117
Horse transport, All Saints . .	119
Grape crop at Merbein . .	121
Vineyard at Glenrowan . .	123
Chateau Yaldara, Lyndoch . .	124
Old hydraulic press, Wendouree Winery, Clare . . .	125
Wine-pressing at Sunbury, 1875 .	127
Vintage time at Yering, 1866 .	143
Wine-tasting in a Melbourne cellar, 1882	146
Auldana Vineyard in the 1880's .	148
Early picture of Auldana Winery	149
Johnston's Vineyard, Sunbury, 1875	170
Francis's Vineyard, Sunbury, 1864	171
At work in the Australian Wine Research Institute . . .	180

FOREWORD

THERE are in Australia a great many wines from fair to fine in quality which are characteristically *Australian* wines. They cannot be anything else: they are members of the great family of wines of the world, just as the men who make the wines are members of the great human family. Both the men and the wines of Australia have characteristics of their own which they owe to the soil and sunshine of their native land, and they have good cause to be proud of the name that is theirs.

The first settlers to grow grapes and to make wine in Australia came from England, where they were born either during the second half of the eighteenth century, or at the beginning of the nineteenth; that is, at a time when Port was rightly known as the Englishman's wine, when much red wine of high alcoholic strength and temptingly low in cost came from the Cape of Good Hope as the poor man's Port, when Hamburg Brandy, Hollands, and Rum were incredibly cheap.

They were drunken times such as there had never been before, and such as, happily, have never been known since. Claret, Burgundy and Champagne also Hocks and Moselles, were the privilege of the rich and the great in the England of the pre-Victorian era; which is why the pioneers of the wine industry in Australia built distilleries as fast as they built wineries, and why there are even today more fortified wines made than table wines, and a slightly greater tonnage of grapes used in the making of brandy and other spirits than in the making of wine.

None of the early settlers who planted some vines and made some wine during the first half of the nineteenth century in Australia had any background or experience as *vignerons* or vintners. Some were granted great stretches of land, and others purchased large estates, but none other than the first comers had the benefit of cheap convict labour. The shortage of labour, unskilled or semiskilled, made it quite impossible, in the beginning, to plant and to care for large vineyards. Many of the early settlers, however, liked to have, usually near the homestead, a vineyard large enough to give them every year a little wine for their own drinking, and a good deal more that they could distil into brandy and fortifying spirit.

Grazing and fattening cattle demanded so much less labour than growing grapes, and it also paid better. But money, happily, is not everything, so the love of the grape and the pride of drinking one's own wine may easily become a fascination, unique and almost irresistible. Which is why more vineyards and larger vineyards gradually came into production in many of the valleys of Australia: those of the Parramatta and Hunter Rivers, in New South Wales, first of all; then those of the Murray and Goulburn in Victoria, before reaching South Australia where there are today more vineyards producing grapes for wine-making than in the other four wine-producing States of Australia put together.

The wine industry of Australia had modest beginnings, and there were a great many obstacles in the way of its progress in a country which had no wine-conscious—let alone wine-loving—population, but a population of spirits- and beer-drinkers. But this is no longer true: wine is now gaining a greater measure of recognition and appreciation than it ever had before in Australia. Today the wine industry is one of the major industries of the country—no less than $Aust. 200 million (£Aust. 100 million) have been invested in it, and the modern equipment of the Australian wineries and distilleries, not only the larger ones, is equal to the finest to be seen in any of the European countries.

Cold, in this scientific age, works miracles, and refrigeration has done more in Australia than in any other of the world's winelands to raise the standard of quality of wine. The high temperature at the time of the vintage, in Australia, was for many years a cause of grave anxiety for the Australian *vigneron*, who was unable to check the tempo of fermentation of the new wine and avoid acetic fermentation and other such-like disasters. Today, happily, there is no longer any such danger, as the winemaker is at all times in complete control of the temperature of the must, or grape-juice, in his vats or tanks as it becomes wine.

From the beginning, in spite of costly mistakes and mishaps, to our own day, in spite of the high cost of modern equipment, Australian wines, the best as the rest, have always been moderately priced by the bottle over the counter, though sometimes (as elsewhere) much too dear in the hotel dining-room. The low basic price was in earlier days a bull point with the masses but a bear point with the classes. No better proof of this do I know than what I was told at the Melbourne Club, Melbourne: during the first one hundred years of the existence of the Club, there never was a single bottle of Australian wine in their cellar, where most of the classical growths of European vineyards and most of the great vintages of the past had been given a bin of their own. Now, of course, things are very different, and the wines of Australia occupy pride of place: they are still much cheaper than imported wines, but very much better than they used to be and much better value.

In Australia, as practically everywhere, the small man in any trade or industry has a poor chance of survival. It is certainly regrettable, but it is no less certainly inevitable.

The cost of labour, of transport, of raw material, and of all else, is bound to rise as population grows and demand becomes more rapidly greater than supply. Mechanical tractors and all manner of modern agricultural equipment are much too costly for the small *vigneron*: the greater the acreage of the vineyard and the greater the load of grapes to be picked and processed at the time of the vintage, the greater will be the benefit of those mechanical aids. Which is why more and more the big and bigger organizations are doing more and more of the planting of vineyards, producing the greater proportions of grapes, wines, spirits and their by-products. The small *vigneron* is by no means doomed: he may and he will, we all hope, continue to tend his vineyards as all good vineyards must be tended, with the loving care that is the only truly intelligent care. The big firms will be only too happy to buy his grapes at a rewarding price because his grapes will be better than those of their mammoth vineyards mechanically cultivated. The little man will gradually disappear as a wine-maker, and the big firms will use the grapes they buy from him to make wine which may not be any better than the little man made—when he was lucky—but they will make wine that will be much more consistently safe and sound. It is true, of course, that standardized wines are bound to lose some of their individuality as wines, but the middleman, the wine-dealer who stocks the wine, appreciates above all qualities in a wine its dependability.

Sunshine galore, fertile soil, and the best classical varieties of grapes to plant are assets shared alike in Australia by all, however small or big they may be; but the big concerns have financial resources which enable them to keep their wines in cask and bottle longer, thus giving them a better chance to reach the consumers when they—the wines—are at their best. They are also in a much better position to make their wines better known in our advertising age, when too few people still bother to think for themselves and so many more are content to have their mind made up for them by newsprint, radio or television.

It is unfortunate that Australian wines have been so cheap for so long: it makes it more difficult to market the better wines which necessarily cost a little more—and they are often worth a great deal more. They all share with all the good wines made in the world the two basic qualities of balance and soundness, just as you would expect any good man, woman, or child to be sound of body and mind. But that is not enough. Good wines, like all good people, must also have a personality of their own: that is, the characteristics which they owe to the land of their birth, its soil and climate, and also to the care and training of their nursery days.

The world is made of all sorts, and there are all sorts of wines for them all. There is no reason why any of the good wines which are better known than others should be jealous of other good wines not so well known as they are themselves: there can never be too many good wines in the world any more than there will ever be too many good people.

THE VINEYARDS

THE vineyards of Australia may be divided into two main groups, the quality group and the quantity group.

In the vineyards of the quality group an important proportion—if not the whole of the grapes—have been chosen from the better varieties of *Vitis vinifera* grapes, the classic grapes, or aristocrats, as they are sometimes called. They are the varieties of grapes from which all the better wines of the world are made, in Australia, as in California, Chile or South Africa, wherever soil and climatic conditions are suitable, and whenever the aim and ambition of the *vigneron* are to make wines that will be the peers of the more famous of the European wines, all of them made from the same varieties of grapes.

Unfortunately, it happens that the more highly bred any subject may be, the less fertile it will be, and all the aristocrats among vines deserve only too well the name of "shy bearers" given to them. Their average production, under favourable conditions, is merely two tons of grapes an acre, whereas some vines in irrigated areas bring forth ten tons an acre; but nobody would expect the quality of their grapes, and of the wine made from them, to be comparable, and it is not. It is only from those "shy-bearing" vines that wines may be made that will stand the test of time, age with grace, reach a high standard of perfection and possess the so rare and so highly valued distinction which we call, for the lack of a better name, breed.

In the vineyards of the quantity group, the majority of the vines belong to the commoner varieties of *Vitis vinifera*. They are usually known as "free bearers" in opposition to the "shy bearers", and they bring forth large quantities of grapes bursting with sugar and water, from which large quantities of wines are made which may have colour and strength, sweetness and a pretty label, but no vinous charm: wines for the thirsty and for the distillery, not for the connoisseur.

However, very recent developments in Australia suggest that one must not be too dogmatic about "quality" and "quantity". There has recently been a notable increase in plantings of the classic varieties of grapes, including the "shy bearers", in what have always been regarded as "quantity" areas: that is, the irrigation areas; and, as a result of the newest soil treatments and improved vine husbandry generally, the classic varieties have shown such a leap in yields that they can be considered to have entered the quantity group; yet, Australian wine men say, they have still retained much of their quality. Advances in wine-making techniques have also played an important part in making possible a remarkable improvement in the quality of light table wines made from Riesling, Semillon, Cabernet and Shiraz grapes grown in Australian irrigated vine-

3

yards. So, apparently, there is not always such a wide gulf as was once thought between quality vineyards and quantity vineyards. Nevertheless, the basic reasons why there should be such great differences between the wines produced from district to district and even vineyard to vineyard still hold good.

The nature of the water and of the sugars in all ripe grapes is exactly the same, just as the nature of the blood in the veins of king and beggar is the same, although by no means identical; but the quantities of water and sugars in all ripe grapes vary from year to year according to the incidence and intensity of rains and sunshine. What is of greater importance as regards the quality of the wine made from all grapes is the nature of the various acids and salts which will be eventually responsible for the distinctive character of different wines. Vegetal acids vary according to the different varieties of vines, and mineral salts according to the geological formation of each vineyard's soil and subsoil.

The more immediately obvious difference, however, between the grapes of "quality" and "quantity" vineyards is water. All "quantity" vineyards are close to a river, and pumps are to them what our heart is to each one of us: these are the vineyards of the "irrigated areas". There are also some "quality" vineyards situated conveniently close to a river, and it gives them the chance of occasional waterings in drought periods, but they are not irrigated, and they retain the right to their title of "quality" vineyards.

There are vineyards in five of the six States of Australia, but South Australia has a commanding lead in production of wine grapes. New South Wales and Victoria are the next two more important wine-making States; Western Australia has now quite a number of vineyards, but Queensland only very few. It was not always thus: up to about a little more than a hundred years ago, New South Wales had more than twice the acreage of vineyards there were in Victoria and South Australia put together, but South Australia took the lead in 1859; Victoria at one stage later shot ahead but was disastrously affected by Phylloxera. (Actually, Victoria produces 25 per cent more grapes of all kinds than South Australia, but more than 90 per cent of Victoria's grapes are dried.)

The number of acres planted in vines is of importance "quantitatively", but the variety of grape selected for planting in each vineyard is of greater importance "qualitatively". Today, the Australian *vigneron* knows the name, the age and the pedigree of all his vines, the date when planted and their yearly yield. In the beginning, however, and for a long time, there was a great deal of uncertainty and confusion regarding the vines imported from Europe, Madeira, and the Cape of Good Hope. We read, for instance, that one of the most enthusiastic amateur *vignerons* among the early settlers in New South Wales, Captain John Macarthur, visited a number of French vineyards, with two of his sons and a French expert guide, in 1815–16, when he bought a large number of cuttings from vines deemed to be the most suitable for growing in New

South Wales. He left those cuttings with a London market-gardener, with instructions to ship them to Sydney after they had rooted and were likely to stand the sea voyage. Then he sailed for Australia, and, calling at Madeira *en route*, he followed a similar plan, selecting suitable cuttings to be shipped to him the following year. Unfortunately, when the French cuttings reached him in 1817, and when he got those from Madeira in 1818, they proved to be quite different from those he had selected and most of them had no identification name of any kind. In 1841, however, one of Captain John Macarthur's sons, William, gave a list of the vines which were in production at the time at Camden Park, the estate near Sydney which his father had named after the then Colonial Secretary, the first Lord Camden. This was the list: Pineau Gris, Frontignac, Gouais (La Folle), Verdelho (Madeira), Cabernet Sauvignon, Riesling, Grenache, Mataro.

In 1825 the Australian Agricultural Company ordered from Chiswick, England, a collection of vine cuttings, but there is no record of what happened to them. It was only in 1831, when James Busby brought back from France and Spain no less than 570 different varieties of grapes, that viticulture made a real start in Australia. Busby gave a specimen of every variety to be planted in the Sydney Botanical Gardens, and he planted the rest in his own vineyard, at Kirkton, near the Paterson River, a tributary of the Hunter River, in New South Wales.

In 1840, a group of Adelaide citizens subscribed to a fund for the purchase and importation of an important collection of vine cuttings from the Cape of Good Hope: most of the cuttings were distributed on arrival among the subscribers, but a specimen of each of the different varieties was planted in the Adelaide Botanical Gardens, at the time on the north bank of the Torrens River, opposite the present Zoological Gardens.

Although the Busby collection at Kirkton was the more important, it appears from records still available that the Camden Park nursery supplied most of the vines for the early vineyards of Victoria and South Australia during the second quarter of the nineteenth century.

In his book *The Vine in Australia*, published in Melbourne, in 1861, Dr A. C. Kelly remarks that "at first little attention was paid to the varieties of the vine suited to the soil and climate of this Continent. Vines from all parts of Europe and the most diverse climates were indiscriminately mixed in the same vineyard. A vine from the cold climate of the Rhine or the Neckar was planted alongside of another from the Tagus or the Douro. The first ripened its fruit in February, the other perhaps in April, making it impossible to have both ripe at the vintage. Much time was wasted in introducing varieties altogether unsuited to our climate, and which might have been saved by a preliminary enquiry into the nature of our own climate and a comparison with the climate of Europe. There are many acres in situations as Adelaide planted with vines of northern Europe, which proved so utterly useless that they have been rooted out after ten years' trial, to be replaced by the more vigorous vines of the south of Europe".

Nearly one hundred years later, in the *South Australian Journal of Agriculture* of November 1958, the then viticulturist of Roseworthy Agricultural College, Mr C. D. Matthews, wrote of the varieties of vines that were first imported into Australia, as follows: "Although the Busby and Macarthur vines provided the start for the vine growing industry in South Australia, it is regrettable that they were used, as in many instances the names of the varieties had been lost or altered prior to or during transit from the Continent, and many had been wrongly renamed".

Today, of course, there is less confusion, but a high degree of specialization, which accounts for the fact that there is but a very small number of varieties of vines cultivated in considerable quantities in the irrigated areas for the making of dried fruit and special wines—Sultanas, Muscat (Gordo), Grenache and Doradillo—whereas there is a greater variety of vines grown in much smaller quantities for the making of the different varieties of dry and sweet wines—chiefly Shiraz or Hermitage, Pedro Ximenez, Semillon, Mataro, Palomino, Riesling or Rhine Riesling, Frontignac, and Ugni Blanc or White Hermitage; also, but to a much smaller extent, Pinot Noir, Cabernet Sauvignon, Verdelho, Chasselas, Malbec and Traminer.

NEW SOUTH WALES

New South Wales was the cradle of viticulture in Australia. The first thing that the first Governor, Captain Arthur Phillip, did, as soon as he had a roof over his head, was to have vines in his garden and grapes on his table. There is no lack of documentary evidence to show that many early settlers planted a vineyard, built a winery and a distillery, usually near the homestead. Thus, Captain John Macarthur, writing in 1793 from Sydney to his brother James, then in London, mentions that he has "built a most excellent brick house" in the centre of his farm, "with three acres given to grapes and other fruit".

There were no book-sellers and there were no book-shelves in the early period, and the pioneers of the pre-Busby days, who had no experience how best to plant vines and to make wine, must have been very grateful to the editor of *The Sydney Gazette* who published on the back page of the first number of his paper, dated Saturday, 5 March 1803, the first of a series of articles to help the amateur *vignerons* of New South Wales with directions on how to plant a vineyard:

"The ground to be turned up, cleared of weeds, and trenched out to the depth of 18 inches; or, should it not be encumbered with stumps or roots of trees, underwood or brambles, the cuttings of vines may be immediately planted without that precaution . . .

The Wine Growing Areas of Australia

Detailed maps of each of the numbered areas appear later in the book.

The key to the numbers is:

Map on page

1.	Hunter Valley . . 14
2.	Muswellbrook . . . 14
3.	Mudgee . . . 14
4.	Rooty Hill . . . 14
5.	Murrumbidgee Valley . 17
6.	Swan Hill . . . 17
7.	Robinvale . . 25
8.	Murray Valley . . 25
9.	Tahbilk . . . 33
10.	Shepparton . . 33
11.	Rutherglen, Wahgunyah, Cowra . . . 33

12.	Glenrowan, Milawa . . 33
13.	Great Western . . . 42
14.	Drumborg . . . 42
15.	Coonawarra . . . 42
16.	Nildottie . . . 50
17.	Langhorne Creek . . 42
18.	Southern Vales . . 50
19.	Adelaide Metropolitan . 61
20.	Barossa Valley . . . 75
21.	Clare-Watervale . . 75
22.	Swan Valley . . . 89
23.	Roma 89

"For the purpose of planting the young vines already rooted, holes are to be made with a strong hoe, or broad pick-axe, at a discretionary distance of about 2 and a half to 3 feet open from each vine, and some mould or old turf must be laid round the foot of each . . .

"The method of dressing the vines after the vineyard has been formed, is principally to prune them well, and to attend to a minute knowledge of their nature; also what influence the change of climate may have operated on them; some will not produce without being propped, others best without; and the situation of the land and temperature of the climate will determine if the branches have to be carried more or less in height, and consequently how to be supported; they may be cut off either in a flat or sloped manner, but care must be taken to clear away all dead or defective parts."

The fact that the editor of the first newspaper published in Australia thought fit to give up space in his journal's first issue to help the *vignerons* of New South Wales proves beyond any doubt that there must have been at the time a very real and widespread interest taken in the planting of new vineyards in New South Wales, and this is confirmed by the records which have survived of early vineyards planted near Sydney—in the Parramatta Valley, the Rooty Hill area, at Minchinbury and Hawkesbury, before 1825. What is much more remarkable is that those early *vignerons* not only managed to make wine for their own consumption, but wine good enough to be sent all the way to London.

Thus the one-time explorer Gregory Blaxland, who grew grapes at his Brush Farm, now Ermington, in the Parramatta Valley, sent some of his wine to London in 1822, and he must have been a proud man when he heard that the Royal Society of Arts had given his wine a Silver Medal. He sent some more of his wines to London in 1828, and this time they gave him a Gold Medal.

During the second quarter of the nineteenth century, a number of vineyards were planted farther away from Sydney, chiefly in the Hunter River Valley, a hundred miles to the north, where there are still today a few of the original vineyards, and many others which were planted more recently. The most famous among the veterans is Dalwood, in the Pokolbin area, which was first planted in 1828 by George Wyndham. He was a migrant from Wiltshire, and the homestead which he built on the left bank of the Hunter River, from stone quarried by convicts, still stands: it had to be a large house since he and his wife, Margaret, were blessed with twelve sons and two daughters. The house has been modernized and the vineyard has been enlarged, but there were, up to 1959, some of the original convict-planted vines, noble centenarians which were then uprooted, as they could no longer pay for their keep. The Dalwood vineyards and estate now belong to Messrs. Penfold, who have also given the name "Dalwood" to a 723-acre estate forty miles from the parent Dalwood Vineyard and fifteen miles west of the dairying centre of Muswellbrook. Three hundred acres of this new Dalwood

The skilled hands of the vine-dresser. Pruning vines is a difficult art. Each variety of grape has different habits of growth and requires different refinements of pruning.

Estate, which was bought in 1960, were, by 1965, planted with the finest table-wine varieties. Here the visitor sees a remarkable sight: vines planted in dead straight rows each nine-tenths of a mile long, giving every facility for the use of tractors, cultivators, mechanical harvesters and so on.

The planting of vineyards and the making of wine were given every encouragement by the early Governors of New South Wales, as well as by urban and rural authorities, for their economic value and also partly, if not chiefly, for their "sobering" appeal. Thus Dr John Lang, whose younger brother Andrew was one of the pioneers of viticulture in the Hunter River Valley, wrote at the time: "There is reason to hope that, if the population of New South Wales could by any means be converted into a

After pruning, the vines are trained on the trellis. This picture and the one of the vine-dresser were taken at a South Australian vineyard.

wine-growing population, they would in due time become a wine-drinking and comparatively temperate, instead of a rum-drinking and most outrageously intemperate population".

By far the most famous *vigneron* of New South Wales in the early days was James Busby, who has often been referred to as the Father of Viticulture in Australia. Before leaving Australia for New Zealand in 1832, he had not only planted a model vineyard of forty acres, at Kirkton, the estate to which he gave the name of his birthplace, but he had distributed over 20,000 cuttings to about fifty of the Hunter River Valley *vignerons*, and he had also published for the benefit of *vignerons* in all parts of Australia the first book to be published in Australia for their guidance and assistance, a book which was for a long time regarded as the Bible of the Australian *vignerons* in its original and successive editions. Its full title was *Treatise on the culture of the Vine and the art of making Wine, compiled from the works of Chaptal and other French writers and from the Notes of the Compiler during his residence in the wine Provinces of France.*

Today, there are no longer any vines growing at Kirkton, but there is a dry white wine made from grapes grown in the Hunter area and marketed by the firm of Lindeman under the name of Kirkton Chablis: it so happened that the son of the Dr Lindeman, who founded the firm, married the daughter of James Busby's niece and heir.

THE VINEYARDS

Today there are still many vineyards in the Hunter River Valley, and they are responsible for many of the better-quality table wines, not merely of New South Wales but of Australia. Most of Hunter vineyards are in the Pokolbin area, a short distance west of Cessnock and Branxton as one comes from Newcastle, where the Hunter flows into the Pacific Ocean. Among the most important of the Hunter vineyards and wineries today, Dalwood (Penfold) is the oldest, Ben Ean (Lindeman) is the largest, Mount Pleasant (McWilliam's) is one of the best known. There are a number of long-established Hunter vineyards and wineries, such as Tulloch's, Tyrrell's, Oakvale, Glendore, Bellevue and Sunshine. Latest in date and smallest of Hunter vineyards is the five-acre vineyard of Cabernet Sauvignon grapes planted in 1963 by an eminent Sydney surgeon, Max Lake.

The vineyards of the Hunter River Valley have had their troubles. Some were washed away by the worst floods of the Hunter, a river which has not too many friends but too many tributaries: when the rains happen to be excessive, so many swollen streams rush into the Hunter that the Hunter becomes a menace.

COROWA, is a long way to the south-west, upon the right bank of the Murray River, which divides New South Wales from Victoria. The vineyards of Corowa suffered

Mount Pleasant Vineyard, in the Hunter River Valley, 100 miles north of Sydney. High quality table wines are produced here.

from the Phylloxera invasion, but many were replanted, and there are still a number of flourishing vineyards, such as Southern Cross and Felton (Lindeman), two of the largest. Most of the grapes from Corowa vineyards are used for making sweet fortified wines, brandy and fortifying spirit.

GRIFFITH is in the valley of the Murrumbidgee, one of the Murray's main tributaries. It is completely surrounded by vines as far as the eye can see: vines which are irrigated by the water of the Burrinjuck Reservoir. These vines produce very considerable quantities of wine.

ALBURY, on the New South Wales bank of the Murray, and on the road from Sydney to Melbourne, used to have some important vineyards, the last of them at Ettamogah, a few miles from Albury. It was owned by J. T. Fallon who did not replant the vineyard when it was blighted by the Phylloxera in 1906; his manager, John Delappe Lankester, born in 1837, was pensioned off and lived on to 1938.

Typical irrigated vineyards. This is the view from the tower of McWilliam's Winery at Hanwood in the Murrumbidgee Irrigation Area, in southern New South Wales.

Max Lake, a Sydney surgeon, at work in the winery of the small vineyard he established in the Hunter Valley in 1963. The vineyard is planted with Cabernet Sauvignon grapes, one of the most famous red wine varieties.

VICTORIA

The cult and culture of the grape in Victoria may be traced to the fortunate accident that Charles Joseph Latrobe, who arrived in September 1839 to take charge of affairs at Port Phillip, had lived for some time in his early twenties at Neuchâtel, in Switzerland, where he had acquired not only some knowledge but a real appreciation of wine, as well as a bride, Sophie, the daughter of Frederick Auguste de Montmillon, Swiss Counsellor of State. Latrobe first fell in love with Jolimont, the Counsellor's enchanting country estate, which stood among magnificent trees some 2,000 feet above the Lake of Neuchâtel, and then he fell in love with the daughter of the house. When they came to Victoria, they named their home "Jolimont" and planted a small vineyard in what was to be the garden of the first Government House in Melbourne. Others followed Latrobe's lead, and he gave them every encouragement: he directed, for instance, the planting of vines at Mayfield, the home of the McCrae family, as appears from an entry in Georgina McCrae's Journal, dated 9 August 1842:

"Mr. Latrobe came to show Osmond how to plant the vine-cuttings obliquely to the sun, each cutting to have three joints and eyes—one of these to be above ground, the second level with the surface, the third to be rubbed off to make way for the root."

At that time, Skene Craig, Commissariat Officer of the Port Phillip District, had a vineyard in what is today Collins Street West, one of Melbourne's principal streets, and it is more than likely that he had had the advice and blessing of Latrobe, who was his chief.

The greatest service that Latrobe rendered to Australian viticulture, however, was

13

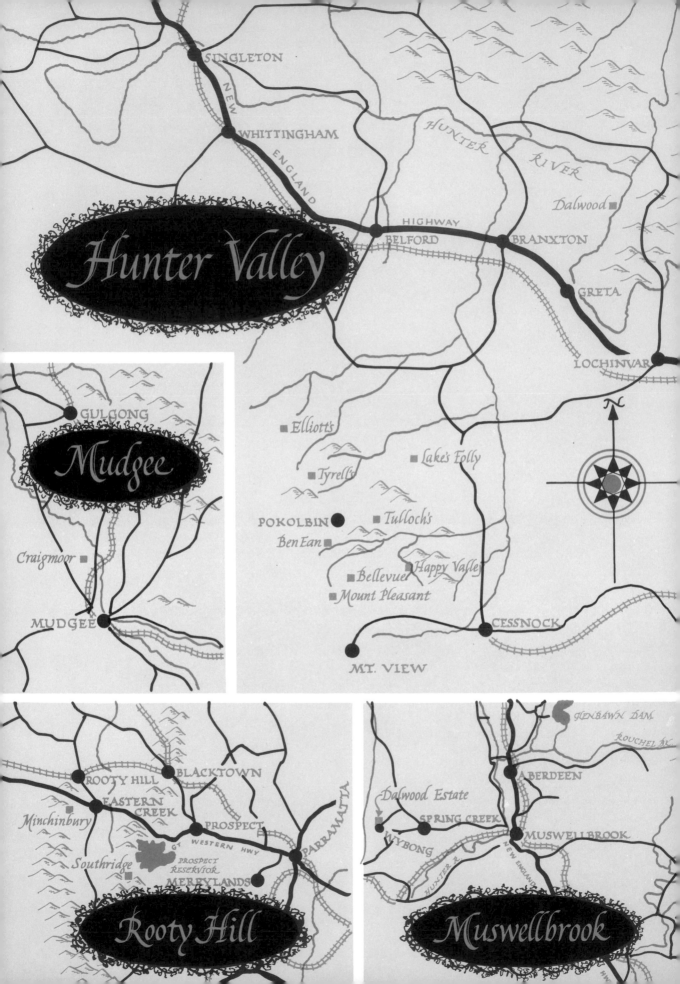

The vintage comes in at Mount Pleasant, one of the best-known vineyards in the Hunter Valley. Most grape-pickers are itinerant workers.

to persuade Clément Deschamps, the son of a head *vigneron* of Neuchâtel, and other of his Swiss friends, to come over to Port Phillip and to grow grapes and to make wine as grapes should be grown and wine should be made. This is how Baron de Pury and his cousins the brothers de Castella came to Victoria: they planted vines in the Yarra Valley and made better wine than had ever been made there before. They were not only much better-educated men than the average Australian settler, but they knew much more about viticulture and wine-making; more important still, they possessed, as an inheritance from their forebears that almost mystical love of the tree of life, the Vine, which all true wine-lovers regard as one of God's greatest gifts to Man.

Another Swiss migrant of more humble station, for whom Latrobe was responsible, was Amict, the husband of Rose Pelet, Latrobe's Swiss housekeeper: he had a vineyard of his own in what would be called today the centre of Melbourne, and his wine was served at the fancy-dress ball given in Melbourne on 28 November 1850 to celebrate the Port Phillip District's separation from New South Wales to become the Colony of Victoria.

The Melbourne "municipal" vineyards, as one would expect, soon gave way to bricks and mortar, but old as they were, they were not the first to be planted in the Colony. Edward Henty has always been credited with the planting of the first vineyard in 1834, when he settled at Portland in western Victoria.

In 1838 William Ryrie, who had a cattle station at Yering, some thirty miles east of Melbourne, in the Yarra Valley, planted a vineyard of thirty acres, which was to

15

grow, not many years later, to 3,000 acres and produce some of the finest table wines of Australia. This was chiefly due to the purchase of some of Ryrie's land by the brothers Paul and Hubert de Castella, and Baron de Pury. It was not long before the de Castella wines, marked under the labels of St. Hubert and Chateau Yering, as well as the wine of Baron de Pury, marketed under the label Yeringberg, gained and deserved high praise from all wine-lovers and connoisseurs. Unfortunately, the number of wine-lovers and connoisseurs was much too small. The wines of the Swiss colony were given more praises than orders, and production gradually declined and finally ceased altogether in the 1920s, when rising land values, among other factors, made it uneconomic to continue.

The coming of Phylloxera to Victoria in the 1880s was responsible for the disappearance of other vineyards of great promise that were planted at an early date—that is, before 1850—in the Geelong and Bendigo districts. The vineyards of the Goulburn River, a southern tributary of the Murray, were planted a little later and fared rather better. The Tabilk run, at Old Crossing Place, where the Goulburn River was first crossed by the explorer Major Mitchell on 9 October 1836, was occupied by Henry Moore from 1842 to 1852, when it was leased to Hugh Glass and John Purcell; Hugh Glass was allowed to purchase the pre-emptive rights of 640 acres, or one square mile of the Tabilk lands. He appointed as his manager a Frenchman, Ludovic Marie, who came from Burgundy: he was well known in the Tabilk district as he had a general store and also ran a punt ferry service across the Goulburn. He planted some table grapes in the garden of his homestead, and they brought forth such beautiful grapes, and such an abundance of them, that Marie could not resist the temptation of experimenting with wine-making grapes. He had no difficulty in persuading Hugh Glass and others that both soil and climate were highly favourable and, on 16 March 1860, the Goulburn Vineyard Proprietary Company was formed, with Ludovic Marie as resident manager, and with Mr R. H. Horne (the poet "Orion" Horne) as honorary secretary *pro tem*.

The prospectus of the new company was drawn up by Horne, who was once upon a time a friend of Charles Dickens and a regular contributor to *Cornhill*. Would-be subscribers were assured: "That Victoria is a country eminently adapted by Nature for the culture of Vines is a fact that has long been generally known. The means that we possess here for making wine of the most delicious quality, and better suited to the inhabitants of these colonies as a healthy beverage than most of the light wines which are imported, has also been equally well known to those who are conversant with the subject. The wines of the Rhine and the Moselle can certainly be equalled, but, in some instances, will be surpassed by vintages of the Goulburn, the Loddon, the Campaspe, and, in fact, of the whole Valley of the Murray.

"Besides the commercial benefits, the best sanitary and moral results may be anticipated because a wine-drinking population is never a drunken population."

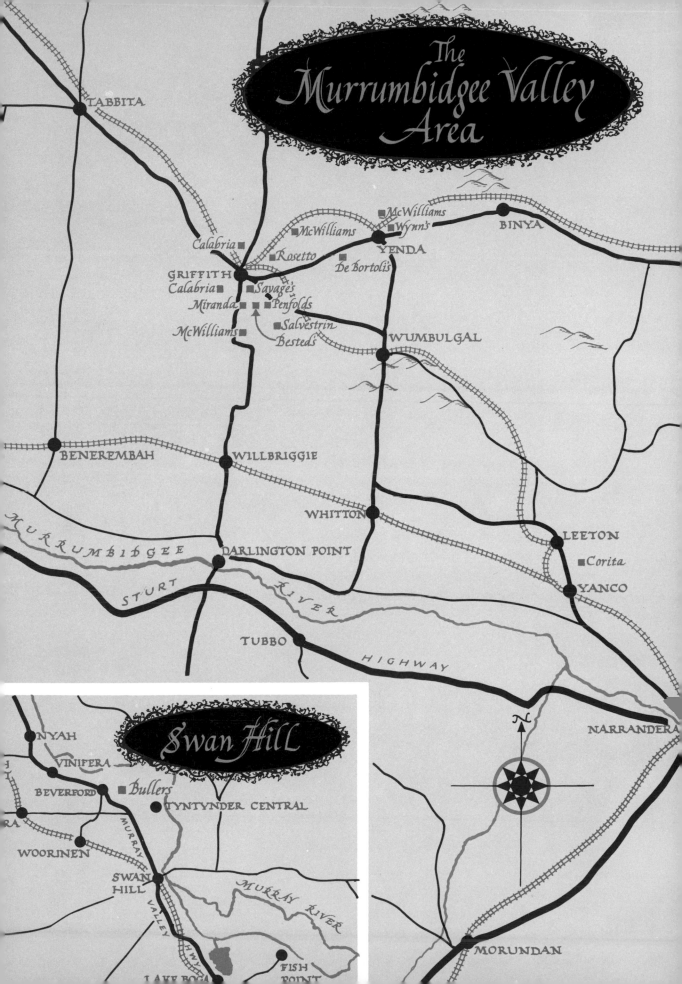

Three months later, on 6 June 1860, at a meeting held at 70 Queen Street, Melbourne, a new company, the Tabilk Vine-yard Proprietary, was formed, with Horne again honorary secretary *pro tem*, and Marie again manager. Mr J. P. Bear, a member of the new board, proposed that an advertisement for the purchase of a million vine cuttings be inserted six times in the leading newspapers of South Australia, Victoria, and New South Wales. Later, Horne wrote that those cuttings were planted by a highly qualified *vigneron*, and that 700,000 of them "took root and produced wine the first year". (Horne, as we mentioned before, was a poet.) By the end of 1860, 150 acres of the Tabilk run had been cleared under Marie's direction, and sixty-five acres had been planted with vines. In the *Kilmore Examiner*, a correspondent wrote in 1861 that he had visited Tabilk where there were 200 acres of vines "all of them healthy and free from blight".

The only considerable township near Tabilk is Nagambie, seventy-five miles north of Melbourne, and, north of Nagambie, on the way to Shepparton, in the Goulburn Valley, there is quite a fair vineyard before Mooroopna; it is known as the Excelsior Vineyard, and it is cared for by George and Trojano Daveniza, great-nephews of the Trojano Daveniza, an Austrian from Dalmatia, who first planted the vineyard in the early 1870s.

Although the vineyards of the Yarra come first in point of seniority, those in a loop of the Murray in the north-east corner of Victoria, have been of much greater importance during the past hundred years or so; that is, from 1851, when Lindsay Brown planted a vineyard at Gooramadda, soon after being followed by John Graham, at Netherby, G. F. Morris at Fairfield, and, in 1864, by George Sutherland Smith, at All Saints, Wahgunyah. The vineyards within a ten-mile radius of Rutherglen added up to 3,000 acres up to 1899, when the Phylloxera struck and disaster followed. Since then, many vineyards have been replanted. There are still grapes today at Fairfield, the Mia Mia Vineyard, and a winery, and members of the Morris family in charge. There are still grapes growing at All Saints and the largest assembly of oak casks there is still lodged in the same old winery, and the two grandsons of the original Sutherland Smith are still in charge, with their sons. But there are no longer any grapes growing at Burgoyne's Mount Ophir.

The soil and climate of Victoria's North-East are, of course, the same as before, which is why the dry red wines of the Rutherglen district today, are mostly what they

The vine is a wonderful plant that can thrive in adversity and often produces the best wine under difficult conditions. The vineyard shown here is high in the hills above Rowland Flat, in the Barossa Valley of South Australia. It was established in 1962 by G. Gramp and Sons, who named it, appropriately, Steingarten (Garden of Stones). The vines are Rhine Riesling.

have always been: big wines, dark, almost black-red wines, of greater alcoholic strength than the Hunter River table wines, with more power than charm: "wines for heroes", as they have been called sometimes. However, some Rutherglen wine-makers are now aiming for lighter wines—and with success.

Besides dry table wines, the vineyards of the Rutherglen area also produce good sherries and a large quantity of dessert wines, which must be better than most, since they are always given top prizes at the Wine Shows.

There is a vine nursery at Wahgunyah and a Government Viticultural Station some ten miles to the south-east of Rutherglen.

South-west of Rutherglen, but still in Victoria's North-East, is Wangaratta, and there are vineyards within eight to fifteen miles of this prosperous industrial town: they produce grapes from which quality wines are made more akin to the quality wines of the Rutherglen area than any other wines made in Victoria.

Milawa lies between the Ovens and King River valleys a few miles south-west of Wangaratta. Its largest vineyard is that of Brown Brothers, who happen at present to be father and son, John Brown II and John Brown III, son and grandson of John Francis Brown (John Brown I), who planted the first vines there in the eighties of the last century. They have now seventy-five acres in production and another fifteen acres newly planted, mostly with Shiraz, Cabernet Sauvignon, Mondeuse, Rhine Riesling, and White Hermitage: the old winery has been completely modernized and fitted with all the latest scientific equipment. At Everton, a few miles away nearer the mountains, the John Brown Senior and John Brown Junior of today also own another vineyard of ten acres, the grapes of which are brought to Milawa at vintage time, to be "processed".

About the same distance as Milawa from Wangaratta, but to the south-west, looking towards the Warby Ridge, there are some veteran vineyards at Bundarra, the two most notable being those of the Bailey Brothers and those of Booth's. Alan and Roly Bailey are the fourth generation in charge of the Bundarra vineyard, which was first planted by Alan Bailey I in the seventies.

Booth's vineyard is some distance away, nearer the Warby Ridge; it was planted in 1892 by a Mr Opie, and destroyed by the Phylloxera ten years later; it was replanted soon after by Ezra Booth, and today there are some fifty acres in full production: they are in charge of two brothers, Clifford and Geoffrey Booth.

In an altogether different part of Victoria, more than a hundred miles west of

At B. Seppelt and Sons' vineyard at Great Western, near Ararat, Victoria, Australian Champagne is matured in underground galleries, which, because they were dug by miners of the gold-rush days, are known to this day as "drives". The galleries provide three and a half miles of stacking space, where more than a million bottles of maturing sparkling wine are kept in shaking-tables and free-standing racks.

Melbourne, the Great Western vineyards are responsible for some of the best quality wines of Australia, still and sparkling. Their soil is mostly lighter and less fertile than the soil of most other Victorian vineyards: it is richer in lime but poorer in all else, and this is the basic cause of the higher standard of quality of their wines. Unfortunately and inevitably, the average yield of the Great Western vineyards is so much poorer than that of other Victorian vineyards that they have almost ceased to be economic in an age of keen competition, which is one reason why many of the early vineyards of Great Western have now ceased to exist.

There is a township called Great Western: it is by no means Great and it is not particularly Western. It was originally called Weston, from the name of a colourful personality in the gold-digging days; then, in 1860, a great deal of publicity was given

At Chateau Tahbilk, in Victoria, the dreaded Phylloxera pest struck in the 1890s. Most of the vines were destroyed, but for some unexplained reason, seven rows survived. This sign commemorates the veterans. The rest of the vineyard was replanted with vines grafted on Phylloxera-resistant stocks.

to the crossing of the Atlantic by a wonder ship called the *Great Eastern*, and it was then that Weston was dubbed Great Western. This has been its name ever since.

Fifty years ago, there were over 2,000 acres of vines in the Great Western area; that is, from Glenorchy, in the north, to about ten miles below Ararat, in the south, the village of Great Western being half way between Stawell and Ararat, with the Grampians Mountains twenty-five miles to the west. Vines were first planted in the area by Messrs. Trouettes and Blampied in 1862: their vineyard was just outside the village and they called it St. Peter. The following year, Joseph and Henry Best each planted a vineyard, the one that was nearest the village being called Great Western, and the other Concongella. A little later on, there were other vineyards planted a few miles to the west, in the Rhymer area, whilst in the north, at Doctor's Creek, nearer Stawell, the Stawell Vineyard Company owned the largest of a number of vineyards. In the opposite direction, south of Ararat, there was the Emerald Vineyard Company, owned by Messrs. J. and M. Mooney; at Eversley there was the Decameron Vineyard Company and Mr Paul Vautravers' Swiss Vineyard, as well as a number of smaller vineyards.

Mr Hans Irvine, who bought the Great Western Vineyard from Joseph Best in 1885, decided to make some sparkling wine in 1887 when he succeeded in bringing out from Champagne a fully qualified expert, Charles Pierlot, and a team of French technicians. It was also Hans Irvine who had underground galleries dug out near his winery in order to give the wine a better chance to have its second fermentation in bottle in the peace of a cool cellar, and also to be binned away under conditions as similar as possible to those existing in France, in Champagne. Incidentally, if those underground galleries are known today, as they have always been, as "drives", it is because "drives" is the mining term for underground galleries in mines and they were made by the miners of the gold diggings.

In 1918 Messrs. B. Seppelt and Sons bought Mr Irvine's property—vineyard, winery and "drives"—and they still own it, but they have greatly improved and modernized the winery, as well as enlarged the vineyards, in recent years. Seppelt's Great Western vineyard has now 650 acres of quality grapes in production, and the "drives" a run of three and a half miles.

Joseph Best's brother, Henry Best, sold his Concongella vineyard of twenty acres to the Stawell Vineyard Company, which eventually sold it to the Thomson family, under whose charge it flourishes today.

Latest in date but greatest in yield, the vineyards of Mildura, in the north-west of Victoria, owe their existence and their fortune to the Chaffey Brothers, George and Ben, two Californians who were the pioneers of large-scale irrigation on the Murray River in the 1880s. Mildura is the name of the town: Mildara is the name of the largest organization responsible for the making and marketing of the Mildura district's wines and brandies.

21

THE VINEYARDS

SOUTH AUSTRALIA

The vineyards of South Australia have had up to now the rare privilege of being Phylloxera-free, which is one of the reasons why there are a great many more wine-producing vineyards in South Australia than in all the other Australian States put together. They may be divided into six main groups as follows:

(1) Adelaide Metropolitan Vineyards.
(2) Barossa Valley, Keyneton, Eden Valley, Springton, Clare and
    Watervale vineyards.
(3) Southern Vales vineyards.
(4) Coonawarra vineyards.
(5) Langhorne Creek and Bleasdale vineyards.
(6) Renmark, Berri, Loxton and Waikerie irrigation vineyards.

ADELAIDE METROPOLITAN VINEYARDS. Many vineyards were planted north and south of Adelaide in the early days in areas where dwellings and factories now stand, but there are still today a number of veteran vineyards in what may be called Adelaide suburbs: vineyards the existence of which is gravely threatened by the relentless tide of bricks and mortar. The more important are the vineyards to the east and south of the City (on what was called once upon a time the Adelaide Plain), and on the foothills of the Mount Lofty Range, but there is no trace left of the first vines that were planted at North Adelaide by J. B. Hack in 1837 and George Stevenson in 1838. Actually, the first large commercial planting was that of A. H. Davis, who obtained cuttings from the Busby collection and established them at his farm in the Reedbeds (now Underdale, a western suburb of Adelaide) between 1838 and 1840. That vineyard has also long since disappeared.

There are still vines, however, at Magill, where the first were planted by Dr Penfold in 1844, and at Auldana, where they were planted by Patrick Auld in 1854.

Besides vines and an up-to-date important winery owned by Messrs. Penfold at Magill, visitors may still see Dr Penfold's little house, religiously kept by his great-grandchildren as it was a hundred and twenty years ago, with the original furnishings and a number of souvenirs of the pioneering days. At Auldana, which now belongs to Messrs. Penfold, the original vineyard is still being cultivated, and the original winery still stands, but has been modernized.

Near Magill, at Burnside, some of the vines which were originally planted by H. C. Clark in 1858 at Stonyfell have been replaced by other and most likely much more suitable varieties than the first; they are now owned by H. M. Martin and Son,

One of Australia's most famous wine-growing areas, the Barossa Valley of South Australia, starts at Lyndoch. The picture shows the entrance to the Wilsford Winery.

as well as the homestead and winery. There are also other more recently established wineries in the same areas, as well as farther north on the way to Tanunda but still close to the last foothills of the Mount Lofty range: at and near Modbury, where Dr W. T. Angove planted a vineyard at Tea Tree Gully in 1884, and in Hope Valley nearby, where Douglas A. Tolley planted a vineyard in 1893; those two vineyards are still in fine fettle (though they have been reduced by urban development).

No further from the centre of Adelaide than Magill, but to the south-west of the City, near Glenelg, is Hamilton's Ewell Vineyard. It is still owned by the direct descendants of the first Hamilton who bought the land in 1837, and who is variously credited with having planted his first vineyard in 1838 or 1840.

A little nearer Adelaide, but to the south-west of the City, at Glen Osmond, Woodley Wines now own the winery on the site of the one-time vineyard which was planted in 1856 by Osmond Gilles.

A few miles south of Adelaide, on the slopes of O'Halloran Hill, a Mrs Horne planted a vineyard in 1892; it belonged from 1921 to 1966 to the Robertson family, who built a modern winery and distillery at Happy Valley. They retained the original name of the vineyard: Glenloth. The business was sold recently to Seager, Evans and Co. Ltd., of London.

A number of attempts were made in the early days to grow grapes in the open on a commercial scale in the wetter parts of the Adelaide Hills, but all failed, with the exception of the vineyard planted at Clarendon in 1849 by John Edward Peake who, incidentally, was the first to import direct from Spain the Palomino, Pedro Ximenez, Doradillo, Temprana, and Mollar Negro grapes which have been grown in South Australia ever since.

Dr R. M. Schomburgk, who became famous as the Director of the Adelaide Botanical Gardens, planted a small vineyard in 1857, at Buchfelde, now called Loos, west of Gawler, on the Para River; it was he who introduced in South Australia the Sultana grape, little knowing that a hundred years later it would be grown—thanks to irrigation—to a greater extent than any other grape (but for dried fruit rather than wine).

BAROSSA VALLEY. The Barossa Valley is the Valley of the Para River; it lies thirty miles to the north-east of Adelaide, and it rises gently during some twenty miles of the Para course; it narrows and expands in turn all the way in a haphazard manner, its width averaging nearly five miles.

The Barossa Valley is an enchanting land of orchards, vineyards, olive groves,

A general view of the Barossa Valley from Mengler's Hill, behind the town of Tanunda.

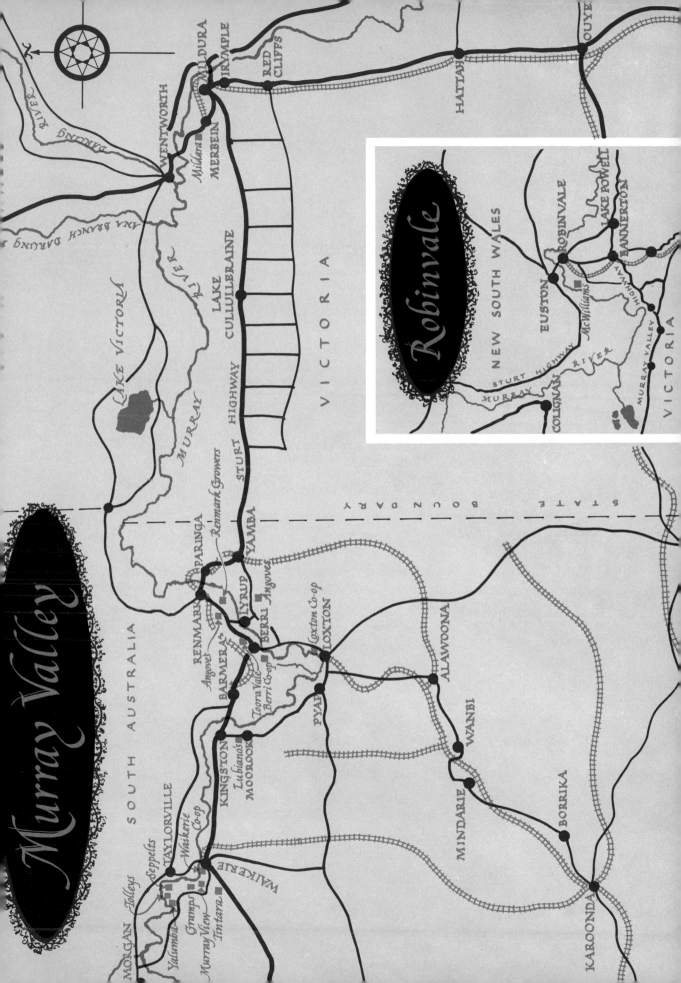

grassy slopes and clumps of trees, not unlike the Barrosa Valley in Spain after which (despite the difference in spelling) it is said to have been named; with this difference also, however: that there are many more *vignerons* and market gardeners, more ease and comfort as well, in the Barossa Valley of South Australia than in the Barrosa Valley of Spain.

There are three principal towns in the Barossa Valley, Tanunda, Nuriootpa, and Angaston, each of them with a population of about two thousand people. There are, however, a number of smaller community centres scattered among the folds of the Valley's rolling downs: flourishing settlements with no sign of poverty anywhere and every token of prosperity nearly everywhere. They bear witness to the foresight and generosity of one of South Australia's early settlers, George Fife Angas—Angaston was named after him—who found the money that made it possible for three shiploads of dissenting German Lutherans to leave Germany, and to find liberty of conscience, sunshine, work and happiness in South Australia. This happened in the forties of the last century, and those early German migrants were followed by a number of their compatriots during the fifties and sixties. Many of them came to the Barossa Valley and had no cause to regret it. Some of their descendants have not only made fortunes, but they have been, and they still are, among the foremost citizens and most public-minded leaders of the State: the Gramps of Orlando, and the Seppelts of Seppeltsfield, for instance, have built organizations of major importance and of world-wide repute.

The Barossa Valley is the most important of all the non-irrigated vinelands of Australia, with nearly 20,000 acres of wine-making grapes, as well as dried-grape vineyards. It produces on an average 38,000 tons of grapes a year, and what is of even greater interest is the fact that the great majority of the grapes grown in the Barossa Valley for wine-making are quality grapes.

As one reaches the Barossa Valley coming from Adelaide, there are many small vineyards and orchards before the great stretch of vines at Rowland Flat, the property of Messrs. Gramp whose homestead, winery and distillery of Orlando are one of the outstanding landmarks of the Valley. Farther on, at no great distance, one comes to Tanunda, where a number of firms have their offices, such as Messrs. O. Basedow Wines Ltd., Messrs. R. H. Binder, Messrs. P. T. Falkenberg Ltd.

There are a number of vineyards, mostly small ones, east of Tanunda, but there are many more to the west; that is, on the right bank of the Para River, such as Rosevale, St. Hallett, Paradale, Tolley's, Chateau Leonay and North Para (where Erwin and Laurel Hoffmann, two of the Barossa Valley's best-known people are to be found). Further to the west there is one of the most spectacular estates of the Barossa Valley, at Seppeltsfield, the homestead, winery and distillery of Messrs. Seppelt, surrounded by many acres of vineyards.

Leaving Tanunda, road, river and railway lead to Nuriootpa, where Messrs. Penfold

Many of the early vine-growers of the Barossa Valley were Silesians, and German influence is apparent in the architecture of the Valley's towns. St John's Lutheran Church at Tanunda was built in 1868.

have, at the edge of the town, a number of well-equipped modern buildings—winery, distillery, laboratory, storage cellars and so on—while Messrs. Tolley, Scott and Tolley have their main distillery close by. The Barossa Co-operative Winery Ltd. has its headquarters at Nuriootpa, where also is the establishment of Tarac Industries Pty. Ltd., which processes the marc of the wineries for tartaric acid, grape-seed oil and fortifying spirit. (The tartaric acid goes to Sydney and becomes cream of tartar.)

The Eden Valley, in South Australia, which is noted for its production of high-quality white table wines.

Proceeding from Nuriootpa to Angaston by road, one passes by a number of vineyards, the oldest of them all being Saltram, a small distance from Angaston; the original vineyard was planted by William Salter in the early fifties of the last century, and it now belongs to Messrs. H. M. Martin and Son Ltd.

Beyond Angaston, one soon comes to one of the finest homesteads, wineries, and vineyards of the Barossa Valley, at Yalumba, where Samuel Smith planted the first thirty acres of vines in 1849. His great-grandchildren still live at Yalumba, but in much greater comfort than their forebear ever knew or dreamt of; it is also quite certain that old Sam would not recognize as his winery the present-day premises replete with the most modern scientific equipment.

The visitor who leaves Yalumba has the choice of two roads. One leads due south to Eden Valley, before reaching Springton, at both of which places Hamilton's have wineries. The other road, at the fork, goes east to Keyneton, once upon a time surrounded by vineyards which produced some very good table wines. The main reason why the Keyneton wines were so good was that the soil of their vineyards was so poor, which is also why there are fewer vineyards now, in an age when quantity pays so much better than quality. Happily, there are exceptions to all rules, and there is still one winery in the area and a large vineyard in fine fettle. There is modern equipment in the winery and none but quality grapes in the vineyard: they are the property of Cyril

28

Henschke whose father, Paul Alfred Henschke, was the son of Paul Gotthardt Henschke, an Australian-born son of a German migrant who farmed land near Keyneton and eventually planted a small vineyard there about a hundred years ago. Although Keyneton may not claim to be geographically speaking within the Barossa Valley proper, the table wines of the Henschke vineyard can claim to be the peers of the best table wines of the Barossa Valley.

Further on, some eighty miles from Adelaide, there are a number of vineyards scattered along the hilly and wooded country upon both sides of the road and railway from Clare to Watervale. The best known of the Watervale vineyards is Buring and Sobels' Quelltaler. A little further on are the wineries of the Stanley Wine Company, the Clarevale Co-operative and Roland Birks.

There is but one survivor of the early Clare-Watervale vineyards, the Sevenhill College Vineyard; it was originally planted by the Jesuit Fathers who came from Austria to South Australia in 1848. They built a college and the Church of St. Aloysius, which still stands and is served by their successors. Other vineyards in the same area, such as the one that was planted in 1853 by John Ward, and another planted by Valentine Mayr in 1859, no longer exist.

SOUTHERN VALES. Next to the Barossa Valley, both in acreage and in beauty, the vineyards of the Southern Vales have produced a considerable quantity of quality wines

Sevenhill Vineyard, eighty miles north of Adelaide, is attached to the Jesuit College of St Aloysius. The vineyard, founded more than a century ago, produces sacramental wine and a small quantity of dry red table wine.

for well over a century. Some of them are nearer Adelaide than any but the Metropolitan vineyards, merely thirteen miles to the south-east of the City.

The oldest of the Southern Vales vineyards was planted about 1838 by John Reynell, and the small township which has in the course of the years grown around what was once John Reynell's homestead has borne his name ever since: it is called Reynella which is also the name under which Messrs. Walter Reynell and Sons market the wines which they make from the nearby vineyards, which, needless to say, are considerably greater than the original one.

If one leaves Reynella and turns one's back on the St. Vincent Gulf, three miles to the west, the first of a jumble of vales and gullies—the Southern Vales—one comes to is Morphett Vale. It was there that R. C. H. Walker planted an important vineyard and built a winery, some sixty years ago; the winery is now the property of the Emu Wine Company.

Next to Morphett Vale, one comes to the very picturesque McLaren Vale, with ironstone in the soil and many vineyards upon slopes facing north, east and west.

The lead given by John Reynell in the early forties was soon followed by others, by none with greater enthusiasm and greater faith in wine than Dr A. C. Kelly. He was an Adelaide medical practitioner who planted a vineyard near Morphett Vale in 1845 and called it Trinity Vineyard. (Later it was owned by John B. Macmahon, but has now been replaced by houses.) Twenty years later, in 1865, Dr Kelly talked some of his rich Adelaide friends into putting up the necessary money to form a company that would buy the first vineyard that was planted in McLaren Vale by W. Manning, in 1850: the vineyard was called Tintara and the company that bought it took the name of Tintara Vineyard Company. It started well, but it did not prosper for very long: in 1873, the Tintara Vineyard Company was in liquidation. There was at the time an acute economic crisis and nobody to bid for the Tintara vineyard and winery. At last, happily, a brave man came forth, Thomas Hardy was his name, and he bought "for a song" the bankrupt Tintara Vineyard Company. He already had a little vineyard at Bankside, near Adelaide, with an orchard, and he had made a great success of both; he also made a great success of Tintara, where his grandson and great-grandchildren now own some of the finest vineyards of McLaren Vale, and make some of the finest wines and brandy of Australia.

Other fine vineyards in McLaren Vale include Seaview, originally known as Hope Farm, which was first planted by George P. Manning in 1850, and is now owned by Messrs. Edwards and Chaffey. There are also in the same area the vineyards of Kay Bros., Osborn's, also Ryecroft (Ingoldby's) and Sparrow further down. Upon the other side of road and rail, the chief vineyard is Johnston's. A newcomer is the Southern Vales Co-operative Winery Ltd.

McLaren Vale, in South Australia, produces high quality dry table wines from its ironstone soil.

COONAWARRA. A long way to the south-east, on the Mount Gambier road, one comes to Coonawarra, before Penola. There is, at Coonawarra, a large patch—about ten square miles—of red soil in which grapes and stone-fruit grow exceptionally well, a fact which John Riddoch was the first to realize and to take advantage of, when he founded the Coonawarra Fruit Colony in 1890. His lead was soon followed by others, so that by the end of the last century, there were 900 acres of vines at Coonawarra.

Unfortunately, the area was off the beaten track and transport was difficult and costly, so that, good as Coonawarra wine was, it proved to be uneconomic to market it. At one stage, £3 a ton was all that the wineries offered to the *vignerons* for their grapes. Most of the *vignerons*, naturally enough, gave up growing grapes, but one of them, W. L. Redman, decided that he would no longer sell his grapes but make his own wine and market it himself. He did so with conspicuous success, at first selling his red table wines in bulk, and later in bottle, under his own trade-mark "Rouge Homme".

In 1965 W. L. Redman and his sons sold the entire enterprise to Lindeman's Wines Pty. Ltd., of Sydney, but this transaction takes us a little ahead of our story, for by then interest in the potential of Coonawarra as a vine-growing area had revived.

By 1950 no less than 650 of the original 900 acres of vineyards had been uprooted, but the excellence of the Rouge Homme Clarets and their high reputation must have attracted the attention of some of the more important wine-making firms. Messrs. S.

31

Wynn and Co. were the first: they bought the bulk of the existing vineyards, 126 acres, in 1951 from Woodley Wines Ltd., together with the big cellar built by John Riddoch; a few years later, they had planted new vines to such an extent that they can count upon a thousand tons of grapes from their Coonawarra vineyards. Then came Penfold, who planted some eighty acres of vineyards; also Mildara Wines Ltd., who built a modern cellar with storage for 40,000 gallons of wine. There are also a number of small growers who sell their grapes at vintage time, and at good prices, to one or the other of the local wineries.

By 1963 the total acreage of the Coonawarra vineyards was about 500 acres— double what it was in 1950.

The vineyards of Coonawarra are the most southerly of all Australian vineyards, which means that their grapes are gathered later than elsewhere; it also means that they are gathered at a time when the heat of the late summer or early autumn is by no means as fierce, and hence much more suitable for the early stages of fermentation. This is all to the good. Unfortunately, it also means that the vines of Coonawarra have more to fear from spring frosts than the vines of more northern location, so that the *vignerons* of Coonawarra are bound to accept greater differences in the quantities of grapes they harvest year by year than happens in most other vineyards of Australia.

LANGHORNE CREEK. Some twenty-five miles east of Adelaide, at Langhorne Creek, on the Bremer River, at no great distance from the northern shore of Lake Alexandrina, a vineyard was planted by Frank Potts, in 1860: he called it Bleasdale. This vineyard is still thriving and produces a great deal of wine, chiefly dessert wines. There is also an important vineyard at Metala, owned by Mr Denys Butler: it is planted mostly in Cabernet Sauvignon grapes which are processed by H. M. Martin and Son at Stonyfell, near Adelaide.

BERRI, RENMARK, WAIKERIE, LOXTON. In the South Australian loop of the Murray River, there are considerable quantities of wine made from the produce of irrigated vineyards. The Berri Co-operative Winery and Distillery is an offshoot of the Berri Co-operative Packing Union. It started in a modest way in 1918 with a grape-crusher handling less than a hundred tons of grapes a year, but by 1948 the Berri Distillery had expanded to such an extent that its crushers dealt with 20,000 tons of grapes a season, and its cellars could take in four million gallons of wine and spirits. There has been more expansion since then and there are in the Berri area today some five hundred growers, many of them veterans of the two World Wars, whose grapes are processed by the Berri Distillery.

Renmark Growers' Distillery is two years senior to Berri in age, but not its equal in capacity. For thirty years, from 1928 to 1957, Mr D. T. DuRieu, O.B.E., was chairman

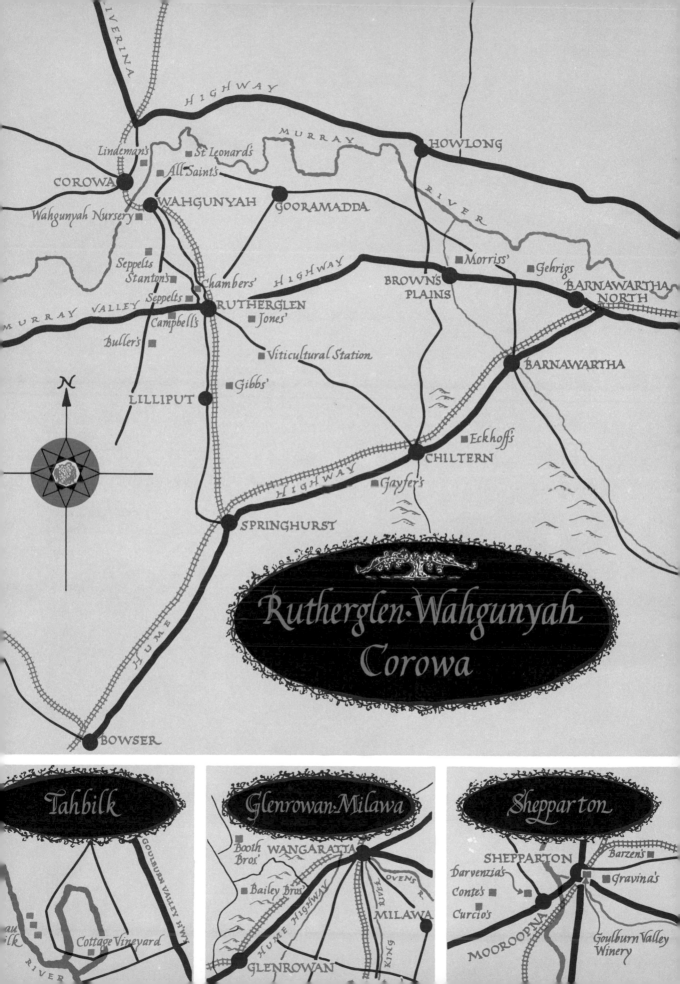

RIVERINA

HIGHWAY

MURRAY

HOWLONG

RIVER

Lindeman's
St Leonards
All Saints
COROWA
WAHGUNYAH
GOORAMADDA
Wahgunyah Nursery

Morriss'
Gehrigs
BARNAWARTHA
NORTH

Seppelts
Stanton's
Chambers'
HIGHWAY
BROWN'S
PLAINS
Seppelts
RUTHERGLEN
Campbell's
Jones'
Buller's
BARNAWARTHA
Viticultural Station

MURRAY VALLEY

N

Gibbs'
LILLIPUT
Eckhoff's
CHILTERN
HIGHWAY
Gayfer's

SPRINGHURST

Rutherglen·Wahgunyah
Corowa

HUME

BOWSER

Tahbilk

GOULBURN VALLEY HWY

Cottage Vineyard

RIVER

Glenrowan·Milawa

Booth
Bros.
WANGARATTA
Bailey Bros.
HUME HIGHWAY
OVENS R.
MILAWA
GLENROWAN

Shepparton

SHEPPARTON
Barzen's
Darvenzia's
Gravina's
Conte's
Curcio's
MOOROOPNA
Goulburn Valley
Winery

of the Renmark enterprise; he was also president of the Federal Viticultural Council for seven years and a foundation member of the Wine Board.

Waikerie Co-operative Distillery, formed in 1919, has given splendid service to its grower-members, though in a less spectacular way than the other Murray River co-operatives.

Loxton Co-operative Winery and Distillery, established as a result of a land-settlement scheme after the Second World War, is one of South Australia's biggest brandy-producers.

Frost pots flare and smoke at Wynn's Coonawarra Estate Vineyard at Coonawarra in the south-east of South Australia. Coonawarra is the most southerly wine-making region of Australia.

The old cellars at Auldana Vineyard, in South Australia. Auldana is named after Patrick Auld, who bought the land on which the cellars stand in 1842 and planted a vineyard there about ten years later.

THE WINES

36

GOD giveth the grapes; man maketh the wine. There are all kinds of grapes, and there are all sorts of men, in Australia as elsewhere, which is why there is such a variety of different wines in Australia and in other countries in which climatic conditions make it possible and economic to grow in the open wine-making vines that will ripen their grapes every year—or nearly every year.

Wine is the suitably fermented juice of freshly gathered ripe grapes. There is in the juice of all ripe grapes more water than anything else: water which the roots of the vine have found in the soil or sub-soil of the vineyard and sent up to the berries of every bunch of grapes. The quantity of water in grape-juice may and does vary a good deal, but its nature is identically the same in all grapes, whether they be grown at Coona-warra or Clos Vougeot. There is also in the juice of all grapes, when ripe, some grape-sugar, and, again, its quantity may and does vary, but its nature is the same. If there are, as we know, so many wines which are so different, it is firstly because there are in the juice of all ripe grapes very small quantities of vegetal substances, mostly acids, which vary with the varieties of grapes; also very small quantities of mineral substances, mostly salts, which vary with the nature of the soil and sub-soil of different vineyards. Although those salts and acids and other substances are there in such very small quantities, their importance is capital: they are responsible for the bouquet and flavour of the wine, and hence for its character, individuality and appeal.

Man maketh the wine, and whatever there may be in the juice of ripe grapes, the raw material from which all wines are made, the quality or the lack of it in any wine depends not only on the acids and mineral substances in the berries, but on the know-ledge, the care, the intelligence and probity of the wine-maker from the moment the grapes are picked and brought to him. It will be for him to decide how those grapes are to be crushed or pressed: whether with or without their stalks; whether in one continuous squeeze that will extract all their juice, or in separate pressings, keeping the juice of each pressing separately.

No sooner has the wine-maker secured the juice of his grapes in vat, tank, tub, cask, or whatever container of his choice, than he must give it his whole attention and make sure that its fermentation will be exactly what he wishes it to be.

Fermentation is a perfectly natural, one might call it an inevitable, phenomenon, which transforms sweet, watery, unstable grape-juice into a dry, heady, and more stable wine. It happens when the molecules of carbon, hydrogen and oxygen of grape-sugar are shuffled or regrouped into two groups instead of one. One group is carbon dioxide, which escapes and loses itself in the air (if we let it), and the other group makes up what we call ethyl alcohol: it stays put, and then there is no grape-juice left—it has become wine. Other readjustments do take place at the same time as this regrouping, but the most important and spectacular of all is the birth of carbon dioxide and ethyl alcohol. None of this would happen but for the presence of what is called a catalyst produced by yeast: the catalyst, like a bandmaster, does not perform but gets the band to play.

Natural as fermentation may be, it is important to keep it under control and make sure that it is not going to be too slow or too quick, as there are a number of accidents that may happen in the course of the molecular regrouping: accidents also are so natural. This control of the fermentation into wine is more necessary in Australia than in Europe because of the relatively high temperature at vintage time in nearly all the vineyards of Australia: high temperature has such a speeding action upon fermentation that the molecular regrouping is rushed in a manner which does not give it a fair chance of doing its work properly.

Today, happily, temperature-control is no longer a problem: it is only an expense. All the great wineries of Australia, and most of the smaller ones as well, have now the necessary equipment for the control of the temperature at all times and practically everywhere.

The control of temperature by air-conditioning methods is an expense which European wine-makers can save, since they never or rarely experience at the time of the vintage temperatures comparable with those of Australia, but the control of fermentation by the Australian wine-maker also applies to the yeasts. When wine-making grapes are ripening, their skin softens a little, enough for microscopic fungi, blown upon them by the wind, to get a hold and to form, in their thousands, a fine dust-like covering that is known as the "bloom". Those strange little fungi stay put until the grapes are crushed; they then get their chance: they get into the juice of the grapes and there they multiply at a very fast rate into very tiny buds which keep on budding—on and on. In Australia, however, the wine-maker calls such natural yeasts "wild" yeasts, "wild" because free, and, if free, a menace or at least a risk. So he kills outright, either by physical or chemical means, the yeasts that come to the crusher or press with the grapes, and he replaces them with scientifically prepared pure yeast: he can thus put in exactly the right kind and quantity, whereas he never could be sure whether the right kind of yeast, or too little or too much of it, had come in with the grapes. Hence his control of fermentation is quite assured.

The modern Australian wine-maker is well informed and well equipped, and an entirely different type of person from his forebears, about whom Dr A. C. Kelly wrote in *The Vine in Australia*, published in Melbourne in 1861: "It is a notorious fact that

Fermentation has just begun in these red-wine grapes at Lindeman's Rouge Homme Winery at Coonawarra, South Australia.

modern science has not found its way into the cellar of the *vigneron*, who follows exactly the same routine his fathers have pursued for centuries."

There can be no doubt whatever today that the great Australian wine firms have the latest and most scientifically devised equipment, which represents an investment of many millions; they also have a highly qualified trained staff, and their technicians regularly visit all the more important wine-producing areas of the world to further their knowledge of any progress made in the technological approach to wine-making. The Australian Wine Research Institute at Glen Osmond, South Australia, is in charge of Mr J. C. M. Fornachon, who is acknowledged by oenologists throughout the world as a master and a leader, particularly in the field of Sherries. In addition, there is at Roseworthy Agricultural College, near Adelaide, a wine-making school which has taught students from overseas, as well as from all States of Australia.

All this means that there is much good wine made in Australia. But it does not mean that all wine made in Australia is fine wine: it is not. In Australia, as in all other wine-producing countries, much the greater proportion of all the wines made are *ordinaires*, or plain wines, that will quench the thirst, clear the bowels and rejoice the heart of us all, plain people as most of us are. In Europe, however, considerable quantities of such *ordinaires* or plain wines are drunk by the people who make them, by their families, their friends and practically all men and women in the lower-income group: these people have always been used to drink, as their forebears have done before them, some kind of inexpensive local wine, and it has become a tradition and a daily communion at mealtime.

There is only a slow development of customs of that sort in Australia. In spite of the fact that many migrants from European wine-drinking lands have settled in Australia, the solid core of people is still made up of two opposite camps: the drinkers and non-drinkers, the hard-liquor camp and strong-tea camp.

Then, there is also the climate of most parts of Australia, which absolutely demands cold beer rather than even the best of wines at certain times of the summer. This is why wine is for the majority of Australians the exception rather than the rule, but there are more and more Australians who welcome and provoke occasions that will justify such exceptions. If most of them prefer sweet wine to dry, it is because they also like plenty of sugar in their tea and coffee: again the climate may be blamed for this fondness for sugar, or it may be due to the physiological need of people who rarely, if ever, think of saving their physical energy. Whatever the reason may be, the fact is that the most popular of the Australian wines, in Australia, is Sweet Sherry.

Quality wine, in Australia as in all other wine producing lands, is a small proportion of the total production of the nation's vineyards. It is inevitable. Quality wines are bound to cost more: they are made with greater care, of none but the best grapes, and they are kept longer so that they may have a chance to show how good they can be if given time. In the more famous wine areas of Europe, quality wines are getting dearer and dearer all the time, although by no means better and better: most of them bear names which have acquired in the course of time a valuable prestige value and their world-wide demand is growing faster than their supply.

In Australia, the number of wine-lovers, wine connoisseurs, and even of wine snobs who would love to be considered connoisseurs, may not be very large at present, but it is growing and it is apparently growing faster than the supply of quality table wines, since the "private reserve" and other high-quality Australian wines command premium

A white-wine ferment at an advanced stage at the Wendouree Winery near Clare, South Australia.

Australian brandy maturing in French oak at the Renmark Growers' Distillery at Renmark, South Australia.

prices and are by no means easy to procure. There cannot be any doubt whatever that the appreciation of quality wines is growing in Australia, and at a rapidly increasing tempo. The demand for dry table wines has grown by no less than 30 per cent during the past few years and the lion's share of the increase has gone to the better-quality "bin" or "reserve" wines, which are worth so much more and yet cost so little more.

When the day comes, as surely it will come soon, when there are a great many more educated consumers in Australia—that is, people who will realize that their senses of smell and taste ought to be trained or educated just as their senses of sight and hearing—the demand for quality wines will soar and so will their supply. Vintners, in Australia more than in many other vinelands, have sunshine, fertile soil, good grapes, modern equipment—all they need to make more of the fine wines which they make now—but they also have shareholders, and they are in duty bound to make wines that they can sell profitably.

If we take a good vintage of recent times, the 1962 vintage, we might well ask what happened to the 42.2 million gallons of wine which official statistics tell us were made in that year.

This is what happened:

    24,200,000 gallons were distilled;

    11,000,000 gallons became fortified wines, mostly "sweet sherry";

    7,000,000 gallons became dry or sweet table wines and sparkling wines.

FORTIFIED WINES. Fortified wines are not weak wines which have been bolstered up by an injection of spirit, but either full-strength wines or wines that would have become full-strength wines of their own accord if left alone but have been given a still higher alcoholic strength by an addition of brandy or fortifying spirit, either during or after fermentation. The two methods of making fortified wines are known as the Port method and the Sherry method.

41

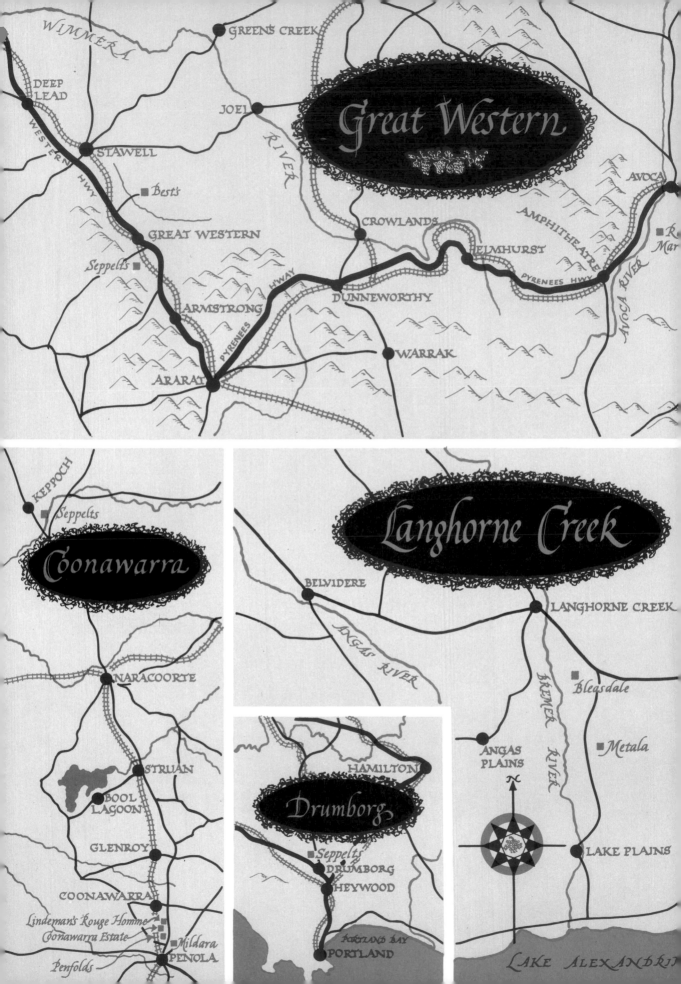

To make fortified wines by the Oporto or Port method, the wine-maker must watch with great care the fermentation of his grape-juice and decide when to check it while there is still a goodly quantity of the original grape-juice sugar left unfermented: he does this by killing the yeast with the right quantity of brandy or spirit. This is the classical way of making a wine which will be sweet because it will still contain some of its original grape-juice sugar, and strong because it will have a double dose of alcohol, one from the fermentation of the grape-juice, before it was checked, and the other from added brandy or spirit.

To make fortified wine by the Sherry method, the wine-maker lets his grape-juice ferment right out and become a wine with the alcoholic strength corresponding to the amount of sugar there was in the grape-juice but none of the sweetness of the original grape-juice sugar left in the wine. He then raises the alcoholic strength of his wine by the addition of as much or as little brandy or spirit as he thinks fit, and he will also colour the wine with caramel or whatever he thinks best to please the eye of his customers.

In Australia, the withdrawals from bond of fortified wines for home consumption, which may be reasonably considered as the quantities of such wines sold and drunk in Australia, averaged 3.4 million gallons a year before the last war; but by 1951-2, they had risen in a surprising manner to 13.4 million gallons a year, the highest figure ever recorded.

After that, although production and consumption of fortified wines remained much greater than production and consumption of unfortified or beverage wines, dry and sweet, still and sparkling, Excise figures for fortified wines showed, for several years, a slight decline in demand. However, from 1963-4, withdrawals from bond for home consumption began to rise again. The figures for recent years are:

1959-60	9,892,294 gallons	1963-4	9,554,676 gallons
1961-2	9,397,204 gallons	1964-5	9,650,476 gallons
1962-3	9,065,214 gallons	1965-6	9,733,722 gallons.

The term "fortified wines" covers a number of wines, most of them rather sweet, which are marketed in Australia as Port (ruby, tawny and white), Muscat, Madeira, Tokay and, of course, Sherry, the best seller of all. There are also a number of such wines which are sold under the registered names or brands of the firms responsible for their making.

43

These oak barrels at Seppelt's Winery at Rutherglen, in north-eastern Victoria, contain sweet wines for which the district is famous.

An indication of the relative importance of the demand for the different types of fortified wines is to be found in Australian domestic wholesale sales statistics:

				Gallons	
				1964–5	1965–6
SHERRY					
Sweet	..	..	..	4,096,000	4,388,000
Dry	..	..	..	1,313,000	1,480,000
DESSERT WINES					
(Port, Muscat, Tokay, Frontignac,					
Madeira, Marsala, etc.)			..	3,017,000	4,110,000

Sherry is the most popular of all fortified wines in Australia, and the name is used for a great many wines of different standards of quality. The best of them are the dry sherries which have been "Flor"-fermented, and also some of the dry and pale Sherries mostly marketed as Flor Fino, Fino Palido, Special Fino, Pale Fino; or else under some registered trade-mark such as Dry Friar, Pale Dry Solero, Extra Dry Solero, Del Pedro, Seaview Dry, and many more.

There are also a number of Sherries which are both sweet and of good quality: some of them are to be found in the "Cream Sherry" class. Half-way between the Dry and the Cream or Sweet Sherries, there are various brands of Medium Sherries which vary in quality, sweetness and price.

For practical purposes, the dividing line between fortified and unfortified wines in Australia can be considered to be 27 per cent of proof spirit, which is almost equivalent to 15 per cent of ethyl alcohol by volume. In Great Britain and Northern Ireland, the

Customs accept as "light" or unfortified wines all Australian wines the alcoholic strength of which is not over 27 per cent of proof spirit, although they will charge the higher rate of duty—that is, the duty on fortified wines—upon any wine from the Continent the alcoholic strength of which is above 25 per cent of proof spirit.

This somewhat curious discrimination in favour of Australian wines is a very small matter, but there is another difference between some of the fortified wines of Australia and the fortified wines of Portugal and Spain that might be considered of more importance because it could be argued that it might affect not only their cost but their quality.

In Portugal and Spain, Ports and Sherries are always fortified with Brandy: that is, distilled wine. In Australia, some are fortified with Brandy and some with "fortifying spirit". However, Australian wine men point out that in Australia fortifying spirit is made only by fermenting grape-sugar and distilling off the alcohol thus formed. By contrast, the fortified wines of Europe, except in certain special areas, including Jerez and the Douro Valley, are often fortified with alcohol derived from sources other than the grape.

Barrels that will soon contain maturing brandy stand under gum-trees outside Horndale Distillery south of Adelaide.

UNFORTIFIED WINES. The unfortified wines of Australia may be classed in four groups: one for red and rosés wines, one for the sweet white wines, one for the dry white wines, and one for the sparkling wines.

None of them are fortified, but none of them are as low in alcoholic strength as the lightest of French and Italian beverage wines. Nevertheless, the old idea that *all* Australian wines are high in alcoholic strength is incorrect: there are many Australian white table wines with strengths between 10 and 11 per cent of alcohol by volume.

It is true that the lightest European wines are likely to contain even less alcohol than the lightest Australian wines, particularly in poor years; it is also probably true that the *average* strength of wines in Europe is rather less than in Australia; but figures published by reputable authorities suggest that the differences are not tremendous. For instance, Dr Peynaud, of the University of Bordeaux, quoted these figures of alcoholic strength by volume in 1947:

39 Bordeaux whites (including Sauternes)	Min. 10.5	Max. 15.4	Mean 13.2
51 Bordeaux reds	9	12.9	11.1
27 Burgundy whites	10	13.8	11.8
19 Burgundy reds	12	15.7	13.5

It may be useful to refer back to these figures when, a little later, we discuss in more detail the alcoholic strength of Australian wines.

The demand for table wines in Australia is steadily growing, as appears from the figures (gallons) of their wholesale sales in recent years:

	1960–1	1961–2	1962–3	1963–4	1964–5	1965–6
Dry Red	1,439,000	1,493,000	1,637,000	1,995,000	2,129,000	2,519,000
Dry White	761,000	909,000	1,034,000	1,166,000	1,241,000	1,411,000
Sweet White	691,000	746,000	1,162,000	1,368,000	1,531,000	1,905,000
Sparkling Wine	262,000	290,000				
Total:	3,153,000	3,438,000	3,833,000	4,529,000	4,901,000	5,835,000

RED AND ROSÉS WINES: The two most popular red wines of Australia are marketed under the names of Claret and Burgundy. They are made in every one of the four main wine-producing States of Australia, irrespective of the nature of the soil of entirely different vineyards.

Most of them are dark in colour and all are fermented with the skins of the grapes. The grapes used are among the varieties known as black in English but called blue in Germany: their outside skin is blue—midnight blue—but they have a crimson lining

A 5,000-gallon cask at Lindeman's Winery at Corowa, New South Wales. This cask came to Australia from Germany after the First World War as war reparations.

which will stain the white juice of the grapes pink at first, then ruby, and eventually very dark red. Thus the alcoholic strength of all red and rosés wines depends upon the ripeness and richness in sugar of the grapes from which they are made, while their colour depends upon the time allowed by the wine-maker for the fermenting grape-juice to extract the colouring matter of the grape-lining.

The majority of Australian dry red wines are wines made from Shiraz or Hermitage grapes, which are good grapes and appear to produce substantial crops in a variety of different soils. The better-quality red wines, whether called Claret or Burgundy, are made from the Cabernet Sauvignon grapes, not only because it is a better grape than Shiraz (though not nearly such a free bearer), but because a Cabernet-made red wine will last longer and improve more markedly than other red wines.

As a rule—a rule with many exceptions—a red wine which is marketed in Australia as Claret is likely to be of lower alcoholic strength than its brother marketed as Burgundy. In the Hunter River Valley, where many of the lighter and better Australian dry red table wines come from, the average alcoholic strength of the dry red wines is 13 per cent of alcohol by volume, whereas it is 14 per cent in the Rutherglen district. Bordeaux red wines average, as a rule, only about 11 per cent and Burgundy reds somewhat more than Bordeaux, though still less than Rutherglen, as indicated by the table quoted earlier.

A number of Australian dry red wines are also marketed under the name of their birthplace and that of the grape or grapes from which they were made, such as Mount Pleasant Hermitage, Coonawarra Cabernet, Dalwood Hermitage, Tahbilk Cabernet, or Mildara Cabernet-Shiraz.

The demand for rosés wines is not very great, maybe because rosés are not generally above 11 per cent or at most 11½ per cent alcohol. Most rosés are made from Shiraz or

47

Hermitage grapes, some from Cabernet, some from Merlot, and the best from Grenache grapes. They are usually marketed simply as rosés with the name of the firm responsible for their bottling and sometimes with the name of the grape from which they were made, such as Angove's Rosé or Lindeman's Grenache Rosé.

Rosés wines are best drunk when young and fresh: unlike red wines, which are more mellow and gracious after from five to ten years at peace in bottle, they have nothing to gain by being kept for a number of years. Rosés wines should be served cold—chilled but not frozen.

WHITE WINES. Most fortified wines are made from Spanish grapes—Palomino, Pedro Ximenez and Doradillo—but all the unfortified white wines are made from French or German grapes, mostly Semillon—which they call Riesling in the Hunter River Valley—and Riesling, which are often called Rhine Riesling to indicate that they are true Riesling grapes.

White wines are made from white grapes by much the same process as red wines are made from black ones, with this difference, however: that the juice of black grapes is fermented with the red-lined, blue-black skins of the grapes, which give them their colour, whereas the juice of white grapes is fermented without any of the grape-skins, which would give them a golden colour. There was a time when the wines which we call white were golden, often deep-gold verging on orange, and their rich colour was greatly admired, but today fashion has decreed that white wines should be as nearly as possible "water-white", or colourless, or at least lighter in colour than they used to be. So there are no skins left in the fermentating vat, and some of the white wines of Australia, like almost all other white wines of the world, are practically colourless, although Australia does have some choice examples that match the beautiful golden glow of Yquem, Montrachet or Johannisberg.

The alcoholic strength of the white wines of Australia—usually 11 or 12 per cent of alcohol by volume—is, as a rule, from 1 to 2 per cent less than the strength of the red wines, and the white wines, also as a rule, are not kept back and matured like the reds: they are at their best when young and lively, nine to eighteen months of age—or of youth. This does not mean, however, that those light white wines will not keep: they will, but they have little, if anything, to gain by age.

Most dry white wines are marketed as Riesling, Chablis, Moselle, Hock, or White Burgundy, and sweet table white wines as Sauterne. There is, however, a generally accepted notion that the names of Chablis and Moselle should be used for the lighter types of white wines, not lighter in colour but of body, and often with a little more acidity: they may be the wines made from the earlier pickings of the grapes; that is, when the grapes are either barely ripe or still wanting a few days of sunshine to have their full quota of sugar. Obviously, the last grapes to be picked from the same vineyard will have had the benefit of an extra week, maybe two or three, of Australian sunshine, and they will be much more suitable for making bigger wines of the Hock type rather than Moselle, and, more particularly, of the Sauterne type.

The practice is gaining ground to market white wines in the same way as many red table wines are now marketed, either under the names of vineyard and grape or of some registered fancy name, such as Lindeman's Sunshine Riesling, McWilliam's Mt. Pleasant Riesling, Penfold's Private Bin Riesling, Gramp's Orlando Barossa Riesling Spatlese, Chateau Reynella Riesling, Seaview Riesling, Lindeman's Coolalta White, or Smith's Yalumba Carte d'Or.

SPARKLING WINES. Sparkling wines are made in Australia, as they are made in many other parts of the world, either by the *Méthode Champenoise* or in *cuve close*. The difference between the two is the difference between anything hand-made and machine-made: the first is better but dearer. The *Méthode Champenoise* means that the wine will have its second fermentation in its bottle, so that each bottle has to be handled separately to be cleared of all "rejects" thrown by the wine in the course of its fermentation; then

Brother Hanlon, who is in charge of wine-making at Sevenhill Winery, in South Australia, in one of the winery's century-old cellars. Sevenhill Vineyard is attached to the Jesuit College of St. Aloysius.

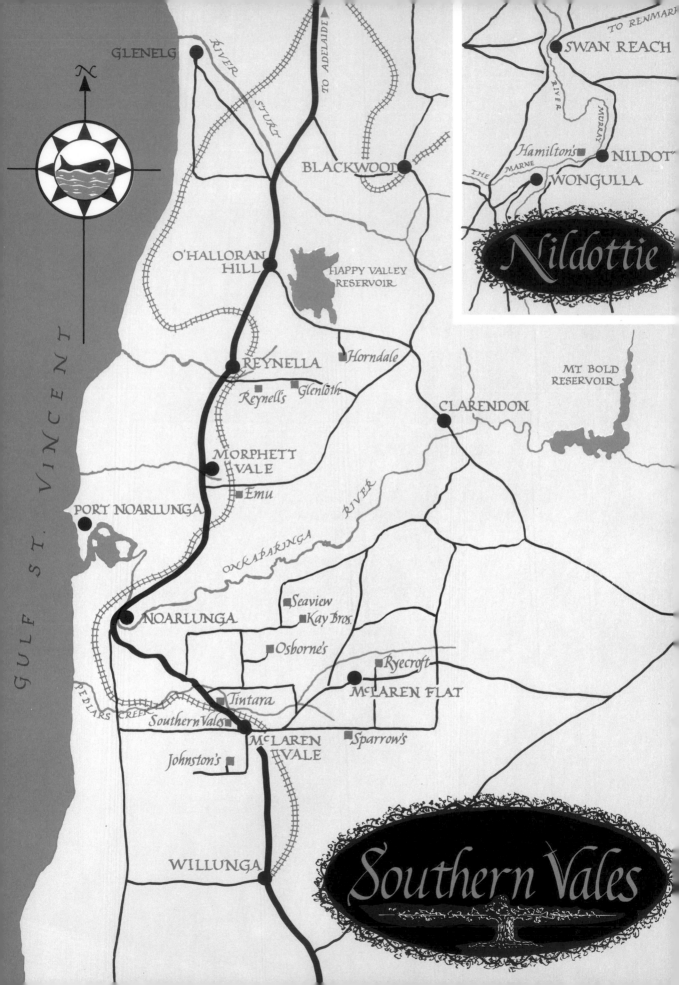

it has to be *dosé* individually, that is, given exactly the right *dosé* or quantity of sweetening. In the *cuve close* method, the fermentation takes place in a great vat, hermetically closed, from which the wine and just as much of its gas that is good for it will be bottled. It saves a great deal in wages to trained staff, not to mention cellar-space and time.

Sparkling wines are made by both methods in Australia, as elsewhere—mostly white, but also red and rosé or pink. White and pink sparkling wines made by the *Méthode Champenoise* are marketed as Champagne in Australia, and some of the white wines as Sparkling Moselle; the red sparkling wines are marketed as Sparkling Burgundy. There are also, however, considerable quantities of sparkling wines marketed in Australia under the names of registered brands such as Gramp's Barossa Pearl, McWilliam's Chateau Gay.

Of all wines, sparkling wine deserves more than any of the others to be called a fancy wine, and since each one of us is entitled to his or her own fancy, the best sparkling wine, be it white, pink or red, sweet or dry, is the one which you happen to fancy.

NOMENCLATURE. It may be regrettable, but it is quite understandable that the vintners of Australia have given for many years to their wines, and still give to many of them, names which belong to very different wines made from grapes grown in European vineyards.

It is obvious that white wines made from Chardonnay grapes grown in the lime-rich and humus-poor vineyards of Chablis, or from Riesling grapes grown on the steep slopes of the Mittel Mosel, cannot possibly have anything in common, save their colour or the lack of it, with white wines made from different grapes grown under entirely different climatic conditions.

It is equally obvious, however, that one cannot be expected to buy a wine with a name that conveys no idea whatever of what it is. There were brave and honest men who did try, and they failed. There was Captain Elder, for instance, who had a vineyard at Glen Osmond, south-east of Adelaide, in 1857: he made a red wine, probably a very nice red wine, which he tried to market as "Red Osmondeau", but he had to call it Burgundy to sell it.

It was inevitable then, but conditions are very different now. As distinct from the people who are quite content to explore no further than sweet sherry, there are now in Australia wine-consumers who are wine-lovers, whose palate is becoming more critical year after year, and who take an intelligent interest in wine. They know perfectly well that Riesling is a quality white grape and Cabernet a quality red grape: give them the name of the grape from which the wine in the bottle was made; give them the name of the grape's native vineyard and the year when the grapes were vintaged, and your modern Australian wine-lover will be much better informed than if he be offered

51

"Chablis" or "Hock", which may be any white wine, and "Claret" or "Burgundy", meaning a red wine incognito.

In Australia, as elsewhere, the big firms are growing bigger and the small firms are getting fewer. We live in an age of publicity, and publicity is costly, which is why the big firms with ample financial resources and large stocks of wine have a much better chance than the little man. But why should they spend their money to advertise names like Chablis and Hock for wines which anybody—including the little man—may offer, quite possibly at a lower price? What it pays them to advertise is their own name coupled with the names of grape and vineyard: it is all that the modern Australian wine-consumer asks for.

This is why the more popular table wines today include Penfold's Dalwood Hermitage, McWilliam's Mount Pleasant Hermitage, Lindeman's Coolalta Red Hermitage, Wynn's Coonawarra Cabernet, Emu's Houghton Cabernet, Reynella Cabernet Sauvignon, Seaview Cabernet-Shiraz, Mildara Cabernet-Shiraz, or Chateau Tahbilk Cabernet, among the red wines; and among the whites: McWilliam's Mount Pleasant Riesling, Penfold's Private Bin Riesling, Lindeman's Coolalta White, Lindeman's Sunshine Riesling, McWilliam's Lovedale Riesling, Wynn's Modbury Estate Riesling, Chateau Reynella Riesling, Edwards and Chaffey's Seaview Riesling, Hamilton's Springton Riesling, Hardy's Old Castle Riesling, Mildara Golden Bower Riesling, Smith's Yalumba Carte d'Or, Angove's Bookmark Riesling, Lindeman's Cawarra Riesling, Gramp's Orlando Barossa Riesling, Chateau Tahbilk Riesling, Buring and Sobels' Quelltaler, Leo Buring's Leonay Rinegolde and so on.

The time-honoured craft of the cooper still has an important part to play in the wine industry. This cooper is at work at Penfold's Magill Winery in Adelaide.

THE
VIGNERONS

A VINTNER is a wine man, a man who makes or buys wine to sell, a man who gives to the wines that he handles, from birth or babyhood, the intelligent care and love to which a young wine, like a young child, is entitled. Most if not actually all Australian *vignerons* were, in the early days of viticulture in Australia, vintners as well as *vignerons*. They had to be: there was nobody to whom they could look who was prepared to buy from them the wine they made and to market it for them.

Considering the many difficulties that faced the early vintners of Australia before they could build up a demand for their wines, it is quite remarkable that, in a country where viticulture and wine-making upon a commercial basis are barely one hundred and fifty years old, there are still a number of vintners who grow grapes where grapes were grown and who make wine where wine was made more than a hundred years ago. There are still vineyards and wineries owned and cared for by the third, fourth and fifth generations of the men who first planted a vineyard and made wine on or near the same spot, and there are a number of others where the original vineyard and winery have changed hands, but are in the good hands of younger owners who carry on the work of the original founder.

The fact that South Australia has had the good fortune to escape the ruinous invasion of Phylloxera must be responsible for the much greater number of centenarians among veteran vineyards there than there are in New South Wales and Victoria. Another reason is the fact that vineyards and wineries have survived, near Adelaide, the relentless rise of the bricks-and-mortar tide of suburban development better than they have done near Sydney and Melbourne: it is not easy to visualize vines growing, as they did, in what is now Collins Street! There are still vineyards that are known as the Adelaide Metropolitan vineyards, although there are now only a few of the many erstwhile Torrens vineyards. There used to be, for instance, in the fifties of the last century, an East Torrens Winemaking and Distillation Company, with vineyards at Stepney, a suburb of Adelaide: there was also an Adelaide Winemaking and Distillation Company, with a capital of £10,000, without any vineyards, the function of which was to buy grapes, process them, and market wines and brandies.

All the more important firms of today have offices and an efficient staff in the chief cities of Australia and in London; the others have agents in charge of the distribution of their wines who are able to let their principals know which are the types of wines likely to have the greatest appeal.

Up to the outbreak of the First World War, the demand for Australian wine in the United Kingdom was for red table wines, "dry reds": wines that were darker than most, stronger than most, and cheaper than most. They did not appeal to wine-connoisseurs who had a traditional or acquired love of the light, dry wines of France and Germany, but they were gratefully hailed by a great many wine-consumers, who thoroughly appreciated the inner comfort which Australian flagon Burgundies gave them at a price within their means. The cost of Australian table wines ranged from 13s. to 28s. a dozen bottles, at a time when the duty was merely 1s. a gallon or 2d. a bottle. The demand for the unfortified wines of Australia rose from scratch to nearly a million gallons a year (963,460 gallons) in 1911.

The declaration of war in 1914 halted the shipping of Australian wine overseas: the allocation of tonnage for war material, foodstuffs, raw materials, and the high rates of marine insurance left little hope to the Australian vintners of selling any quantities of wine overseas.

Immediately after the war, however, shipments of wine from Australia began to gather momentum, rising from 176,029 gallons in 1918, to 4,224,504 gallons in 1927, and then became stabilized at an average of 3¼ million gallons a year up to 1940, when the Second World War and submarine terror far worse than during the first war halted all shipments of wine from Australia.

During the "between-the-wars" period, the Australian vintners were faced with the fact that they had far too large stocks of fortified wines, in spite of very much greater demand for that type of wine in Australia. This was due to the mass-production of fortified wines in the irrigation areas, where an acre of Doradillo grapes could yield

Although Australia was one of the last countries to start making wine, it already has a remarkable number of vineyards that have been in the hands of one family for three, four or five generations. Here Robert Potts, a member of the fifth generation to live at the Potts family's Bleasdale Vineyard, tries his hand at shovelling the marc. Bleasdale is at Langhorne Creek, South Australia.

as much as ten tons of grapes, when an acre (non-irrigated) of Cabernet or Rhine Riesling grapes could not be expected to yield more than two tons of grapes.

It was only natural that the Australian vintners would turn to the United Kingdom as the country where they had the best chance of marketing their surplus fortified wines, mostly Port and Sherry types. At the time, the consumption of Port and Sherry was much greater in the United Kingdom than that of all other wines. It was, however, unfortunate for the Australian vintners that the Anglo-Portuguese Treaty of 1916 had given the protection of the law in England to Port and Madeira, restricting the use of those two names to the wines of Portugal and Madeira.

In 1924, Australia's Wine Export Bounty Act became law, because "the vital need for Australia was to get rid of bulk stocks". (H. E. Laffer, *The Wine Industry of Australia*, 1949, p. 77.) Those bulk stocks were all sweet, fortified wines from the irrigated areas, which is why the bounty for which the Act provided applied only to wines of at least 34 per cent proof spirit. The bounty was 2s. 9d. a gallon, to which had to be added a refund of 1s. 3d. a gallon paid in Excise for the fortifying spirit used in the making of the wine: this meant that the sweet, fortified Australian wines of the Port and Sherry types had a start of 4s. a gallon F.O.B.

In 1925 the Australian vintners had another present, this time from the British Chancellor of the Exchequer, who announced in the House of Commons, when introducing the year's Budget, that Empire wines not exceeding 27 per cent of proof spirit would pay in future a duty of 2s. a gallon, and that the Empire fortified wines not exceeding 42 per cent of proof spirit would pay 4s. a gallon, whereas the wines of non-Empire countries would pay 3s. a gallon if not exceeding 25 per cent of proof spirit and 8s. a gallon if not exceeding 42 per cent.

In 1927, rather meanly, if we may say so, the Australian Government cut down its bounty by 1s. a gallon.

In 1929 a helping hand was offered to the Australian vintners when the Wine Overseas Marketing Board Act was passed by the Commonwealth Parliament. This Act provided, among other things, for the creation of a Board to be known as the Wine Overseas Marketing Board (later to be called, more simply, the Australian Wine Board), and one of the first things that the Board did was to open a London office in 1930, and to appoint Mr H. E. Laffer its first manager, with the title of overseas representative.

In 1930 also, the Australian Federal Government imposed steep increases in the rate of Excise duty on fortifying spirit, and the wine industry asked that the increase in revenue should go into a fund for payment of the bounty. The Government agreed to establish the Wine Export Encouragement Trust Account, to which part of the Excise charges was credited, and from this account the amounts due for the bounty on export were paid.

In the early years of the Trust Account, there was no accumulation of funds, but during the Second World War, when wine exports fell sharply, a considerable credit balance was built up, amounting, at the end of 1946, to £1,100,000. Then, however, the Government decided to discontinue the bounty (from 28 February 1947), claiming that increased prices being obtained overseas for wine and a rise in consumption of wine in Australia made it no longer necessary.

Of the £1,100,000 in the Trust Account, £600,000 went into Commonwealth Consolidated Revenue and £500,000 into a new account called this time the Wine Industry *Assistance* Trust Account. Eight years later, in 1955, it was decided to use this £500,000 to establish and maintain the Australian Wine Research Institute.

The Institute took over scientific research work which had been begun in a small way as far back as 1934 under the control of a body known as the Oenological Research Committee, which consisted of representatives of the University of Adelaide, the Wine Board and the Federal Viticultural Council.

The research done under the committee's guidance was conducted in the buildings of the Waite Agricultural Research Institute at Glen Osmond, South Australia, with the co-operation and support of the Commonwealth Scientific and Industrial Research Organization.

The new Institute, however, built laboratories of its own, with a pilot winery, across the road from the Waite Institute; its control is vested in a council responsible to the Commonwealth Minister for Primary Industry and the Wine Board.

Mention has already been made of the world-wide recognition that has been given to research on Flor Sherry for which the Director of the Wine Research Institute, Mr J. C. M. Fornachon, was responsible. But the work of the Institute is, of course by no means confined to studies on Flor: it covers many aspects of vine-growing and wine-making.

One of the most interesting and ambitious projects on which the Institute is currently engaged is being carried out in co-operation with the Soils Division of the Commonwealth Scientific and Industrial Research Organization, the Commonwealth Bureau of Meteorology and the South Australian Department of Agriculture. It is a long-term project, now in its eighth year, and it has a very important objective: to discover precisely how variations of soil and season influence the major and minor constituents of grapes, which, in turn influence the quality of the wine that is made from them.

For this experiment the Institute has established no less than forty-two experimental plots of vines scattered over the wine-producing areas of South Australia: in the Barossa Valley, the Springton and Eden Valley area and the Murray Valley. Grapes from the plots are brought to the Institute at vintage time each year and made into wine under standardized conditions in the Institute's pilot winery. Both the grapes and the

*Many Australian
wineries "buy in" more
grapes than they produce
themselves. This grower
has just delivered his
load to a South Australian
winery.*

wines made from them are chemically analysed, and, at intervals during maturation, the wines are evaluated and compared by tasting. When the experiment is completed, it seems certain to provide basic information that will be of first-rate value to vintners and *vignerons* everywhere.

The Australian wine industry is thus quite highly organized on the scientific side; it is no less well organized on the marketing side.

Not only are Australian wines selling in increasing quantity in Australia; they are becoming better known in other countries, and for this much of the credit must go to the Australian Wine Board, working in co-operation with the Australian Trade Commissioner Service.

An important decision by the Board was to establish a central supply point in the United Kingdom, with the aim of ensuring that quality Australian wines and brandies would always be available under the makers' labels.

The result was the opening in 1960 of the Australian Wine Centre at 25 Frith Street, Soho, which was financed by seventeen leading Australian wine firms and the Board itself.

The Centre sells wine retail direct to the public and will accept orders by letter or phone for wine or brandy to be sent anywhere in Britain. In addition there are agents for the Centre in all Australian capital cities who accept orders from people who wish to have Australian wines sent to relatives or friends in Britain.

The Centre also organizes wine-tastings and many types of promotion to encourage the sales of Australian wines and brandies in Britain.

Britain remains the Australian wine trade's best overseas customer: she takes well over a million gallons of Australian wine a year. Canada comes next, with imports of about 300,000 gallons of wine a year and fifty to sixty thousand gallons of brandy.

Australian wine is now going also to many countries in south-east Asia, the Pacific Islands and the West Indies, and even Japan, not traditionally a wine-drinking country, is today beginning to buy Australian wine.

Australia's total exports of wine and brandy in recent times have ranged between one and a half to two million gallons: a modest figure indeed when compared with the exports of the world's great wine-producing countries, but a figure on which Australian wine men are thoroughly justified in hoping to improve.

The time has now come to consider the vintners of Australia individually, and it is of interest to ask, first of all, which is the oldest Australian vineyard still in the hands of the family that founded it.

No clear-cut answer can be given. Hamilton's Ewell Vineyards and the Reynella Vineyards, both south of Adelaide, are the oldest surviving vineyards in South Australia. Richard Hamilton and John Reynell were among the early settlers in the Colony of South Australia, which was founded in 1836; but we cannot be sure today whether it was Richard Hamilton or John Reynell who made the first cask of wine: the two companies that own the vineyards today are still disputing the matter, though in a good-humoured and gentlemanly way.

Walter Bagenal, in *The Descendants of the Pioneer Winemakers of South Australia* (1946) favours the Reynells' claim; so does an article in the November 1958 issue of the *South Australian Journal of Agriculture* by C. D. Matthews, who was at that time viticulturist of Roseworthy Agricultural College.

On the other hand, the Hamiltons are able to produce evidence in rebuttal. They point out that the official *Archives of South Australia* record that Richard Hamilton arrived in South Australia in the *Catherine Stewart Forbes* on 17 October 1837, and that John Reynell arrived in the *Surrey* almost exactly a year later, on 16 October 1838. Furthermore, private letters in the possession of the Hamilton family state that Richard Hamilton planted vines late in 1837 and that John Reynell did not plant vines until late in 1838. Admittedly, there are no official records to substantiate the statements in the letters. However, the records of the South Australian Land Titles Office show that Richard Hamilton took up land (Country Section Grant Number 148) on 6 June 1838. The same records show that Land Grant Section Number 524, at what is now Reynella, was originally taken up by Thomas Lucas, of Armagh, Ireland, on 12 March 1839 and was transferred to John Reynell on 6 July 1839.

Thus, it seems certain at least that Richard Hamilton came to South Australia a year earlier than John Reynell and received his land grant also a year earlier, but precise evidence about which of the men planted the first vines and made the first wine is at present lacking, and the case of neither family is helped by the fact that dates given in the writings of contemporary and near-contemporary observers are contradictory.

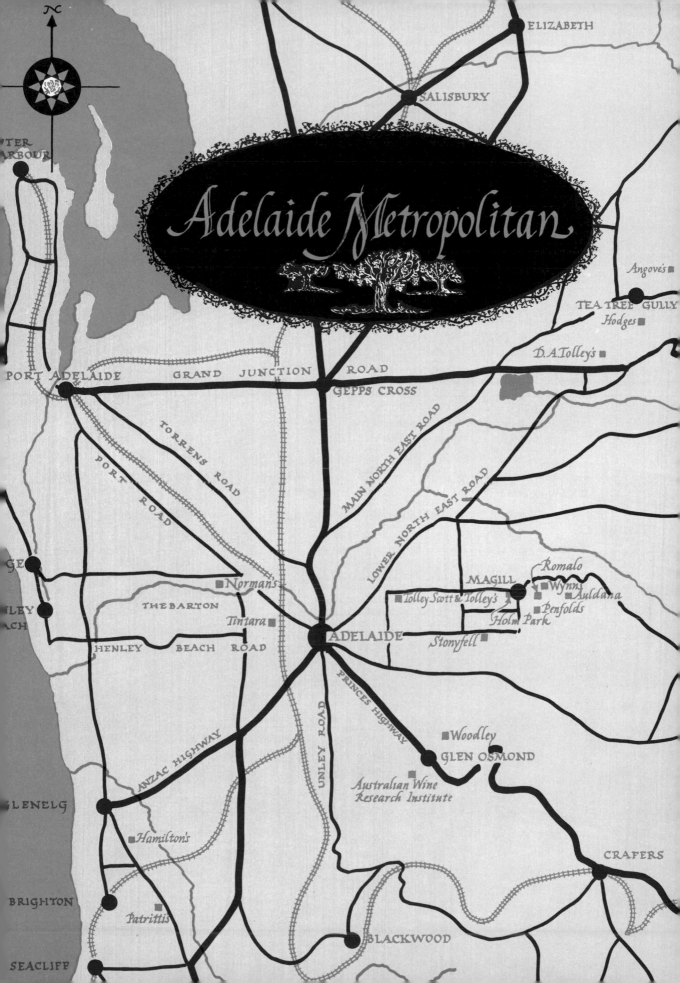

The 125-year-old Cave Cellar at Reynella, in South Australia, is the oldest underground wine-cellar still in use in Australia. It was excavated by John Reynell, who settled in South Australia in 1838.

REYNELLA

Jonn Reynell, a scion of the Reynells of Newton Abbot, in Devonshire, was born at Ilfracombe in 1809, and, although of farming stock, he must have had more than a farmer's usual share of wanderlust: he spent some time in Egypt and in the United States of America, and he paid a number of visits to France, Spain, Italy and other countries of the Continent, before he decided to sail, in February 1838, from Plymouth to Port Adelaide via the Cape. He was not alone: two of his brothers, Harry and Thomas, and one of their cousins, James Reynell, were also aboard the good ship *Surrey*, 461 tons, Captain G. Sinclair. There was also a fair passenger, Mary Lucas, the daughter of Admiral Lucas, V.C., who became John Reynell's wife soon after the *Surrey* reached South Australia.

John Reynell and his wife, Mary, settled upon a site thirteen miles south of Adelaide and three miles east of the St. Vincent Gulf—"good sheep country"—where they farmed and had a dairy, twenty-eight cows and heifers. Bennett's *South Australia* refers to John Reynell as one of the seven largest stockholders operating within four years of the proclamation of the new Colony of South Australia.

Whatever room there may be for doubt and disputation about whether Reynella is the oldest vineyard, it is certain that the cellar known as the Cave Cellar that John Reynell excavated, not under his house, but very near to it, can claim to be the oldest of the underground cellars still in use in Australia. A sloping broad alley runs from the house to the cellar entrance, which is almost concealed by a grassy bank.

The year 1854 was one of the most important in John Reynell's life, since it was in that year that he sold that part of his property where the township which bears his name to this day, Reynella, was built, and it was also in that year that his son Walter was born, who was to devote his remarkable intelligence and energy to building up the highly successful firm which we know today as Walter Reynell and Sons Ltd.

John Reynell died on 15 June 1876, and Walter, his only son, died in April 1919, four years after *his* only son, Carew, who was killed at Gallipoli, in 1915, when colonel commanding the Australian Ninth Light-Horse Regiment. Carew had one son, Richard, who was born in 1914. Richard was at Oxford, in 1939, when the Second World War was declared; like his father, he joined the Forces, and, like his father, he was killed in action (in 1940) as flight officer, and, again like his father, he left a baby son, who was born a year before Richard's death. This last heir in the male line of the Reynells of Reynella, has no intention of ever having anything to do with business; his ambition is to make his career in the R.A.F., in which he now serves.

Walter Reynell had two sisters, one of whom married Mr Ross Reid, the maternal grandfather of Mr Ian Thomas, the present chairman of Messrs. Walter Reynell and Sons Ltd. Other members of the Reynell family own some 40 per cent of the company's shares, but they take no part in the management of its affairs, leaving it to a team of experienced directors to deal with the conduct of the business. The managing director of the company is Mr Colin Haselgrove.

It is quite exceptional for the registration of any brand to be accepted using the name of a town, but "Reynella" could be and was accepted as the registered name of the wines marketed by Walter Reynell and Sons Ltd. because it was the name of Reynell's vineyard and farm long before there was a town of Reynella.

From the beginning to this day, there has never been any attempt made at the Reynella vineyards to increase the yield of the grapes at the expense of the quality of the wine, which is why the wines of Reynella enjoy in the Australian wine industry a reputation for fine quality second to none.

HAMILTON'S EWELL VINEYARDS

The founder of the Hamilton wine and spirit enterprise was a Scot who had lived in England and had a country seat near the village of Ewell, in Surrey; later he was to give the name of the village to the vineyard he planted in South Australia.

Richard Hamilton was born on 13 February 1792, maybe in a hurry, since he was a

A wagonload of grapes stands on the weighbridge at Hamilton's Ewell Winery at Glenelg, a suburb of Adelaide. A few small vine-growers still prefer horse-drawn transport.

hasty man all through his life: he married before he was twenty-one and died at the relatively early age of sixty; he had nine children, and he was certainly too hasty when he sold fifty acres of land in Long Island, New York, in 1835 or 1836, and bought a Land Order, dated 7 June 1837, signed by Robert Torrens, whose name still flows through Adelaide, and Rowland Hill, the Father of Penny Post.* The Land Order gave Richard Hamilton the right to take up land south of Adelaide on arrival. One must remember that there were wars and trouble ahead in plenty in the United States, far from "united" yet, so that Richard Hamilton had good cause to think that his large family would have more space and more peace in Australia than in New York, and also more sunshine and better opportunities than at Dover, where Richard Hamilton, his wife and family lived, in 1837, at 119 Margate Road.

When Richard Hamilton and his wife, Ann, landed at Port Adelaide with their children (all but Henry, who was born in 1826 and had been left in England at the Bluecoat School), they chose a block of land near Glenelg, seven miles south-west of Adelaide, near the sea, and they must have planted a vineyard at once if we are to believe that there were 1,200 gallons of wine made at Glenelg in 1840.

Today, there are still at Hamilton's Ewell Vineyards a few of the original vines kept for show, and quite a number of others that were planted in 1860, but, of course, the great majority of the vines are of much more recent plantation. Some were planted by Henry Hamilton, the Bluecoat boy, and others by Frank Hamilton, his son, whose son, Eric Hamilton, was until recently in charge of the vineyards, winery and distillery responsible for a million gallons of wine and spirits every year. Eric's son Robert is now general manager.

Besides the wines of different sorts which are made at Glenelg from the Hamilton's Ewell Vineyards, as well as Brandy, fortifying spirit and liqueurs distilled, rectified and compounded there, the firm owns wineries at Eden Valley and Springton, on the fringe of the Barossa Valley. At the Eden Valley cellars, purchased in 1964 from another company, Hamilton's crush grapes from the new Nildottie vineyards near Swan Reach, on the River Murray. At Bridgewater, in the Mount Lofty Ranges, the Old Mill Bond, formerly a flour-mill operated by water, is used for maturing the firm's Brandies and Whiskies.

LINDEMAN'S WINES PTY. LTD.

Henry John Lindeman must have been an exceptionally brilliant medical student to have become a member of the Royal College of Surgeons in London in 1834, when he was only twenty-three years of age. Besides being brilliant, he must also have been of a somewhat restless disposition since, instead of becoming a general practitioner, as his

---

* Torrens was chairman of the Colonization Commissioners for South Australia and Hill was secretary.

father was, he joined the Royal Navy. His first appointment must have been a disappointment: they sent him no farther than Greenwich, to H.M.S. *Dreadnought*, the sailors' hospital ship. Presently, however, he had his heart's desire, spending eighteen months as a surgeon on board *Marquis of Camden* in Indian and Far East waters. By then the Napoleonic Wars were a fading memory, the world was at peace, prospects of promotion for a naval man were particularly dim and when the young doctor fell in love and married in 1840, he decided to give up his career in the Royal Navy and to emigrate to Australia. Dr Lindeman and his bride, Eliza Bramhall, reached Sydney in September 1840, and they soon after proceeded to the Paterson River, a tributary of the Hunter. It is rather a curious coincidence that both Dr Lindeman, in New South Wales, and Dr Penfold, in South Australia, almost at the same time, in 1843 and 1844, had the same urge—almost a passion—to have a vineyard of their own, in spite of the fact that so much of their time and energy was devoted to their professional duties.

Dr Lindeman planted his first vineyard in 1843, and he named it "Cawarra", a name which the Aborigines used for "by running waters", and a name which has been better known than most during the past hundred years as that of a very popular Australian table wine. All went well for a few years, and the doctor, who was a great believer in quality and not in quick profits, built up a sizeable stock of Cawarra wines which were given a chance to mature in a great storage cellar built of gum-tree slabs.

Then, in 1851, a catastrophe wiped off everything: a disastrous fire destroyed the whole of the wood-built winery and cellar. It was a terrible blow, and Dr Lindeman felt it so much that he left Cawarra and went to the gold-diggings in Victoria, both as a surgeon and a miner. But he was soon back by the Paterson River and busy rebuilding his winery and his cellar. Year by year, Dr Lindeman planted more vines and made more wine, and he decided, in 1870, to transfer the headquarters of his wine business to Sydney, in Pitt Street, where all his wines were also bottled.

At Cawarra, all the wines produced were dry table wines, but the demand for the heavier and sweeter types of wine was growing all the time; it was in order to meet the demand that Dr Lindeman bought, in 1872, a property at Corowa, known as Haffner's Vineyard. Since then, the firm has acquired much land and built large cellars, so that today Corowa is the firm's major winery, specializing in sherries, ports and muscats.

Dr H. J. Lindeman had three sons and he took them into partnership in 1879, only two years before his death, when Mr Charles Frederick Lindeman succeeded his father and greatly expanded the firm's business. In 1900, the Porphyry Vineyard was acquired: it was an old vineyard originally planted in 1838 by Henry Carmichael, near Raymond Terrace in the Newcastle district: it is no longer in cultivation, but the name has been registered by Lindeman for one of their white wines of the Sauternes type.

In 1910 Lindeman acquired a property in the Hunter River Valley, near Branxton, west of Maitland, which was named "Sunshine" and it is now one of the company's most important Hunter River vineyards, famous for its dry white table wines and "Sunshine" Riesling.

In 1912 Lindeman acquired the Ben Ean vineyard, which had been planted in 1870 by Mr J. McDonald when the Pokolbin area was thrown open to settlement by the selectors. It is today the centre of the firm's operations in the Hunter River Valley, with a large winery and semi-underground cellars. In or about the same year, the firm acquired from the Wilkinson family the Coolalta vineyard, at the back of Ben Ean, upon even steeper hillsides. It had first been planted in 1866.

Kirkton, the name of the vineyard originally planted by James Busby in 1839, is now one of Lindeman's registered wine names. The vineyard came to the Lindeman family by the marriage of James Busby's nephew James Kelman and Mathilda, the daughter of Dr Lindeman. As late as 1924, some of the original Kirkton vines were still bearing fruit from which a few casks of wine were made.

In 1959, Mr R. H. Kidd was present when the last two bottles of the late Leo Buring's stock of Kirkton St. Cora Burgundy, as the red wine was labelled, were opened, and Mr Kidd has written: "The first bottle was received with dismay, as the cork had given out, but the second bottle was truly magnificent, a thirty-five-year-old wine from the vines which were then ninety-four years old".

During the two World Wars and the period of the World Depression, Lindeman's had more than its fair share of troubles and difficulties, but since 1947 it has gone from strength to strength without any setbacks. In 1953 the firm became a public company, and in 1960 it moved its headquarters to the Sydney suburb of Marrickville, where one of the most modern bottling plants in Australia has been installed.

PENFOLDS WINES PTY. LTD.

No greater oak ever rose from a smaller acorn than did the great trading organization known as Penfolds Wines Pty. Ltd. today. Its story begins with a little ship, the *Taglioni*, 361 tons, listed A1 at Lloyds, and skippered by her owner, casting anchor in the South Australian port of Largs Bay, in August 1844. It is not difficult to imagine how grateful all aboard must have been to the captain who had brought them safely half way round the world and how pleased they must have been to turn their back upon him and his little ship for ever. The arrival of *Taglioni* at Largs Bay was duly reported in the *Adelaide Register* of 8 August 1844, with an editorial comment welcoming Dr Penfold, one of the *Taglioni*'s passengers, and informing the *Register*'s readers that Dr Penfold was "the fortunate purchaser of the delightfully situated and truly valuable Estate of Makgill at the sum of £1,200".

Ulliade grapes at Penfold's Kalimna Vineyard, in the Barossa Valley of South Australia. Ulliade, also known as Oeillade, Cinsaut and Blue Imperial, is used for making Ports and red table wines.

Dr Christopher Rawson Penfold was a Sussex man and he had been a general practitioner in Brighton. What prompted him to leave England, to buy an estate near Adelaide, and to live there with his wife and daughter for the rest of his life, nobody will ever know. Besides Mary, the doctor's wife, and Georgina, their infant daughter, there was another and a very important member of the household, Ellen or Elise Timbrell, who was in turn Mary's personal maid, Georgina's nurse, and Dr Penfold's assistant wine-maker. For the doctor, a very busy and greatly valued general practitioner, was also a great believer in the therapeutic properties and excellence of wine: so much so that he had no sooner built a house—a small house which is still there and religiously kept as near as possible as it was in the beginning—than he planted a small vineyard.

As the years went by, he planted more vines, made more wine, and finally gave up his practice and devoted himself to the making of still more and better wine. Dr Penfold died in 1870, at fifty-nine, but his widow, Mary, proved to be an excellent business woman who carried on most efficiently the work which the doctor had so much at heart. She enlarged the winery and increased the demand for the wine she made with the help of her faithful Ellen Timbrell.

Her daughter, Georgina Ann, her only child, had married in 1861 Thomas Francis Hyland, an Irishman who was an officer in the Civil Service of Victoria and was stationed at Castlemaine. When the doctor died, Hyland resigned from the Civil Service and came to Magill to give his mother-in-law all the assistance he could in the conduct of the wine enterprise, as well as the great happiness of having her daughter and grandchildren with her.

In 1881, Mary Penfold handed the management of her vineyard to Joseph Gillard, whose own vineyard and cellar she had recently bought, but she remained at The Grange, the name given by the doctor to the original homestead that he built in 1844, to the day of her death in 1895; she was a highly respected and well-beloved figure for many miles around.

Some idea may be had of the importance Magill had acquired under Mary Penfold's rule from an entry in her stockbook for 1881: there were at the time 107,000 gallons of wine, mostly if not wholly fortified wines of the port and sherry types, when the total stocks in South Australian cellars were estimated to add up to 312,000 gallons.

Under Gillard's management, however, it was decided to plant varieties of grapes more suitable for the making of dry table wines, both red and white, as the demand for lighter, unfortified wines had been growing, and, in 1891, the total acreage of the

Because the demand for Australian table wines is growing remarkably, many Australian vine-growers are increasing the acreage of their vineyards. Seaview Vineyard, at McLaren Vale, South Australia, has already established large-scale new plantings.

Grape-pickers at work at Penfold's Kalimna Estate Vineyard in the Barossa Valley.

Magill vineyard had reached 12,314 acres: they produced on an average a million gallons of wine a year, wines of different types for which there was a demand in various parts of Australia and even in New Zealand.

Thomas Francis Hyland and his wife had four children, two sons and two daughters. One daughter died young, at Magill, and her sister married and lived for the rest of her life in England. The two sons, Frank Astor Penfold Hyland, born in 1873, and his brother Herbert Leslie Penfold Hyland, born in 1875, served the family firm with devotion and skill. Frank bought the Dalwood homestead, vineyards and winery, near Branxton, in the Hunter River Valley of New South Wales in 1904.

Leslie Penfold Hyland moved to South Australia in 1900 to take control of the South Australian section of the company. He purchased the McLaren Vale cellar, south of Adelaide, a property worked for many years in conjunction with the Magill establishment. A year later, he decided to build at Nuriootpa, in the Barossa Valley, between Tanunda and Angaston, a winery, distillery and laboratory, which has made it possible for the firm to buy and process the grapes of a large number of Barossa Valley grape-growers.

In 1912 Frank Penfold Hyland bought the vineyard and winery which had been first planted and built by Captain William Minchin, at Minchinbury, north of Sydney, beyond Parramatta, at Rooty Hill. It was part of the original 1,000 acres given to Captain Minchin on his retirement from the army in 1819.

In 1913 the business was formed into a company, and Frank Penfold Hyland was chosen as its first managing director.

An entirely new venture for Penfold's was the building of a winery, distillery, and storage facilities eventually to cater for a million gallons of wine and brandy at Griffith, in the Murrumbidgee area of New South Wales. This was in support of the Australian authorities' decision to settle in the River Murray and Murrumbidgee areas a large number of soldiers who were returning from the First World War, and who, it was planned, should grow grapes under irrigation conditions. About the same time Penfolds also bought the Sparkling Vale property in the Hunter River Valley.

Leslie Penfold Hyland died in 1940, and his elder son, Francis William (Bill) died in 1946. Frank Penfold Hyland died in 1948, and his widow, Mrs Gladys Penfold Hyland, became chairman of the company. Jeffery, second son of Leslie, returned from active service in 1945, when he rejoined the company, became a director, and now holds the position of deputy chairman and managing director of the organization, which has become a public company.

Meanwhile the company's purchases of vineyards continued, including some 100 acres at Magill, all that was left of the original 232 acres acquired in 1842 by Patrick Auld and planted about ten years later. The original winery of the Auldana Company is also now the property of Penfold's and used by them mainly for their sparkling wines.

In 1945, Penfold's added two more properties to their group: the Modbury vineyards of 195 acres, a few miles north of Magill, and the Kalimna Estate, formerly owned by D. and J. Fowler Ltd., which is situated at Moppa, in the Barossa Valley, a few miles from Nuriootpa. Kalimna's 900 acres of vines gives it the distinction of being the largest vineyard in Australia.

In 1948 Penfold Vale, in the Hunter River Valley, was purchased by the company, and fifty acres were planted with various species of fine-quality white grapes. Penfold's

A steeply sloping site and stony ground were deliberately selected by G. Gramp and Sons for this experimental planting of Rhine Riesling grapes in the hills above Rowland Flat in the Barossa Valley in order to simulate as closely as possible the conditions in which the same variety of vine grows in its native Germany. The vineyard is called Steingarten.

also acquired, in the same year, the Matthews vineyard of fifteen and a half acres in the Hunter River Valley.

In 1960, Penfold's acquired the 723 acres of Wybong Park, now known as Dalwood Estate, between a creek which has never been known to dry up and the foothills of a range of mountains, forty-five miles west of Dalwood. After seeing the results from the new vines planted, they purchased in 1966 a neighbouring property of 555 acres. A new winery, built at a cost of $330,000, came into production in 1967 to process grapes from this area.

G. GRAMP AND SONS PTY. LTD.

Johann Gramp was born in 1819 at Eichig, close to Kulmbach, in Bavaria; his father was a well-known landowner and farmer, but, in 1837, young Johann left him and his brothers to see the sea and the world beyond. At Hamburg Johann joined the barque *Solway*, 400 tons, as a passenger, crossed the Atlantic to Rio de Janeiro and then back to the Cape of Good Hope, eventually reaching Kangaroo Island, off the South Australian coast. He stayed on Kangaroo Island for a while, but later moved to the mainland, where he first worked for the South Australian Company and then joined a baking business before taking up land of his own at Yatala, near Adelaide, where he built a house of red-gum logs.

In 1847 Johann Gramp moved to Jacob's Creek, a mile north-east of the site where the Orlando Winery now stands in the heart of the Barossa Valley. It was there that he planted a small vineyard, and in 1850, when his son Gustav was born, Johann Gramp made his first octave of wine: it was a white wine of a hock type, the forerunner of one of Gramp's popular *Carte Blanche*.

Slowly but steadily more grapes were planted and more wine was made until 1877, when Johann's eldest son took over from his father the conduct of affairs, moving to the present site of the Orlando Winery at Rowland Flat. By 1912 Gustav, ably aided by his two sons, Hugo and Fred, had built up a remarkably successful business which became a limited company under the name of G. Gramp and Sons Pty. Ltd. In 1920 Hugo Gramp became managing director of the company, and when he was tragically killed in an airliner that crashed near Melbourne in 1938, his brother, Fred, became managing director. Today, Fred's two sons, Sid and Keith, and Hugo's son Colin, the fourth generation, are giving the firm the benefit of their youth and industry.

In 1953 Orlando revolutionized the table-wine production in Australia by adopting the temperature- and pressure-controlled fermentation technique which had been developed in West Germany and Austria. It meant the construction of new buildings and the installation of the latest scientific wine-making equipment, but now the storage capacity at Orlando has reached four million gallons.

On 5 November 1956, Orlando again made history when it introduced the first naturally sweet effervescent wine in Australia under the name of Barossa Pearl.

Major developments also took place in the viticulture side of the business, and the company has now over 1,000 acres of vines in production, some in the Barossa Valley and some near Ramco, on the Murray River. Except for a little irrigating, the vineyards of the Barossa Valley depend upon natural rainfall and intense cultivation: the Ramco vineyards rely on irrigation by the overhead permanent-sprinkler system.

In addition to the grapes of its own vineyards, the firm purchases each year, at the time of the vintage, thousands of tons of grapes from hundreds of growers who find it much more satisfactory to sell out their ripe grapes than to attempt to process them.

The firm has its headquarters at Rowland Flat, South Australia, and its own offices in all the capital cities of Australia, as well as agents in New Zealand, Great Britain, Canada, the United States of America, Fiji, the Near East, the Far East, and East Africa.

S. SMITH AND SON PTY. LTD., YALUMBA

Samuel Smith was no boy of eighteen, like Johann Gramp, when he turned his back on his native land and sailed for Australia, in 1847; he was a man of thirty-five, a brewer at Wareham, in Dorset, with a wife and five young children, who, of course, were not asked but had to go.

After a long and most uncomfortable voyage round the Cape, the Smith family landed in South Australia. They squatted for a time by the River Torrens, at Klemzig, and then packed themselves and their few belongings into a bullock-wagon and slowly

Part of the port store at S. Smith and Son's Yalumba Winery at Angaston, South Australia. Port is matured in oak in a relatively warm part of the winery for twenty years or more.

trekked on and on for some fifty miles along the Barossa Valley until they came to a collection of shacks upon a site that has now become one of the three chief urban centres of the Barossa Valley, Angaston. The town was named after George Fife Angas, who was, in 1848, when the Smith family arrived, the "lord of the manor", or chief land-owner of the district.

Samuel Smith was given a job by Mr Angas in his garden and orchard, and Samuel soon realized that the soil and the climate were what most vines would love and that they would bring forth large quantities of grapes every year. It was then that he decided to plant a vineyard and that he bought from Mr Angas thirty acres of land: he called his property Yalumba, which is the Aboriginal word for "all the country around". Working by day and by moonlight, he planted his first vineyard in 1849, recording in later years that "it was a year of struggle—but God gave me wonderful strength, and my wife helped me in every possible way".

In 1852 "gold fever" hit the Colony, and Samuel Smith joined the rush to the neighbouring Colony of Victoria, leaving his wife to look after the children and the vineyard. It took him five weeks to reach Bendigo, in central Victoria, with two companions and a six-oxen team: they travelled for most of the way along the Murray River, where they were able to find fish and game for food.

Samuel Smith did not make a fortune when he reached the gold-fields, but after he had sunk sixteen shafts without success, on the seventeenth attempt—to use his own words—"the Lord prospered my labours". Four months later he returned to Adelaide, where he sold his gold for £300, which gave him the chance to buy another eighty acres, a plough, two horses and harness.

During her husband's absence, Mrs Samuel Smith, who was surely worth more than all the gold in Bendigo, had taken good care of the five children—one boy and four girls—as well as of the vineyard, and, on his return, Sam could and did go straight ahead with planting more vines, building storage cellars, making wine that was each year just a little better than the year before; so much so that within ten years "Yalumba" had become well known throughout South Australia as the name of one of the Colony's best wines. The fame of Yalumba reached England in 1866, when some Yalumba wines were sent to the International Exhibition in London and were awarded a bronze plaque.

In 1888, when Samuel Smith died, his only son, Sydney, who had been his father's partner for a number of years, took over the management of the estate. He was ably supported at first, and later succeeded by, his two sons, Percy, who managed affairs at home, and Walter, who travelled the world in search of markets for Yalumba wines. Walter, became affectionately known to a very large number of friends in many countries as "Tiger Smith" on account of his prowess as a big-game hunter.

In 1923 Percy Smith retired and a company was formed: two sons of Walter became directors, Sidney Hill Smith and Wyndham Hill Smith. Sidney Hill Smith was one

The winery at Yalumba, where the first grapes were planted in 1849 by Samuel Smith.

of the victims of the same air disaster in which Hugo Gramp was killed on 25 October 1938, and his brother Wyndham then became managing director and chairman of the company; he is now ably assisted by his late brother's two sons, Mark and John.

The 1938–40 period was one of particular importance to the company; it was then that Yalumba first produced Brandy on a large scale, and also secured overseas agencies for the distribution in South Australia and/or Western Australia of such spirits as Gilbey's Gin and Dewar's White Horse Whisky, thus becoming for the first time, general wine and spirit merchants.

Mark Hill Smith, after his return from service in the Navy during the Second World War, joined the company, the first of the fifth generation of the Smiths of Yalumba, and he is at present sales director.

At Yalumba, the scientific and technical aspects of the business are in charge of Rudolph Kronberger, a Viennese wine chemist who has now been with the company for more than thirty-five years and has done much to place the light table wines and the sherries of Yalumba in world class.

Upon the retirement of the late Harold Yates, who was with the company for fifty years as secretary, Mr Alfred A. Wark, a chartered accountant who joined the company upon his discharge from the R.A.A.F., became secretary to the main company and to various associate companies.

An important and encouraging new venture in which S. Smith and Son Pty. Ltd. have become interested is the re-establishment of the Pewsey Vale Vineyards, in the Barossa Ranges, near Lyndoch.

Pewsey Vale, 1,700 feet above sea-level, is one of the highest areas in which grapes are grown commercially in Australia. In 1847 a vineyard of Rhine Riesling, Semillon and Cabernet Sauvignon grapes was planted there by Joseph Gilbert, who, in his winery set amid gum-trees and gigantic outcrops of rock, produced red and white table wines of very high quality.

Gilbert's interest in table wines was remarkable in an era when most of the wine-makers of the Colony of South Australia were concentrating on sweet fortified wines. His wines were twice awarded the Gold Cup at the Adelaide Show, where he also won many first prizes, and in an international exhibition in 1886, a wine from this area won a Gold Medal and was acclaimed as "possessing true Rhine wine character".

The original Pewsey Vale Vineyards went out of production in 1927, but have now been redeveloped by a partnership between S. Smith and Son Pty. Ltd., and Mr G. Angas Parsons, the present proprietor of Pewsey Vale Station.

In 1961 an area of 150 acres was surveyed and contour-farm planned at Pewsey Vale, and by 1965, 110 acres had been planted on steep, sloping country with Rhine Riesling and Cabernet Sauvignon grapes.

The high altitude, rainfall higher than the local average and a relatively cool climate, account for the high quality of the grapes produced. The first young wines vintaged by Yalumba from the new vineyards in 1965 and 1966 are already remarkably soft and full, but are retaining their delicate character.

B. SEPPELT AND SONS PTY. LTD.

Near-famine conditions in most parts of Europe during the "Hungry Forties" of the nineteenth century led to a great deal of unrest and wholesale migration to lands of plenty in North America, and also to lands of mirage and hope in far-away Australia.

Joseph Ernst Seppelt was born in Silesia in 1813, and he was quite an important person in the forties at Wustewaltersdorf as the head of the family business engaged in the distillation and compounding of various liqueurs and cordials, as well as the making and selling of snuff, at a time when cigarettes had not yet been thought of and when snuff was considered the best if not the only preventive and cure of the common cold.

Joseph Ernst had a sizeable staff who had not been affected so far by the radical political propaganda of the day and who agreed, as business went from bad to worse, to accompany their chief when he decided to give up the struggle at home and try his luck in Australia. Which is how it happened that on 9 September 1849, Joseph Ernst Seppelt, his wife, their three children (two sons and one daughter), a group of skilled and semi-skilled employees and thirteen families from Wustewaltersdorf sailed together from Hamburg.

They reached Adelaide safely on 17 January 1850, and although Joseph Ernst had bought in London, through an agent, two eighty-acre blocks at Golden Grove and two acres of the new capital of South Australia, he parted with the two city acres, what might have been his "kingdom" for a horse. The whole party moved to nearby Klemzig, a settlement of German Lutheran migrants—three shiploads of them—who had been able to get away from Prussia and Frederick's religious intolerance in 1838 under the guidance of Pastor Augustus Kavel.

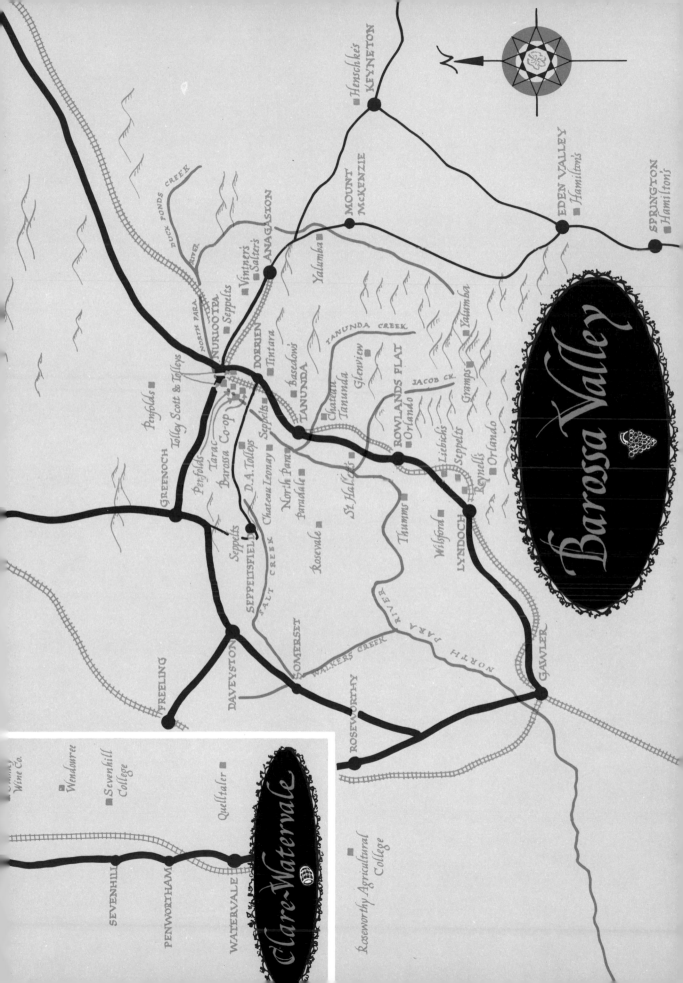

Joseph Ernst Seppelt, realizing that Golden Grove was not suitable for his purpose, took his time, being a sensible man, before deciding where to settle, and it was nearly a year after his party's arrival that he bought from Hermann Kook, a farmer at Tanunda, and probably one of Kavel's migrants, two Sections in the Hundred of Nuriootpa, Numbers 108 and 109, as well as Lots 21 and 24 in the township of Tanunda. The deal was registered in February 1852, Joseph Ernst being described as farmer and his address being given as Seppeltsfield.

Although Seppeltsfield might have been at the time the correct legal address, it was no home, and a great deal of work had to be done before it became the Seppelt homestead. In the meantime, the women and children of the new Silesian migrants were settled at Tanunda, while the men went to Seppeltsfield, four miles away, returning to Tanunda for the week-end and a well-deserved rest. Unfortunately, the young men from Wustewaltersdorf heard of the booming goldfields of Victoria, and most of them deserted their chief to try their luck on the diggings.

Joseph Ernst did not go to Bendigo or Ballarat: he stayed at Seppeltsfield and planted tobacco, and the plants grew only too well, bearing outsize leaves of great beauty but of no use at all for the making of tobacco and snuff. So Joseph Ernst gave up tobacco and planted corn, like the other farmers of the Barossa Valley, and he also planted a small vineyard, as most other farmers had done before him. He must have realized from the beginning that red wine needed keeping for a few years before being drunk, since he built a storage cellar immediately after he had built the dairy for his wife to make butter and cheese.

Joseph Ernst was only fifty-five years of age when he died in 1868. His son, Benno, was one of those rare men who have no wild oats to sow. He was twenty-one when he took up the work left unfinished by his father, and by the time he retired, in 1916, he had built up Seppeltsfield's vineyards, winery and distillery into the showplace that it has been ever since; by then also interstate branches had been opened and a vineyard and winery bought at Rutherglen, in Victoria.

Benno Seppelt's nine sons inherited their father's industry and business ability, steadily increasing the wealth and importance of their firm. Chateau Tanunda was purchased in 1916 and a property at Great Western in Victoria in 1918.

Oscar, eldest of the nine sons, was chairman of directors for twenty-three years, and was a great figure in the wine industry generally. He was followed in the company chairmanship by Leo for three years. Waldemar was for many years secretary and then general manager, and then finally chairman of the company following the death of Leo. Of the fourth generation, Ian, son of Waldemar, is now the senior executive of B. Seppelt and Sons and is also chairman of the Australian Wine Board. Robert, a past president of the South Australian Wine and Brandy Producers' Association, and of the Federal Wine and Brandy Producers' Council of Australia, and his brother John

Seppeltsfield Winery near Tanunda in the Barossa Valley, was founded in 1852 by Joseph Seppelt, a German settler. From modest beginnings Seppeltsfield has grown so large that it is almost a township in its own right.

(sales director of Seppelt's) are sons of Leo. Their cousins Bill and Karl are production manager and vineyard manager respectively and Benno is secretary. The fifth generation is now also represented in the business.

In recent years properties have been bought by Seppelt's at Qualco, near Waikerie; at Keppoch, twenty-five miles north-west of Narracoorte, in the south-eastern part of South Australia, and at Drumborg, near Portland, in the south-west corner of Victoria. New plantings at all these places are coming along well. Grapes from the latter two places will go to Great Western.

All told, the company owns 5,500 acres of land in South Australia, Victoria and New South Wales.

THOMAS HARDY AND SONS PTY. LTD.

Devonshire and Somerset appear to have been a particularly happy hunting-ground for the Colonial Land and Immigration Commissioners to recruit immigrants for the

Stacks of maturing sherry at Mildara Winery, Merbein, Victoria.

The underground cellars at B. Seppelt and Sons' vineyard at Great Western, Victoria, are known as "drives" because they were dug by gold-miners in the last century. Each "drive" is named after a famous Australian.

Colony of South Australia during its formative years. Most of the 243 migrants embarked at Plymouth in April 1850, under the Commissioners' authority, on the 640-ton barque *British Empire*—thirty-nine married couples with 169 children, and ninety-one single adults—were West of England folk. Two of the male single adults, Thomas Hardy and John Holbrook, who were entered as labourers in the ship's papers, were in fact young farmers of Gittisham, near Honiton, and two of the "single female adults" were sisters, Joanna and Mary Anna Hardy, cousins from Somerset of Thomas Hardy. Three years later Joanna married her cousin Thomas, and Mary Anna married John Holbrook.

Thomas Hardy was twenty years of age when the *British Empire* reached Adelaide on 14 August 1850: he had to stretch his legs after the 106 days' voyage, and he had to get a job.

It was John Reynell, also a Devon man, who gave Thomas Hardy a job on his farm thirteen miles from Adelaide, but, after twelve months, Thomas moved to Normanville, a cattle station thirty-five miles from Adelaide. It was there that he heard of the booming goldfields of Victoria and that he came to what proved to be a very profitable arrangement with a firm of butchers operating on the diggings: he contracted to drive cattle from Normanville to the goldfields where the hungry, hard-working gold-diggers were all beef-eaters. After eighteen months, Thomas Hardy had amassed sufficient capital to buy some land by the River Torrens, near Adelaide, build a home, and marry his cousin Joanna. They called their homestead "Bankside". The sixteen and a half acres that he bought in 1853 had never been cultivated before, but Thomas Hardy was not long in clearing the first three acres to plant Shiraz and Grenache grapes in one acre and fruit trees in the other two acres. Where and how Thomas learned to grow grapes and to make wine we cannot tell (it may have been during the year he spent with John Reynell), but we do know that by 1857 he was making wine that he no doubt enjoyed drinking, and that in 1859 he actually shipped two hogsheads of his wine to London.

By 1862, the little vineyard at Bankside had grown appreciably, and Thomas made 1,500 gallons that year, when the total yield of the South Australian vineyards added up to 312,000 gallons.

During the sixties, the quantity of wine that came from the Bankside Winery increased prodigiously from year to year. It doubled from 1863 to 1864, and reached 14,000 gallons in 1865. Half the grapes crushed at Bankside during the latter year had been purchased from a number of small growers, and these purchases gave Thomas Hardy a better chance to improve the quality of his wines through the judicious blending of different grapes.

Unfortunately, the demand for wine did not grow nearly as fast as the supply: both New South Wales and Victoria put up high tariffs to protect their own vine-growers from competing South Australia wines, and sales of Australian wines in London had fallen alarmingly. Many vine-growers failed to sell their grapes at anything like the right price and pulled up their vines: the vineyard acreage of South Australia fell from 6,630 acres to 4,340 acres between 1865 and 1885.

A great enthusiast and apostle of wine at the time was Dr A. C. Kelly, a popular general practitioner in Adelaide who had talked a number of his rich friends into providing the money for the purchase of a property of some 700 acres five miles to the north-east of McLaren Vale, with a vineyard that had been planted in the early fifties by a Mr Manning.

The property was called Tintara and the new company formed to buy it was named the Tintara Vineyards Company. It had a good start, but came to grief at a time of depression during the late sixties. In 1873, the Tintara Vineyards Company was bankrupt and there was no bid for its vineyards, winery and storage cellar full to overflowing with big, black, sound, strong "Burgundy", which was the type of wine Dr Kelly had always preferred to all others and had always recommended to his patients.

As a matter of fact, it was the "wine for heroes", which was more popular than any other at the time: there was a demand for it, if only one knew where the demand happened to be. Thomas Hardy evidently knew. He was the one and only bidder for the bankrupt Tintara Vineyards Company and he paid for the property with the money he made by the sale of the company's own stock of wine.

Thomas Hardy appears to have gained not merely greater experience with age, but even greater energy. He set about to make the best of his new and very much larger property, clearing more ground and planting more vineyards with none but the choicest varieties of vines. He built homes for the permanent staff and huts for the grape-pickers employed temporarily at vintage time, and also constructed a bigger cellar. In 1878 he bought the disused McLaren Vale flour-mill, sold the machinery and turned it into a new winery.

Thomas Hardy had a full life and a happy one: he was blessed with three sons who all inherited the love of the grape that their father had acquired in the sunny land of his adoption. Those three young men each dealt with the many problems of production and salemanship of what had become the Hardy Empire, and they did so in such an efficient manner that their father and mother were able to pay visits to their native land and once to the United States of America.

By 1895, Thomas Hardy's firm had become the largest South Australian wine-producing concern, and it is still one of the largest. When Thomas Hardy died in 1912, on the eve of his 82nd birthday, two of his sons had predeceased him, but one of his grandsons and four of his great-grandsons are now in charge and carry out the Hardy tradition of quality and enterprise.

The surviving grandson is Kenneth T. Hardy, chairman of directors, whose services over many years to wine industry organizations, notably the Australian Wine Board and the Australian Wine Research Institute, led to the award of an O.B.E. by the Queen. Fourth-generation Hardys in the business are Tom (managing director), Jim and David, the three sons of the late T. M. Hardy; and Robert, son of Kenneth. (T. M. Hardy, a distinguished member of the third generation, was killed in the same 1938 plane crash that took the lives of the then chief executives of Orlando and Yalumba.)

The head office and sparkling-wine cellars are at Mile End, just across the parklands from the City of Adelaide; and there are Tintara wineries in the Barossa Valley and at

Waikerie in the Murray Valley. The company has offices and cellars in Melbourne, Sydney and Launceston.

CHRIS HOFFMANN

Samuel Hoffmann was born in 1795 at Richenau, in Silesia, and was a trooper in the Prussian army under General Blucher, at Waterloo in 1815. Then he became a farmer and a father, apparently a better father than farmer, since he had one daughter and eight sons but did not make a success of farming. He applied time after time for a migrant permit, so that he could escape from religious persecution, but did not get one until he was fifty-three years of age. So, in 1847, Samuel and his wife and their nine children left Hamburg on the sailing-ship *Gellert* and reached Adelaide a few days before Christmas, a very different Christmas from any of the white Christmases they had known before.

Grapes coming in at Thomas Hardy's Winery at McLaren Vale, South Australia.

In 1848 Samuel Hoffmann took up the land by the Para River, near Tanunda, in the Barossa Valley, which his descendants own to this day. Sam's daughter Johanne remained single, and seven of Sam's sons went to live and to work elsewhere, but Christian, the baby of the family, who was only four years old in 1848, stayed at home until his father's death in 1878, and to the day of his own death in 1915. It was he who planted the first vineyard, a small one. His son, however, Christian II, who was born in 1868 and died in 1947, not only built a winery, but greatly enlarged the vineyard: he really devoted the whole of his life to viticulture and winemaking. So did his only son, Erwin, who was born in 1898, and is head of the firm today. Erwin also has a son, Bruce, born in 1930, and now Bruce also has two sons, the sixth generation in the direct male line.

EDWARDS AND CHAFFEY PTY. LTD.

Seaview Wines is the name under which the wines of the centenarian Hope Farm are marketed today by Edwards and Chaffey Pty. Ltd., the present owners of the Hope Vineyards, renamed by them Seaview after the name of the summer residence of a former Chief Justice of South Australia, Sir Samuel Way, whose estate happened to be close by.

Hope Farm was first built and named by a Cambridgeshire man, George Pitches Manning, who came to Adelaide with his family, in 1850. He bought 160 acres of virgin land south of Adelaide, four miles north of the townships of Bellevue and Gloucester, in McLaren Vale. He built a house, cleared the scrub, tilled the ground and planted some wheat. Some nine miles nearer Adelaide, at Reynella, there were flourishing vineyards planted in 1838, and they were too good an example not to be followed. So, in 1850, George Manning planted a vineyard of thirty acres and built a winery at Hope Farm, and, soon after, there was also a still on the edge of the bamboo-fringed duck-pond, between the house and the cellars, with a cooling-pipe under the water.

Whether George Manning had the benefit of some expert wine-maker's guidance or not we cannot tell, but he managed somehow not only to make wine, but wine for which there was a ready sale among the farmers for miles around. The brandy which Manning made was no liqueur brandy, but his vinous pride was his "Port": it was made from both Shiraz and Cabernet Sauvignon grapes and, probably, a stunning dose of new brandy.

The winery at Chateau Tahbilk, in Victoria. Chateau Tahbilk vineyard was established in 1860 and is now owned by the Purbrick family. The winery and cellars have been classified by the National Trust of Australia as buildings of historical and architectural interest.

Manning died in 1872, a poor man, as many another good man has died since then. His sons, however, managed to save Hope Farm from the clutches of the mortgagees, and they carried on their father's good work for twenty years. In 1892 they sold Hope Farm to a young Englishman, Walter H. Craven, who enlarged, improved, and modernized the homestead, winery, cellars, and vineyards: it was during his lifetime that the name of Hope Farm was changed to Hope Vineyards. Walter Craven's only son was killed during the First World War, and he, himself, died soon after, when Hope Vineyards became the property of Craven's former manager, Mr G. W. Kay, and was sold by him, in 1948, to Ferguson and Chaffey—Edwards and Chaffey, since 1951.

One of the Seaview Estate's distinctions, besides a whole range of wines from fair to fine, is their plantation of olive trees responsible for a yearly harvest of olives.

WOODLEY WINES PTY. LTD.

On the spurs in the Glen Osmond Hills, and among the "Dimples", or the hollows between them, some "whitish, quartzy-looking stones" were picked up in 1838, according to J. W. Bull, in his book *Early Experiences of Colonial Life in South Australia*. This Mr Bull had at the time obtained an option to buy the location, but, on second consideration, thinking that the place was too stony and would be very difficult to clear and to plant, he gave up his option to his friend, Mr Osmond Gilles, Colonial Treasurer for the Colony of South Australia, who proposed to build on the site a "suburban residence". The next year, 1839, galena—that is, lead sulphide, the chief ore of lead—was found on the spot; Mr Osmond Gilles then resigned his Treasurership and leased the site to Woodley, a company formed to mine the silver–lead deposits which proved to be there.

Mr Osmond Gilles received large sums of money every year as royalties from the company, and he gave the location his name, Glen Osmond, by which it has been known ever since. He also planted a vineyard at Glen Osmond in 1856, and he appointed his friend and benefactor Mr Bull manager of his winery and vineyard.

Rich as the Woodley silver–lead mine was, it was to peter out after only a few years, and the Cornish miners who had been employed there went back to Cornwall, leaving behind to Mr Osmond Gilles and his heirs a remarkable system of tunnels cut deep into

Good, mature oak plays an important role in the production of fine table wines, brandies and sherries, and Australian wineries have invested millions of dollars in the importation of French and American oak for vat storage. The photograph was taken in the storage area at the Stanely Wine Co. at Clare, South Australia.

Ben Chaffey sampling one of the wines made at Edwards and Chaffey's Seaview Vineyard, McLaren Vale, South Australia.

the hillside, with occasional shafts for ventilation. Mr Osmond Gilles found that these tunnels made wonderful cellars in which to store and mature, under ideal conditions, the wines of his nearby vineyards, wines which have been called Woodley wines for the past one hundred years.

Mr Osmond Gilles must have been a red-wine man: he planted mostly Shiraz, Malbec and Mataro grapes, but some Grenache and Verdelho as well. After his death, his nephew Mr Osmond Horne Gilles succeeded to the property, and at Mr O. H. Gilles's death, it passed to Mr Lewis W. Gilles. In 1892 Mr Benno Weidenbach purchased the property and extended the vineyard as far as Milne's Road; he also planted a hedge of olive trees on the northern and western boundaries of the vineyard, and the trees are still there. In 1900 Glen Osmond was purchased by Mr H. V. Pridmore, who was president of the Vignerons' Association. At his death, his widow married Mr Ernest Whitington, who was on the staff of Adelaide's chief morning daily, the *Advertiser*.

In 1924 Lieutenant Colonel David Fulton, former commanding officer of the Third Light Horse during the First World War, bought the property, and, in 1926, when Captain C. E. Hawker joined the firm, the Woodley Wines Company Ltd. was floated.

When Colonel Fulton retired, Mr Tony Nelson became managing director. Vienna born and an expert wine-maker, he had joined Woodleys on 1 July 1940.

In 1963 Woodley Wines Ltd. was sold to a Melbourne company which has retained Mr Nelson as its consultant.

H. M. MARTIN AND SON PTY. LTD.

Sir Rowland Hill will always be remembered as the Penny Post man, and nobody remembers that in 1834 he was a member of the Provisional Committee of the South Australian Association, and that in 1835 he was secretary to the Colonization Commissioners for the Colony. It was he who must have given to one of his nieces, Caroline, the wife of Francis Clark, of Hazelwood, in the Hagley Road, Edgbaston, Birmingham, the idea of leaving England and coming to settle in South Australia with her large family.

They reached Adelaide in 1850, and it was their seventh son, Henry Septimus Clark, only fifteen years of age at the time, who planted the first vines of the original Stonyfell Vineyard in July 1858, with a friend of his called Robert Slape, probably where the Stonyfell Quarry office now stands, about a mile from the Auldana Vineyard at Magill. They planted only one acre and a half of Mataro the first year, and two years later twenty-five acres of Black Portugal, two and a half acres of Muscat, and five acres of Sercial from Madeira and Doradillo from Spain. The two-storeyed cellars which Henry Clark built at the time from locally quarried stone are still in an excellent state of preservation. The wine was made in a lean-to building adjoining the top floor, and there was during the first years no machinery of any kind. The grapes were picked in the daytime and trodden underfoot in the cool of the evening. The wine was stored in 300-gallon casks, some of them made from imported timber and others from local red-gum, some of them still in use.

Keen as Henry Clark was about his vineyard and his wine, they were more a hobby for him than a wholetime and profitable occupation, which is why he held an official position as secretary and engineer to the East Torrens District Council, a district embracing a large area of the adjacent hilly country. This made it all the more imperative for Henry Clark to have a reliable partner who would give the whole of his time to vineyards and cellar. Joseph Crompton, aged twenty-two, lately arrived from England with a letter of introduction to the Clark family, was appointed manager, at a salary of £120 a year, of the firm formed in 1862 by Henry Clark, his brother Algernon and Joseph Crompton, under the name of Clark and Crompton, wine-growers and wine-makers of Stonyfell. In 1864 Henry Clark died; in 1866, Joseph Crompton married Susan Mary, a sister of his remaining partner, Algernon Clark, and in 1873 he bought out Algernon Clark's share in the partnership and became sole owner of Stonyfell, but the name of the firm remained Clark and Crompton until 1880.

During the seventies and early eighties, production continued at Stonyfell at a steady rate of about 9,000 gallons of wine a year, but Joseph Crompton experienced great difficulties in selling his wine through travellers and agents who sometimes played false, and at a time when means of transport were practically non-existent. During the financial crisis of the early eighties, Joseph Crompton lost the fruit of so many years of hard work, although he remained in his business under the supervision of trustees appointed by the Bank of Adelaide, until the bank succeeded in finding a buyer; that is, until 1888, when the bank transferred Stonyfell to Henry Dunstan, a quarryman and road contractor who took no interest whatever in vineyards and cellars but devoted all his energy to working the Stonyfell quarries.

The new owner took as his secretary Henry Maydwell Martin, who came from England in 1851 and married one of Henry Clark's sisters: he was Joseph Crompton's brother-in-law. When, in 1892, Henry Dunstan decided to separate, in a business manner, the quarries and the vineyards of Stonyfell, Henry Martin was appointed manager of the new firm of H. Dunstan and Co., winegrowers, Stonyfell Vineyards. Under Henry Martin's management new and choice vines were planted, and many improvements were carried out in the buildings of the winery. Means were also found to organize the sale of Stonyfell wines in the different States of Australia, and overseas: the Stonyfell wines won a high distinction in 1889 at the International Paris Exhibition and at the Franco-British Exhibition of 1908 in London.

In 1902 Ronald H. Martin, younger son of Henry M. Martin, joined his father as partner at Stonyfell, and they bought the stock and plant at Stonyfell from Henry

Many vineyards close to Adelaide have been submerged under the advancing tide of bricks and mortar. There are some survivors, however, such as Stonyfell, owned by H. M. Martin and Son.

Another view of Stonyfell Vineyard. The first vines at Stonyfell were planted in 1858 by Henry Septimus Clark, son of an English immigrant. Clark was only fifteen at the time.

Dunstan, leased the cellar and vineyards, and traded as H. M. and R. H. Martin Stonyfell Vineyards, until 1926, when it was decided to form a limited liability company as H. M. Martin and Son Ltd.

Henry Martin died in 1936, aged eighty-nine, and his son Ronald then became chairman of the board; during Ronald's regime Stonyfell became well equipped with modern buildings and efficient machinery. Ronald was killed in a car accident in 1950.

The present management of Stonyfell is in the hands of Ronald's son, Henry M. Martin II, as chairman and managing director. One of the directors is Michael Auld, O.B.E., great-grandson of Patrick Auld, of Auldana, who had been general manager, and then managing director, from the time of Ronald's death until January 1962.

W. SALTER AND SON PTY. LTD.

William Salter was born at Exeter in 1804, and he evidently saw little hope of a success-ful career in England, since he accepted, in 1839, an offer from Messrs. King and Co., merchants, of London, to be their agent in the Colony of South Australia, barely three years old at the time. So William Salter landed at the embryo city of Adelaide, in December 1839 with a young wife and three very young children. Conditions must have been primitive—and more than William Salter's wife could stand: she died, but he married another and tougher one who looked after his three young children until they were able to look after themselves.

William Salter must have heard a good deal about the fortunes being made in those days by watching cattle and sheep growing fat on fertile virgin lands; so much so that in 1844 he decided to try his luck as a farmer and trekked fifty miles from Adelaide to a spot near Angaston, well up the Barossa Valley. He built a good house of stone, which stands to this day as a monument to the incredible faith and good luck of a merchant's agent becoming architect, builder and farmer without, apparently, any training whatever.

William Salter first went in for cattle, but too many others were doing the same and there was a glut of meat, with the inevitable consequence of a fall in prices. So William Salter turned to sheep, with the help of his eldest son, Edward, aged ten, as shepherd and night-watchman. (There was no fencing at the time.) Wool prices were good, and William Salter became one of the local worthies, being made treasurer of the first District Council of Angaston in 1853.

Soon after—what appeared to be a great stroke of luck—copper was found on some of the land of Mamre Brook, the name which William Salter had given to his estate. Machinery was imported and Cornish miners also; mining started, and some copper there was, but not enough to pay after a dozen years, and the mine was closed in the late sixties.

In the meantime, the young shepherd of ten had become a man of twenty-two when, in 1859, he entered into a partnership with his father, and founded the firm of W. Salter and Son, vine-growers. After cattle, sheep, and copper, why not grapes? There were others in the Barossa Valley who grew grapes and made wine, so that the Salters, father and son, might as well try their luck at the game.

That is just what they did, and they won. They first planted a vineyard of ten acres at the eastern end of the property with Shiraz vines. Near it they built a shed where the wine was to be made, and a cellar where it would be kept. The degree of adaptability displayed by the men of those heroic days is simply fantastic; for instance, young Edward, who had very little schooling of any kind, kept a "Vigneron's Journal" much better than many a prize-winner of South Australia's Roseworthy Agricultural College of today.

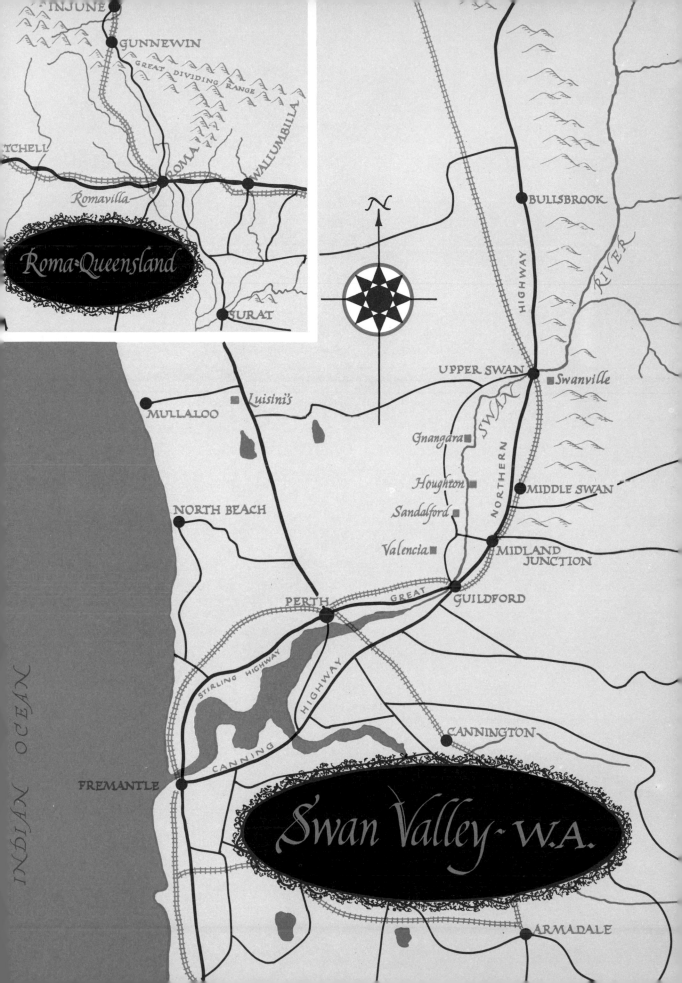

INJUNE

GUNNEWIN

GREAT DIVIDING RANGE

TCHELL

ROMA

WALLUMBILLA

Romavilla

Roma·Queensland

SURAT

N

BULLSBROOK

HIGHWAY

RIVER

UPPER SWAN

Swanville

MULLALOO

Luisini's

SWAN

Gnangara

NORTHERN

Houghton

MIDDLE SWAN

NORTH BEACH

Sandalford

Valencia

MIDLAND
JUNCTION

PERTH

GREAT

GUILDFORD

STIRLING HIGHWAY

HIGHWAY

CANNING

CANNINGTON

INDIAN OCEAN

FREMANTLE

Swan Valley · W.A.

ARMADALE

The first vintage of Salter *Père et Fils* was that of 1862, and Edward recorded that eight pickers, between 20 March and 31 March, gathered enough grapes to keep three treaders fully employed crushing the grapes, from which four hogsheads of must a day were obtained. Fermentation went on merrily during three days in casks of various shapes and sizes which happened to be available, and the first vintage brought in 1,800 gallons—quite an auspicious start.

It seems strange that the Salters went on making wine, as recorded in Edward's Journal during ten years, before devising means to cool the overheating of the fermenting must in vats and casks: they did this in 1891 for the first time by running cold water from a deep well through copper pipes in the vats. It appears that they bought a screw-press and tried it for the 1863 vintage, but they found it unsatisfactory, and treading continued to be the rule up to and including 1884. Treading was done in treading-boxes by men wearing knee-high boots specially made by a local boot-maker named Schulz, who charged twenty-five shillings a pair.

The Salter partnership took no risks about the keeping quality of their wines; from the 1863 vintage onwards all their wines were fortified soon after the end of fermentation or just before fermentation was completed; their early wines all had over 17 per cent of absolute alcohol, and some had as much as 19 per cent. They were no nursery wines.

The Barossa Valley has many rural charms, but it is not in an ideal situation for reaching overland and overseas markets, which were all the more indispensable to the Salters because too many people in the Valley made wine for themselves and their friends. Edward Salter, writing to one of his friends, in 1890, gives a clear picture of the difficulties he had to face: "One of our first transactions in wine was to send 50 hogsheads of wine to London, and after waiting two years for account of sales, we had to supplement the loss of all the wine and the casks, which cost 20s. each, with a cheque for £50. This transaction brought us into debt. Besides this shipment, we sent trial lots to Calcutta, Mauritius, and Brisbane with the result that we got no returns whatsoever. The wines sent were good and sound but were unknown and not after any well-known type. Two other pioneer wine-growers, who like our own firm have since succeeded very well, had the same experience on a larger scale."

Edward Salter then decided to visit all the more populous cities of Victoria and New South Wales to sell his wine himself; this he did until his father's death in 1871, and in 1872 he engaged a traveller, Alfred Birks, who introduced the Saltram wines in New Zealand. An arrangement which was made in 1882 between W. Salter and Son and Thomas Hardy and Sons, wine-merchants of Adelaide, opened the London market for the Saltram wines, the Adelaide firm paying a flat rate for all the wines made by Salter, and being responsible for their marketing. This arrangement lasted ten years: the sale of Saltram wines in England had been firmly established by then.

Quelltaler Vineyard is situated among rolling hills at Watervale, South Australia. The vineyard, first planted in 1865 is owned by H. Buring and Sobels.

In 1913, when Edward Salter died, aged seventy-six, the management of the firm which he had built with such courage and foresight had been in the hands of one of his sons, Leslie Salter, since 1902, and it was he who remained responsible for the fortunes of the firm until 1937. As a member of the South Australian Wine-Makers' Association and of the Federal Viticultural Council, Leslie Salter and Ronald Martin of Stonyfell, another member of both bodies, became great friends and eventually partners. In 1920, when W. Salter and Son became a limited liability company, Ronald Martin was its first chairman and Leslie Salter its first managing director. In 1941, the firm of W. Salter and Son Pty. Ltd. became a subsidiary of H. M. Martin and Son Pty. Ltd. when the latter purchased the shares of the former.

RYECROFT VINEYARDS PTY. LTD.

Ryecroft Vineyard at McLaren Flat was known as Ryecroft Farm when it was bought by Frederick Wilkinson in 1884. Wilkinson planted his first vines in 1886 and had his first vintage in 1895. In 1919 Ryecroft was sold to Jim Ingoldby, who "inherited" Wilkinson's wine-maker, Aubrey Chapman. Chapman was wine-maker until his death in 1957, when Jim Ingoldby Junior took over the job of wine-maker.

Ryecroft Estate covers 200 acres, of which 160 acres are under vines. About 100,000 gallons is the normal average output of wine. About 60,000 gallons of sweet wine are sold in bulk for the overseas market, but Ryecroft's main preoccupation has always been its dry red wines, of which about 34,000 gallons are made annually from Shiraz grapes and about 8,000 gallons from Cabernet. Ryecroft once used to sell its entire output to one or other of the great wine organizations, but since 1954 has been marketing pure Cabernet and Shiraz wines as estate bottlings. About 5,000 gallons of Cabernet and 6,000 gallons of Shiraz are now bottled on the estate each year and released only after at least three years' ageing in wood and bottle. Ryecroft has plans to market the whole of its Cabernet as a prestige estate wine.

H. BURING AND SOBELS LTD.

It was the explorer Edwin John Eyre who chose the site, seventy-five miles north of Adelaide, where Captain John Ainsworth Horrocks settled in 1840, with a mountain at the back and a gentle valley before him—a valley which the Aborigines called Manoora, meaning "The Vale of the Spring". The mountain is now called Mount Horrocks and the flourishing vineyards in the valley, now called Springvale, are the vineyards of Messrs. H. Buring and Sobels.

The first vineyard of Springvale was a small one planted in 1865 by Francis Treloar. The soil is chiefly calcareous, the altitude is 1,300 feet above sea-level, and the average rainfall twenty-six inches—three highly satisfactory conditions for the growing of quality grapes in the open. Francis Treloar sold his property, the vineyard and the grazing land, to Walter Watson Hughes (later Sir Walter Hughes), who left it at his death, to one of his nephews, James Richman. In 1889 T. G. Hermann Buring and Carl A. Sobels, entered into partnership, bought the Springvale Vineyard from Richman and founded the firm of H. Buring and Sobels.

The partners were men of courage and vision: they uprooted most of the grapes in the vineyard and replaced them with much better ones, bent as they were from the start on making none but the best wine that the location of their vineyard was suited for: it was this policy ,which was also that of their sons, and is now also that of their grandsons, which has gained for the wines of Quelltaler, the name under which the firm markets its wine, the world-wide reputation which it deserves and enjoys.

In 1900 the twenty-one-year partnership of Hermann Buring and Charles Sobels was changed to a limited liability company, when the eldest sons of the two senior partners were admitted to the board, A. W. R. Buring and E. E. Sobels, and they, in their turn, could count on the assistance of their sons in due course. Hermann Buring died in 1919 and Charles Sobels in 1923.

For many years now it has been the tradition of the firm for the Sobels family to attend to the production of the wines at Springvale, while distribution and marketing throughout Australasia, as well as many parts of the world, are handled from Quelltaler House, Adelaide, the firm's headquarters in Australia.

LEO BURING PTY. LTD.

After having served for thirty-two years in various wine-making businesses as manager, technical adviser, and governing director, Leo Buring in 1931 formed his own business, Leo Buring Pty. Ltd. This company helped bring about a more widespread interest in the drinking of light wines by its production and mass-selling of a semi-sweet white table wine, Rinegolde, in a broad-based green bottle—quite a novelty when it was introduced.

Leo Buring was later honoured over many years as the doyen of the Australian wine industry; he died in 1961 at the age of eighty-five. The company he founded is now a subsidiary of Lindeman's Wines Pty. Ltd.

Incidentally, the name Rinegolde is adapted from the German *"reines gold"*, meaning "pure gold"—a reference to the wine's colour, the makers disclaiming any association with Rhine wine. A semi-sparkling pearl-wine type of Rinegolde was recently introduced.

Chateau Leonay at Tanunda, in the Barossa Valley, is an important cellar of this company; it produces some very fine white and red table wines.

BLEASDALE VINEYARDS PTY. LTD.

Frank Potts was born in the South of England in 1815 and died in South Australia in 1890. He never had an Old School Tie: he learnt to use brain and brawn at sea. A "powder-monkey" on board one of King George's warships when only nine years old, he was given his discharge in 1836 from H.M.S. *Challenger* at twenty-one, and very soon after, on 23 July 1836, he was aboard H.M.S. *Buffalo*, one of the 176 passengers who sailed from Plymouth on that day with Captain John Hindmarsh, the first Governor of South Australia.

H.M.S. *Buffalo* reached Holdfast Bay in December 1836, and Frank Potts was most likely present on 28 December, at the ceremony of the proclamation of the new Colony at Glenelg, now a suburb of Adelaide.

Ships were the first and the lifelong love of Frank Potts, but he also loved the Australian red-gums. He was never happier than when tackling a rough red-gum log in his sawpit, turning out length after length of quartering, joists, slabs, and so on, with which he not only put up houses and sheds, but built fast yachts and a river paddle-boat, as well as carts, footbridges, ploughs, wine-vats and casks, and a monumental wine-press.

An old lever press at Bleasdale Winery, Langhorne Creek, South Australia. The press, built in 1895, was originally powered by a two-man capstan. Its dimensions are: Overall height, twenty-three feet; overall length, forty-three feet; weight of lever, three and a half tons, capacity of each cage, two and a half tons.

Like most early settlers, Frank Potts had a farm: he also had eight sons and four daughters, but he was nearly fifty years of age when he planted a vineyard. The site that he chose, on both banks of the Bremer, at Langhorne Creek, was on rich alluvial soil which had to be cleared of giant gum-trees, and Frank Potts also built a weir in order to control the flood-waters of the river when in spate. He had the benefit of the guidance of his friend, the Reverend John Ignatius Bleasdale, D.D.—whose name he gave to his estate—a prominent Member of the Royal Society of Victoria. Dr Bleasdale had spent most of his early life in Portugal and possessed an intimate knowledge of viticulture, and it was probably on his advice that Frank Potts built up a pumping device, worked by bullock-power, that enabled him to irrigate his river-side vineyard and to harvest from six to ten tons of grapes an acre.

Today, the vineyard that Frank Potts planted a hundred years ago still bears witness to his foresight and enterprise: it is still owned and managed by some of his descendants, who, in 1948, formed a company under the name of Bleasdale Vineyards Ltd.

C. A. HENSCHKE AND CO.

Leaving Angaston and the Barossa Valley behind, the road to Clare rises for a dozen or so miles to the eastern fringe of the Barossa Ranges, and the flourishing district of Keyneton. But Keyneton has known better days; it once had a brewery of its own—Krieger's—and many more well-to-do and more thirsty citizens and farmers than there are now.

The land around Keyneton is more open than that of the Barossa Valley: by no means flat, but a jumble of billowing downs, sparsely wooded, with poorer soil—hence not so good for general farming, but much better for the planting of vineyards and the making of quality wines. This is why there were five wineries—and all of them had large vineyards—some fifty years ago in this area, which was called by the early settlers, all of them German origin, North Rhine because it reminded them of the open and rather barren country north of Aachen. Today there is still a Keyneton church known as the North Rhine Church, and the only winery is still known as the North Rhine Winery. Evidently competition from Barossa Valley wineries, with their greater yield of grapes to the acre and their greater facilities of transport to Adelaide, was too much for all of the old wineries but one—Henschke's.

Although Henschke's Winery is the only winery left in the Keyneton district, there are still a number of farmers who grow grapes and sell them to Henschke's to be processed into wine, and the area under vines is now gradually increasing again.

Cyril Henschke is the managing director of C. A. Henschke and Co. today, and it was his great-grandfather who first bought the land where the winery stands, and who first farmed it, about one hundred years ago. Great-grandfather Henschke's son, Paul Gotthard Henschke, greatly improved and enlarged his father's farm, and, in the sixties, he planted the first vineyard as a side-line; he made just enough wine for his own large family, and for nearby farmers, who, most likely, also had large families of their own, as was the fashion in those days: they used to call those local wine sales the "cottage-door" business, which was unrecorded and untaxed.

Paul Gotthard Henschke lived to a ripe old age, and when he died in 1914, his son Paul Alfred Henschke greatly developed the vineyard of his father's farm, and he decided that he had better make wine on a right and proper commercial basis to meet the rising cost of living: he had to feed, clothe and educate seven daughters and four sons. Ten of his children left him: they went in search of easier and more engaging prospects in other parts of Australia, but his son Cyril stayed with him, and together they built a new capacious fermenting cellar in 1949, and additions to the older premises.

Cyril Henschke, in sole charge of C. A. Henschke and Co. since 1955, has no ambition to sell all sorts of wines and to make a fortune; he is quite satisfied to make the best dry reds and dry whites that can be made from the grapes of his own vineyard and those which he buys from growers of the district. His Mount Edelstone Claret, for instance, is a dry red wine with a distinctive character of its own, due partly to the care with which it is made from Shiraz grapes, but chiefly to the fact that the three hundred feet higher altitude of Henschke's vineyard is responsible for Henschke's dry red having less body but more bouquet than Shiraz-made dry reds of the Barossa Valley.

The white grapes, mostly Rieslings, which other growers of the district sell to Henschke to be processed, do not lose their identity: each pressing's wine is kept by itself until ready to be bottled, and when the time comes for the bottle to be labelled and marketed, the label bears the name of the grower from whose grapes the wine in the bottle was made, besides, of course, Henschke's name.

One of Cyril Henschke's own favourites is his White Frontignac, a pleasant, semi-dry white wine, made from specially selected bunches of white Frontignac grapes from Cyril Henschke's own vineyard.

STANLEY WINE COMPANY PTY. LTD.

The Stanley Wine Company was established in 1894 in a highly suitable stretch of the Clare country, a district of South Australia long known for the high quality of its dry table wines. In 1903, the directors of the company were Dr O. W. Smith, Mr John Christison (managing director), Mr J. H. Knappstein, Mr Magnus Badger, and Mr Alfred Basedow (general manager). J. H. Knappstein gradually bought out his partners: by 1912 he had gained full control, and he retained it until his death in 1919. Since then, his one daughter and his sons have owned and managed the company. In 1948 the company established vineyards in the Watervale area, south of Clare.

There are now six members of the Knappstein family working for the company,

*Peter Weste, wine-maker
for the Stanley Wine Co.,
drawing off a sample of one of
his 1965 reds for testing.
The company's vineyards
are at Clare, South Australia.*

which accounts for the fact that its vineyards now cover no less than 540 acres, and its winery has become one of the largest and most up-to-date in South Australia.

In 1962, the company announced that £30,000 had been spent upon new plantations, refrigeration and other modern equipment, such as two 12,000-gallon Flexiglass-lined steel tanks, six 10,000-gallon concrete and six 1,000-gallon oaks. Fermenting facilities were also improved by twelve 1,400-gallon tanks and the installation of two Willmes presses from Germany and a new grape-crusher from F. Miller and Co., of Rosewater. Since then, six more 11,000-gallon fermenting-tanks, one stainless-steel tank of 20,000 gallons capacity, and four steel glass-lined 12,700-gallon tanks have been added, while underground storage has been provided to keep pace with the growing productivity of the winery. A centrifuge for clarification of the juice before fermentation has also been installed.

Fully 95 per cent of the Stanley Company's wines are dry table wines, both red and white, the red wines being chiefly made from Shiraz grapes, dark of colour and stout of body, whereas 80 per cent of the white wines are made from white Rhine Riesling grapes, and 20 per cent from Clare Riesling which is a "stranger" to ampelographers.

ANGOVE'S PTY. LTD.

When Dr W. T. Angove, a Cornishman, came to Adelaide, in the early eighties of the last century, with his family, he settled at Tea Tree Gully, near Modbury, some twelve miles north of Adelaide. He was a lover of the open country who enjoyed riding his horse to visit patients who could not come to his surgery. And he certainly was a sensible man, since he planted a small vineyard and made a Burgundy-style red wine for his own family and maybe for some of his patients. Little did he think that the day would come when his name would be known throughout Australia and in many countries of the world in connection with all kinds of wines, vermouths and spirits, but above all Angove's St. Agnes Brandy. (There was a dual reason for naming the brandy after St. Agnes: she is a saint whose name is associated with purity, and the lovely village of St. Agnes in Cornwall was the home of the Angoves' ancestors.)

There is still a vineyard and there is still wine made at Tea Tree Gully, but the headquarters of the firm are now at Renmark, on the Murray River, to which the doctor's eldest son, Thomas Carlyon Angove, moved in 1910, and where Thomas Carlyon Angove's son, Thomas William Carlyon Angove, is now the firm's managing director. T. C. Angove is recognized as having been the "father" of Murray River wine-making.

The more popular products marketed by Angove's Pty Ltd. are first and foremost St. Agnes Brandy, then Marko Vermouth, Angove's Fino Dry Sherry, Bookmark Riesling, Tregrehan Claret, Brightlands Burgundy, and Angove's Special Vintage Port.

TOLLEY, SCOTT AND TOLLEY LTD.

On 23 August 1858, the East Torrens Wine Making and Distillation Company Limited was formed with a capital of £2,000 in 400 shares of £5 each. The objects of this company were to purchase grapes from the growers of the surrounding district for the manufacture of Brandy, fortifying spirit and methylating. The venture was not a success and the gates of the firm were closed for a few years.

They were reopened by a Mr H. Linde, who carried on the business of wine-making and spirit distilling under the name of The Phoenix Distilling Company until the year 1888, when he sold the business to Messrs. Thomas Scott and Ernest and Douglas Tolley, who specialized in the manufacture of brandy, gin and rectified spirits for fortifying wines. Mr Thomas Scott had had a distillery of his own in London, and Messrs. Ernest and Douglas Tolley had been trained by him there. The first thing the

Although Australian wine-makers have not been slow to adopt new techniques and processes, traditional craftsmanship is still needed and valued in the wine industry. Here an employee at the Stanley Winery at Clare, South Australia, is cleaning and resealing an oak storage-cask.

three partners did was to fit in more modern equipment and to make sure of greater bonded storage accommodation.

Ernest A. Tolley was born in Adelaide in 1862, and was sent to London in 1879, when he was entered at King's College and studied under Professor Thompson and Professor Bloxham for three years; he then spent some time in France, more especially at Epernay and Narbonne, before returning to London, where he learnt about distilling under Mr Thomas Scott, at his Abbey Street Distillery, in Bermondsey.

Douglas A. Tolley was born in Chertsey, Surrey, during one of his parents' periodical visits to England; after spending his early years in South Australia, he was sent to London, like his brother, and spent five years at King's College, after which he was apprenticed to Mr Scott's distilling firm.

The brothers returned to Adelaide in 1887, and persuaded Mr Thomas Scott to leave London and to launch them in the career of their choice as distillers. This he did, and the history of the Tolley, Scott and Tolley firm is one of sustained progress during the seventy-five years that followed.

During the nineties, the old Phoenix Distillery in Nelson Street, Stepney, a suburb of Adelaide, was enlarged and improved, and in 1904 a completely new and up-to-date distillery was erected at Angas Park, Nuriootpa. Four years later the firm purchased a winery belonging to Messrs. S. and W. Sage, also at Nuriootpa, with forty acres of vines, and, as opportunity offered, they bought or planted a number of vineyards which eventually added up to 600 acres.

In January 1921, the firm of Tolley, Scott and Tolley was formed into a limited liability company with a capital of £150,000; this made it possible to let different members of the family participate, if and when they wished to do so. Albion James Tolley, father of Ernest and Douglas Tolley, helped to finance the venture. Two brothers of Ernest and Douglas Tolley, Albion Everard Tolley and Frederic Osborne Tolley, were also financially interested in it: they were the founders of an important firm of general merchants, A. E. and F. Tolley.

Both Sam Tolley, Ernest Tolley's son, and Len Tolley, Douglas Tolley's son, carried on the good work after the deaths of their fathers.

Tolley, Scott and Tolley made no secret of the fact that much of the credit for the

S. Smith and Son's Yalumba Cellars at Angaston, South Australia, have the largest bottle-storage area in Australia. More than 100,000 dozen bottles of red wine are kept in huge bins during maturation.

unique excellence and characteristics of their brandies was due to the number of different stills which they had. Some of the older ones would not have had any sale value whatever, and yet the firm would not have parted with them at any price.

For some years past the whole of the grape-crush has been processed at Nuriootpa and the output has ultimately gone by tanker to Stepney for storage, blending and bottling. The modern Stepney bottling-plant is among the most up-to-date in Australia.

It may be regretted, but it cannot be surprising, that the great Distillers Company of Great Britain now owns Tolley, Scott and Tolley Ltd.

DOUGLAS A. TOLLEY PTY. LTD.

In 1893, as an addition to his interest in Tolley, Scott and Tolley Ltd., Douglas A. Tolley established a vineyard and winery at Hope Valley in the foothills of the ranges several miles eastward from the distillery at St. Peters.

In later years this vineyard and winery was fostered by Douglas's son, Len, who developed substantial wine-making operations there, the wine going, mainly in bulk, to all States of Australia for bottling.

The company also has extensive vineyards at Tea Tree Gully, Modbury and the Murray Valley, in addition to vineyards and a winery at Tanunda, in the Barossa Valley.

Len died in 1965, and now his three sons, Peter, David and Reg, look after the company's affairs.

Gradually a trade in bottled table wines is being developed. The company's distinctive brand name, Pedare, is formed from the first two letters of the Christian names of the three sons.

KAY BROTHERS

The Kay Brothers, Herbert and Frederick Walter Kay, bought some land in McLaren Vale in South Australia in 1890, and they built a cellar and winery on the lines of a model exhibited at the Chamber of Manufactures, Adelaide, by Dr J. G. Kelly. They called their winery the Amery Winery and they worked happily together for fifty-seven years; that is, until death claimed F. W. Kay in 1947, and Herbert in 1948 and thus broke up a partnership between brothers which must be extremely rare, if not unique, in the history of the wine industry in Australia. The winery is now in charge of "Cud" Kay, Herbert's son.

The cellars were improved and enlarged in 1927 and again in 1938 and their storage capacity is now of 250,000 gallons.

The vineyard of the Amery Winery covers 130 acres, Shiraz and Mataro grapes being grown to greater extent than other grapes: there are also twenty acres of Cabernet Sauvignon grapes and rather more of Rhine Riesling.

The dry red wines of the Kay Brothers have enjoyed a sustained reputation of many years, an important proportion of the output being regularly shipped to P. B. Burgoyne, in England. Burgoyne's became part of the Emu Wine Co. Pty. Ltd. in 1956, and since that year some dry red has been shipped through Emu, but not since 1961.

There are also comparatively small quantities of dessert wines and Vermouths made at the Amery Winery.

A. C. JOHNSTON LTD.

This firm's property in McLaren Vale is known as the Pirramimma vineyard; its 200 acres of vines produce chiefly dry red wines of the Burgundy type and some sweet red wines. Besides this vineyard, the firm owns thirty acres of almonds and 500 acres of farm-land and grazing. The manifold activities of the company are attended to by two brothers, Messrs. Lex and Digby Johnston, and Lex's sons, Messrs. Ian and Alex Johnston.

The property was originally bought by Mr A. C. Johnston, the father of Lex and Digby Johnston, in 1892, but there were merely a few Grenache grapes growing in a corner at the time. Wine was made in 1900 for the first time, and thenceforth progress was rapid, both in planting more vines and improving conditions in the winery and its cellars.

From 1916 to 1946 the whole of the output of the winery was sold to Messrs. W. and A. Gilbey Ltd., London. Since 1946 Messrs. W. and A. Gilbey Ltd. have continued to purchase the major portion of the wine production from the property.

The grapes now being grown in the Pirramimma Vineyard are as follows: Shiraz (98 acres), Grenache (34 acres), Pedro Ximenez (31 acres), Palomino (13 acres), and Cabernet (3 acres).

W. L. AND O. D. REDMAN
(ROUGE-HOMME WINES PTY. LTD.)

During the eighties and nineties of the nineteenth century, John Riddoch was one of the largest, if not actually the largest, landowner of the Penola district, at the extreme south-east of South Australia next to the extreme south-west part of Victoria.

In 1890, John Riddoch set apart some 1,000 acres of a 60,000-acre property of grazing land which he owned at Coonawarra, north of Penola, about fifty miles from the sea, for an assisted fruit colony known as the Coonawarra Fruit Colony. The soil mostly chocolate-coloured loam, well-drained, with fresh water from six to ten feet below the surface, was most suitable for every kind of fruit, including, of course, vines.

John Riddoch planted a vineyard, but not a large one. His vineyard was, and still is,*

---

* Except for three recently planted experimental vineyards in Tasmania.

the southernmost vineyard of Australia, if not of the world—about as far from the South Pole as some of the Rhineland vineyards are from the North Pole; that is, at the limit of lands where the vine can be expected to bring forth fully ripe grapes every year. This means that they have in Coonawarra their "ice saints" in November, instead of in May, as in Germany: saints who let the *vignerons* down now and again when late spring frosts bring ruin to the crop.

John Riddoch had the good fortune to secure the services of a very able man, a Mr McBain, who had been trained at Roseworthy Agricultural College, and who managed to make good wine with nothing like the equipment which is now to be seen at Rouge-Homme winery. Yet, in a booklet entitled *The Coonawarra Fruit Colony*, W. Catton Grasby, editor of the magazine *Garden and Field*, and at one time headmaster of Roseworthy Agricultural College, wrote, in 1899: "Coonawarra Claret promises to have a very high and wide reputation. Indeed, there is no doubt but that it will be a beautiful wine, of good body, fine colour, delicate bouquet, and low alcoholic strength". Words written sixty-five years ago could not better describe the Rouge-Homme Clarets of today save the last feature, "low alcoholic strength".

As John Riddoch was lucky in McBain, so was McBain lucky in the young assistant, William Leonard Redman, whom he trained and who remained with him for seven years, from 1899 to 1906. Two years later, in 1908, Bill Redman took over the Riddoch Coonawarra vineyard of forty-six acres in production and twenty-six acres of new plantations.

Since then, Bill Redman, now an octogenarian, and his two sons Owen and Don, have enlarged the vineyard, built a winery and underground cellarage; they have now the most modern equipment, but they still stick to the rule which has been the solid foundation of their reputation: to make no wine other than Clarets. The soil of their vineyard and the climate of Coonawarra are ideally suited for the growing of Shiraz and Cabernet Sauvignon vines, as well as for the slow but perfect ripening of their grapes, if and when the sun co-operates, of course. Which is why the date of the vintage on a bottle of Rouge-Homme Claret is no mere ornament, but a reliable warning of the standard of perfection of the wine in the bottle.

As noted earlier in this book, Rouge-Homme Wines Pty. Ltd. has now been purchased by Lindeman's Wines Ltd., of Sydney.

THE EMU WINE COMPANY LTD.

It was in 1883 that the trade-mark "Emu" was registered by one James Cox, manager of Auld, Burton and Co., the company established in Mill Street, Hanover Square, London, in 1871 by a Magill vintner, Patrick Auld, and his English partner, a retired Excise officer named Burton. Shortly after 1879 this company changed its name to the

Australian Wine Company and was bought in 1885 by Mr Aylwin Whately Pownall. The Australian Wine Company, was the first concern to popularize and distribute Australian wines in the United Kingdom: not merely the wines of the Magill Auldana Vineyard, but those of all Australian producers able to offer wines of the right quality at the right price.

This is also what the Emu Wine Co. attempted to do, and succeeded in doing between, the two World Wars, so much so that, by 1925, the company was the largest importer of Australian wines both in the United Kingdom and in Canada.

Before 1930 the company had no vineyards and no cellars of its own in Australia, but in that year it purchased the former property of R. C. H. Walker, in the Morphett Vale of South Australia, a property which has been considerably enlarged and improved, as well as modernized, in the last thirty-five years. There is now at Morphett Vale the best possible storage conditions for one and a half million gallons of wine and a quarter of a million gallons of brandy.

A proportion of the wines and brandies stored and matured at Morphett Vale before being shipped by the Emu Wine Company are wines and brandies made from grapes other than those of the company's own vineyards, and purchased by the company from other producers. All the wines which the company ships to the United Kingdom are shipped in tanks and casks, but those shipped to Canada are in casks and bottles.

In 1945 the company extended its interests to Western Australia, purchasing the vineyards and cellars of the Valencia Wine Company, which had been established at Guildford, in the Swan Valley, in 1890. Four years later, in 1949, the company purchased Houghton, also in the Swan Valley, established in 1859, one of the earliest of the vineyards and wineries of Western Australia.

A novel method of stacking sparkling wine is used at the winery of Australian Wines Pty. Ltd. at Magill, east of Adelaide.

AUSTRALIAN WINES PTY. LTD.

Better known as Romalo, Australian Wines Pty. Ltd. has a sparkling-wine cellar at Magill, east of Adelaide. The company had its beginning in 1919, when Frenchman, Léon Edmond Mazure, former manager of Auldana Winery, set up his own wine-making establishment, calling his property La Pérouse. Two stables housed shaking-tables for the first La Pérouse sparkling wine before Mazure built the winery, which, as it stands today, has room for a half million bottles.

To help with the wine-making, Léon Mazure employed Hurtle Frank Walker, who at the age of twenty-one had been put in charge of the sparkling-wine cellars at Auldana. In 1926 Hurtle was appointed manager of the wine-making company, then known as Australian Wines Export Pty. Ltd. because 200 hogsheads monthly, mainly of fortified wine, were being exported to London at that stage.

The present company, Australian Wines Pty. Ltd., was formed in 1930, when all the wine produced was purchased by S. Wynn and Co. Ltd., and marketed in Melbourne.

By 1944 Romalo was producing large quantities of sparkling-wine each year, and production has continued to increase since then.

Today Hurtle's son Norman manages the company, although Hurtle, now seventy-five, is still a director and still actively associated with the business.

BAROSSA CO-OPERATIVE WINERY LTD.

A progressive merchandising policy and sound technical direction have led to a big advance in recent years in the activities of the South Australian Grapegrowers Co-operative Ltd., the name of which was changed in 1966 to Barossa Co-operative Winery Ltd. The company, which has its headquarters at Nuriootpa, was founded thirty-five years ago, and its latest annual report showed assets of £650,000.

This winery is well known for its production of sparkling wines by the transfer method—and for pearl wines. It is also specializing nowadays in the production of quality table wines, some of which bear the name of the particular member of the co-operative who grew the grapes.

The co-operative's brand name, Kaiser Stuhl, is derived from the name the early German settlers of the district gave to a flat-topped hill overlooking the Barossa vineyards; the shape of the hill reminded them of a hill of the same name in the valley of the Rhine. The meaning of the name is roughly "seat of kings".

CLAREVALE CO-OPERATIVE WINERY

A flourishing Growers' Co-operative Winery has operated at Clare since 1928, known as the Clarevale Co-operative Winery. It had for quite a while a few years ago the unique distinction of having a Cabinet Minister, the then Minister of Lands in the South Australian Government, Mr P. H. Quirke, as managing director. Clarevale is noted for its brandy, and it markets much of its wine output in New South Wales.

RENMARK GROWERS' DISTILLERY LTD.

The beauty of the undulating country in the loop of the mighty Murray River, some two hundred miles north-east of Adelaide, appealed, in 1887, to the brothers W. B. and George Chaffey, as it still appeals today to anybody who has eyes to see, but those two brothers also realized that the land might be made to bring forth untold wealth, as, indeed, it has done since then through irrigation.

The irrigation vineyards of the Murray River and its tributaries are highly prosperous now; they produce a great deal more wine than all other vineyards, but it was not always thus: two World Wars that practically stopped all shipments of wine from Australia brought hardships and ruin to many vineyards, irrigated and others. It was thus that the ruined owner of a Renmark winery left and that its derelict property was acquired on a co-operative basis by thirty-five small local growers who formed the Renmark Growers' Distillery Ltd. in 1916.

In 1917, for their first vintage, they brought about 1,000 tons of grapes to be processed at the winery; today there are over 500 shareholders and they never send in less then 10,000 tons of grapes to be processed at vintage time.

As there are a great variety of grapes grown by different growers, the Renmark Growers' Distillery Ltd. can and does make many kinds of wine, still and sparkling, dry and sweet, fortified and not, as well as Brandy and other spirits.

The brand name is "Renmano".

LOXTON CO-OPERATIVE WINERY AND DISTILLERY LTD.

Although the Loxton Co-operative Winery and Distillery was formed in only 1949 and did not begin production until 1953, it has made such spectacular progress that it is today one of the most important producers of wines and brandies in Australia. It functions in South Australia, by the Murray River, in the Loxton Irrigation Area, which was established by the Commonwealth and State Governments for the development of horticultural properties by ex-Service men under a War Service Land Settlement scheme.

An area of approximately 6,000 acres was developed and more than 250 settlers are now growing the grapes which the Loxton Co-operative processes for them.

BERRI CO-OPERATIVE WINERY AND DISTILLERY LTD.

Berri stands by the Murray River practically half way between Renmark and Loxton, due east of Waikerie, in South Australia.

In 1918 a small distilling plant was set up at Berri, but the Government scheme of settling soldiers from the First World War in the irrigated areas led to so large an increase in the acreage of vineyards in the Berri area that it became obvious that the original plant would have to be replaced by a much larger and more up-to-date distillery. A Berri man, Mr H. R. Curren, and a few of his friends worked among the other growers until they secured sufficient support for a petition to form a separate co-operative company; it was then that the present company came into being and a new distillery was built on its present site, opposite Karoom Siding. The South Australian Government provided most of the finance through the State Bank.

Mr W. Gillard was the only grower in the district who had had any experience in the wine industry, and he was, naturally, chosen as the first chairman of the Berri Co-operative Winery and Distillery.

The plant handled less than 100 tons of grapes in its first year, but by 1948, the Berri crushers could and did deal with 20,000 tons of grapes during that year's vintage. By that time, the original storage capacity had been extended considerably, three 2,000-gallon tanks had been replaced by larger storage tanks, and, with oak vats and smaller vessels, the total storage capacity was 4,000,000 gallons of wine and spirit. The value of the company's buildings and plant now exceeds a quarter of a million pounds.

In 1958 a major decision of the board of management resulted in an outstanding development in the wine industry of South Australia. At a cost of £100,000 from 1958 to 1961, a separate winery unit was erected for the processing of grapes for fine dry wines and their conditioning and storage. This development had become necessary because there had been increased plantings of such varieties of grapes as Shiraz, Riesling and Palomino: they were the varieties of grapes the growing of which had become indispensable to meet the rising demand for dry red and white table-wines and for dry sherries.

The company now has a capacity sufficient to deal with more than 20,000 tons of grapes during a vintage. Average daily intake during vintage is 400 tons, and on one well-remembered day the intake soared to a peak of 804 tons.

The Berri Co-operative Winery and Distillery, like the other wine co-operatives, is really co-operative. The grapes processed are supplied by the 500 members, many of whom are returned soldiers.

The two more popular brands under which wines and brandies of the Berri Co-operative Winery and Distillery are marketed are "Karooma" and "Mine Host".

WAIKERIE CO-OPERATIVE DISTILLERY

Situated on the central reaches of the River Murray in South Australia, the Waikerie Co-operative Distillery was formed in 1919, when only a few hundred tons of grapes were treated. Mr Elliot Miller has been its chairman since 1922; he has also served continuously as a member of the Australian Wine Board since its inception in 1929. The tonnage of grapes handled at this distillery has steadily increased since the Second World War from 1,900 tons in 1947 to around 5,000 tons now. The output of wine and brandy is disposed of in bulk.

GLENLOTH WINES PTY. LTD.

Tout est possible and there may still be an old sportsman somewhere who remembers that the Melbourne Cup was won in 1892 by Glenloth, a five-year-old gelding, at fifty to one. The name is known today to a very much greater number of people than it ever was before, not necessarily, however, to people interested in racing, but to those interested in good wine.

This is entirely due to a Mrs Horne, who in 1892 planted a small vineyard in the O'Halloran Hill district, south of Adelaide, and called it Glenloth for luck. The original vineyard is still bearing first-class table-wine grapes.

In 1922 Mr and Mrs J. Harper Robertson built a winery in the centre of the Glenloth vineyard, and in 1923 began vintaging various types of table and dessert wines. In 1942 an obsolete winery and distillery at Happy Valley was taken over and fully modernized with the latest technical equipment for making a full range of table and dessert wines, as well as brandy and other spirits.

In recent years much further development has been guided by Mr J. R. W. (Bob) Robertson.

The company has had a substantial trade with Britain, and this trading connection led in 1966 to its acquisition by Seager, Evans and Co. Ltd., of London.

S. WYNN & CO. PTY. LTD.

A pair of newly-weds, whose ages added up to just over forty, and their worldly wealth to four golden sovereigns, walked down the gang-plank of a Norddeutscher Lloyd mailboat from Bremen at Port Melbourne in 1913. It had cost them £18 each to get away from the cruel treatment which Jews had to expect at that time in Poland from a Jew-baiting populace and official repression. They little knew that they were also escaping from the nightmare of the First World War.

Their name might have been a joke or a prophecy: Weintraub—Winegrape—and they promptly changed it to Wynn, which certainly proved to be a winner.

There are no vineyards in Poland, but young Weintraub's father was nevertheless a wine-maker: he made wine of some kind from imported raisins and currants. Many migrants had come to Australia and made good before those two young Poles, but none of them could have had a grimmer start and made a more spectacular success of their lives in Australia. Barely forty years after arriving, as he did, friendless and almost penniless, Samuel Wynn had become one of the more important wine-growers, wine-makers, and wine-exporters in Australia, a man of wealth and a proud man who had every right to be proud of what he had achieved in so short a time. He has three sons, two of them doctors and the third, David, the managing director of Messrs. S. Wynn & Co. Pty. Ltd., the family firm, Samuel Wynn, being the governing director.

The firm has its administrative headquarters and bottled-wine storage-cellars in Melbourne, and its four main wine-producing properties at Magill, Modbury and Coonawarra in South Australia, and Yenda in New South Wales.

MODBURY ESTATE. The Modbury Estate vineyards of 500 acres grace the tableland at the foot of the westerly slopes of the Mount Lofty Range, thirteen miles north-east of Adelaide. The soil is partly of red loam, with limestone subsoils from a few inches to as much as three feet below, and partly of a darker brown-red loam over a quartz-rock subsoil.

At vintage time, in March or early April, the Modbury Estate grapes are harvested with care and promptly delivered at the firm's Magill cellars, only eight miles away: there they are crushed and fermented, their wine is processed, conditioned and kept before being transported to the firm's main storage cellars in St. Kilda Road, Melbourne, for final conditioning and bottling.

The Modbury Estate vineyards are planted in white grapes, mostly Palomino and Pedro Ximinez where the subsoil is rich in lime, and Riesling and Semillon over the quartz: the first are used for the making of Sherries and the others for quality dry white wines.

COONAWARRA ESTATE. The vineyards of this estate, near Mount Gambier, at an elevation of 200 feet above sea-level, and about fifty miles inland from the sea, are at the limit beyond which the vine cannot be expected to ripen its grapes. This means that the grapes of the Coonawarra vineyards take longer to mature and that they are harvested at a later date, when the hottest days of the autumn are over, hence when wine can be made under more favourable conditions than in most of the other vineyards of Australia. This is all to the good for the making of quality dry red wines, but unfortunately the location of the Coonawarra vineyards is also responsible for the vulnerability to frost of the vines at the time of their flowering.

Of the 377 acres of the Coonawarra Estate vineyards, seventy acres are planted in Cabernet Sauvignon, some of which are used exclusively in the making of the quality dry red wine which the firm markets under the name of Coonawarra Estate Cabernet; 140 acres are planted in Shiraz or Hermitage, which, blended with some of the Cabernet, are used for the making of the quality dry red wine marketed under the name of Coonawarra Estate Hermitage; twenty acres are planted in Rhine Riesling for the

The old tower at Chateau Tahbilk in Victoria. No one can say for certain what use the tower was put to originally. Some people believe that it was used to keep watch for marauding Aborigines; others that it enabled the original owners to supervise work in the vineyard. Nowadays the tower is featured on the label of Chateau Tahbilk wines.

making of quality dry white wines; sixty acres are planted in Doradillo, Palomino and Pedro Ximenez for the making of the firm's quality Sherries.

OVENS VALLEY BURGUNDY. S. Wynn & Co. Pty. Ltd. have for the past thirty years bought the total output of a small wine-maker in the Ovens Valley and have developed the wine to a distinctive type under this label.

The vineyards of the Ovens Valley are in the north-east corner of Victoria, where the soil is heavy, the winter rains copious and the heat of summer intense—all conditions responsible for the bigger, fuller and more alcoholic red wines made from the Shiraz or Hermitage grapes grown there—wines which are marketed under the name of Ovens Valley Burgundy. This wine, however, is kept in the firm's cellars in wood for at least two years, and it is not released for sale before it has been in bottle for at least another two years, thus giving a big wine a chance to lose some of its original roughness and become gracious.

The quaint structures in the foreground are the ventilators of one of the cellars at Chateau Tahbilk. Tahbilk was first planted in 1860 by a company whose secretary was R. H. Horne (the poet "Orion" Horne), a friend of Charles Dickens and the Brownings.

CHATEAU TAHBILK

There never had been any shortage of lush green grass on the Tabilk "run", a square mile or 640 acres of farm land by the River Goulburn, seventy-six miles north of Melbourne, but it was only in 1860 that a company was formed, with a capital of £25,000, to plant a vineyard, build a winery and a cellar where Chateau Tahbilk stands today. When and why the letter "H" slipped in the original "Tabilk", which is still the way the name of the nearby township is spelt, nobody seems to know, but it is usually accepted that the "H" was put in so that the accent should be on the first syllable "TA", and not on the last "BILK".

By the end of 1860, 150 acres of woodlands had been cleared and sixty-five acres of vineyards were planted. More remarkable still, vaulted underground cellars had already been built, which have been known ever since as "the old cellars", fully three years before there was any wine to be laid to rest in their cool darkness.

From 1860 to 1875 more land was cleared and fenced, more vineyards were planted, a winery was built and equipped, and more cellars were built, which are known as "the new cellars", bringing the total cellar storage to 200,000 gallons of wine. All went well until the last few years of the nineties, when the dreaded Phylloxera pest came to Tahbilk and destroyed 200 of its 360 acres of vines—all but those nearest the river, where seven rows can still be seen today: they have been, and they will continue to be carefully, one might say "religiously", looked after as honoured veterans of the early days. Grafted Phylloxera-resisting vines have been planted in the rest of the vineyard.

In 1925 Chateau Tahbilk, its vineyards, cellars and broad acres were acquired by a Mr Purbrick. His son, Mr Eric Purbrick, returned from a visit to England in 1931, at a time of acute economic crisis, to take charge of the property. With dynamic energy and wisdom remarkable in a young man, Eric Purbrick achieved the complete rehabilitation of Chateau Tahbilk single-handed. Since 1955, however, Eric Purbrick has been able to leave to his son John the responsibility of crops and livestock; this has enabled him to devote most of his time and attention to his vineyards and to the wines of Chateau Tahbilk.

The old homestead had to be pulled down in 1936, but a new house has been rebuilt upon the old foundations and in an attractive style. The avenue of white mulberry trees that leads to the house is an uncommon sight; it appears that they were planted many years ago by a Swiss manager of the old Tabilk Vineyards Company, who had the bright idea that silk-worms fed on the leaves of the mulberries would give the wives and daughters of his employees the profitable pastime of spinning silk in their spare time.

In 1959 the National Trust of Australia (Victoria Branch) classified the cellars of Chateau Tahbilk as rural buildings of historical and architectural interest to the people of Australia. The following year the centenary of Chateau Tahbilk was celebrated with a ceremony at the vineyard at which Sir Robert Menzies, then Prime Minister of Australia, gave an address.

The wines of Chateau Tahbilk are mostly sold under the name of their birthplace and the name of their parent grape, such as Chateau Tahbilk Marsanne, Riesling, or White Hermitage, for the dry white wines; Chateau Tahbilk Cabernet or Shiraz, for the dry reds.

Bottles being sterilized at Best's Great Western Winery, near Ararat in western Victoria. The vineyard was founded by Henry Best in 1886.

BEST'S WINES PTY. LTD.

Eric F. H. Thomson, the managing director of Messrs. Best's Wines Pty. Ltd. has two partners: his brother, W. H. Thomson, and his son, E. V. H. Thomson. The firm has owned two different sets of vineyards in central west of Victoria since 1930.

The oldest and more important of their vineyards are those near the village of Great Western; they were originally planted by Henry Best in 1866, and the name was too good to lose, so that Messrs. Thomson have never sold and never will sell any wine other than Best wines.

Their other vineyard is near Lake Boga, in the Valley of the Murray River, near Swan Hill: most of that vineyard has been planted by Messrs. Best's Wines Pty. Ltd. and it yields quite different grapes from those of the Great Western vineyard. None but dry reds and dry whites are made by the firm from its Great Western grapes, whereas fortified dry wines, fortified red and white sweet wines, as well as fortifying spirit and Brandy are made from the Lake Boga vineyard.

C. H. MORRIS & SONS PTY. LTD.

This is one of the smaller centenarian vineyards of Australia—one of the few to live through economic depressions and the Phylloxera invasion without ever changing hands: it is today in charge of the direct descendants of the founder in the male line.

The Morris Mia Mia vineyard, of Rutherglen, Victoria, was first planted by George Francis Morris in 1859, and it was replanted by his son Charles some forty-five years later, after the disaster of the Phylloxera invasion.

The Mia Mia Vineyard of 110 acres is planted with quality vines only, and the wines for which Messrs. C. H. Morris and Sons are chiefly famed are their Muscats, and their red and white sweet wines.

Charles Morris had three sons, Charles, Gerald and Frederick; in 1953, Gerald retired, and the business has been conducted since then by Gerald's brothers, Charles and Frederick, and his two nephews, Charles Henry (Charles's son), and Frederick John (Frederick's son).

MILDARA WINES LTD.

Mildura, on the Victorian side of the Murray River, was founded in 1887 by two brothers, W. B. and George Chaffey. They planted a vineyard and built a winery in 1888 at Irymple, near Mildura, and they made wine for the first time in 1891. Year by year more and more vines were planted, and in 1914 the Mildura Winery Pty. Ltd. moved its headquarters to Merbein, on the top of the cliff overlooking the river. It has now become Mildara Wines Ltd., a public company with a very large number of shareholders, and agents in most of the chief towns of Australia. W. B. Chaffey was the chairman of the company from the day of its inception to that of his death, while his son, W. H. Chaffey, was the company's secretary from 1917 to 1963. Mr H. R. Haselgrove, O.B.E., is chairman and managing director.

Mildara Wines Ltd. is best known for the range of its Sherries, dry, medium, and cream, but it also produces dry table wines, dessert wines, and brandies.

The most popular Sherry of Mildara Wines Ltd. is that which is marketed as Mildara Supreme Dry, a flor-type Sherry first laid down in 1936. As regards dry table wines, the two most popular are, for the reds, their Cabernet-Shiraz, and for the whites, their Golden Bower. The Cabernet-Shiraz is a dry red wine skilfully blended from the grapes from which it is named: the grapes are grown in South Australia, in which State Mildara owns one of Australia's largest vineyards of Cabernet Sauvignon grapes, at Coonawarra. Mildara Cabernet-Sauvignon, when bottled, is given a bin number as well as a vintage date: Bin 30, for instance, for 1961 vintage. The same applies to Golden Bower, a quality dry white wine which is bottled with the bin number of its vintage. A Brandy of fine quality distilled at Mildara is a pot-still Brandy marketed as Mildara Supreme Brandy.

Mildara's White Opal, a quality dry white wine, a blend of Coonawarra and Mildura grapes, is now available in Great Britain.

ASHMAN'S VINEYARDS

Murray Tyrrell, who is now in charge of the Ashman's Vineyards Estate, a show place of the Hunter River Valley, is the grandson of one of the pioneers of viticulture in New South Wales, Edward Tyrrell, and the nephew of Dan Tyrrell, an even more remarkable man. Dan took charge of the vineyards at the early age of fourteen, in 1883, when his father's health failed, and he was still very much "the boss" in 1959, when he died, a few days before his ninetieth birthday.

It is by no means strange, yet most interesting, to detect the same streak of independence and originality of thought in the three generations. The first thing that Edward did when he bought the land in 1858 was to build for himself a shack of gum-tree slabs, which still stands today, complete with Old Man Tyrrell's square slab chimney-pot; it is possible, but by no means certain, that he lined the shack with tin sheets. He cleared the ground and planted a vineyard, making wine for the first time in 1864.

During nearly twenty years he gradually increased and improved his property. An important stretch of vines which Edward Tyrrell planted in 1879 is still producing good crops—not as many grapes as younger vines do, of course, but grapes more likely to give wines of finer quality. This strip of 1879 vines at Ashman's is believed to the the oldest in production in the Hunter River Valley.

Dan Tyrrell was only a boy when he took charge of the Ashman's Vineyards, but a boy who knew his own mind and who had a mind of his own. He did not believe that great cellars and handsome wineries improved the quality of wine, and he persisted all through his long life in giving to the growing of his grapes and to the making of his wine all the time, skill and money he had to give.

Murray Tyrrell, Dan's nephew, has very much the same mentality as his uncle had. He is not in the least impressed by the very costly, scientifically perfected equipment now in use in nearly all Australian wineries. He believes that the hand-press is better

Cabernet Sauvignon grapes at the Viticultural Research Station at Griffith, New South Wales. Cabernet, the famous grape of Bordeaux, produces red wine of very high quality, but unfortunately the vine is a "shy bearer". This variety has been grown in Australia for many years, and in recent times, as a result of a rising demand for premium-quality dry reds, Australian wine-makers have shown an increasing interest in encouraging its cultivation.

for the making of fine quality wines than a press-button hydraulic or electric press—a more brutal press. "You can feel," he says, "when you have screwed the hand-press down to just the right pressure that will get the best out of the grape and no more."

All grapes at Ashman's are crushed in hand-presses made of oak, and none but the first pressings are used for the making of table wines. Second pressings are used for the making of sweet sherry. Murray Tyrrell is convinced that the age of the vineyard is of great importance, as a vineyard improves with cultivation, which is eventually responsible for the higher standard of quality of the wine made from grapes grown thereon.

Like his uncle before him, Murray Tyrrell is no believer in show: he is convinced that no machinery, however perfect it may be, can replace the skill, experience and constant attention of the man who owns, knows and loves his wine.

At Ashman's the black Shiraz or Hermitage is grown more than any other grapes for the making of dry red table wines of the Burgundy type. For the white wines, they grow mostly, almost exclusively, the Hunter Riesling; that is, the Semillon.

McWILLIAM'S WINES PTY. LTD.

It was at Corowa, on the New South Wales side of the Murray River, that J. J. McWilliam planted his first vineyard in 1877, but it was as the pioneer of the Murrumbidgee Valley viticulture that he brought the firm that bears his name to the forerank of the great organizations in control of the wine industry in Australia. In 1913, the year after the main canal of the Murrumbidgee Irrigation Area had reached the Hanwood District, two fifty-acre farm blocks were bought and planted with about 35,000 cuttings by J. J. McWilliam; three years later, in 1916, the grapes of his vineyard were processed at Junee, where he had built a winery and cellars in 1900, but during the following years the Murrumbidgee Valley grapes were processed first of all at Hanwood, where a winery was built in 1917, and later at Yenda, near Griffith, where a winery was built in 1920, as well as a distillery, and later on, cellars for the storage of the firm's sparkling wines.

While the McWilliam vineyards of the Murrumbidgee Valley are the most important quantitatively speaking, the reputation of the firm's table wines is due to the quality wines from its Hunter River Valley vineyards, more especially the wines of Mount Pleasant.

The Waikerie Co-operative Winery, on the banks of the Murray River at Waikerie, South Australia. More than 7,000 tons of grapes are used each year at this winery for production of sweet wines and brandies.

The site of the Mount Pleasant vineyard, in the Pokolbin area, five miles from Cessnock, was selected and planted in 1880 by Charles King, and sold by him to an Irishman, John Augustus O'Shea, who had a French wife, and a son, Maurice O'Shea. Maurice was sent to France by his parents, first to the famous Agriculture College at Grignon, and then to the still more famous University at Montpellier. When he returned to Australia after the First World War, he took charge of the family vineyard, at Mount Pleasant, consisting at the time of 120 acres. In 1932, the property came under control of Mount Pleasant Wines Pty. Ltd., a company the directors of which were members of the O'Shea and McWilliam families, with Maurice as manager as well as one of the directors.

Subsequently, the O'Shea shareholders sold their shares to McWilliam's Wines Pty. Ltd., but Maurice remained both the manager and a director to the day of his death in 1956. Thus Maurice O'Shea was responsible for the quality of the Mount Pleasant wines for no less than thirty-five years, during which he won the respect and admiration of all wine-lovers in Australia; he had the reputation of being the best wine-maker in New South Wales. He had an unorthodox but rather nice habit of giving to various cuvées of table wines the christian names of some of his friends instead of an

Maurice O'Shea, who was in charge of Mount Pleasant Vineyard, in the Hunter Valley of New South Wales for thirty-five years, died in 1956, but he is remembered as one of the greatest of Australian wine-makers.

identifying number or letter: "George", "Mary", or "Henry", instead of XII9 or Y654. This practice has been retained at Mount Pleasant since Maurice's death.

Since then also, the winery has been not only enlarged but modernized in order to cope with great quantities of grapes from new vineyards which were planted in more recent years.

Lovedale is another property of the firm in the Hunter River Valley, on the Cessnock-Branxton Road; its development was delayed during the last war because the Commonwealth Government decided to use some of the land for the construction of an emergency military landing air-strip; it was not returned to the firm until 1950, but such progress has been made since then that a new and larger winery had to be built there in 1960.

Last in date, but not in importance, is the McWilliam Winery at Robinvale, on the Victorian side of the Murray River loop south of Euston, which is on the Sturt Highway, in New South Wales. Its construction was begun in 1961, with plans to process 5,000 tons of grapes annually, and provision for further expansion to bring this figure to 10,000 tons a year.

All Saints Vineyard at Wahgunyah, in north-eastern Victorian, as seen from the top of the remarkable battlemented winery that the vineyard's founder, George Sutherland Smith, built in 1884. The vineyard had been planted twenty years earlier.

G. SUTHERLAND SMITH & SONS' ALL SAINTS WINERY

George Sutherland Smith came from John o'Groats to Port Phillip in the early fifties of the last century. What made him leave his native land nobody knows, but if it had been work that he wanted, he found plenty of it in and near the fast-rising new city of Melbourne.

There is no existing documentary evidence of how George earned a living then, but, according to tradition, he had some knowledge of building and a taste, backed with some skill, for architecture: he is also credited with the sale to a railway company of a large number of wooden sleepers, but whether he had been personally responsible for the cutting down of the red-gums from which the sleepers were made is uncertain. There cannot be any doubt, however, that he prospered, and that, as all good Scots have always been expected to do, he saved money, since in 1860 he owned two ferry steamboats operating on the Murray River from Echuca.

There is no clue to the reason why he decided to leave Melbourne and its amenities for the rough life more than a hundred miles up country; it is even more difficult to understand how a canny Scot chose to invest his money in a river ferry at a time when he must have known that the railway to Albury was being built and would soon compete with the river ferry.

As a matter of fact, it was not long before this did happen, and when it did, in 1864, George decided to quit, and to look round for something else to do. As Noah, when he left the Ark, planted a vineyard, so George Sutherland Smith, when he left his ferryboats, planted a vineyard, at Wahgunyah; it has been greatly enlarged by his grandsons, David and George, who still lovingly look after old George's venture, with the help of their own sons, David Junior, George Junior, and Peter. The All Saints Vineyard graces the left, or Victorian bank of the Murray River on a three-mile front, facing the Corowa vineyards upon the other side of the river, in New South Wales.

There were a number of vineyards in that north-east corner of Victoria, between Rutherglen and the Murray River, in 1864, when George Sutherland Smith decided to have a vineyard of his own, and as several of those existing vineyards had taken the name of some saint, Old George decreed that his vineyard would be called All Saints, which has been its name ever since.

What did George know about viticulture and wine-making in 1864? Nothing. But

Horses are still used for transport at G. Sutherland Smith and Sons' All Saints Vineyard because soft, marshy land between the vineyard and the winery makes the use of motor vehicles difficult.

he was a good learner, or else he managed to get the right people to work for him, since the first Australian wine ever to be given a Gold Medal at an International Exhibition in Europe was given at the Vienna International Exhibition of 1873 to an All Saints "sweet red wine".

George Sutherland Smith may have been a more fortunate *vigneron* than some of his contemporaries, but he would not have claimed to be a better one; he could claim however, to be a better builder than any of them, and the proof of his skill and imagination as an architect and builder stands today at All Saints. There is no other winery in Australia, or anywhere else in the world, like the monumental All Saints winery with its thick cavity walls and castle-like battlements: it was built over the original pise-walled winery without disturbing any of the wine maturing in the great oak casks still there today, where they have been for nearly a century. This unique example of Victorian taste, Old George's legacy, was built in 1884, and he died soon after. According to the Smith family tradition, Grand-dad George had in mind, when he built his winery, the Castle of Mey, near his native village in Scotland, where his father, a carpenter, used to work: the castle now belongs to Queen Elizabeth the Queen Mother.

During the nineties the vines of All Saints were destroyed by the Phylloxera louse, but they were replanted soon after with varieties grafted on to Phylloxera-resisting stocks, and these have been grown at All Saints ever since.

The chief variety of grapes now being grown at All Saints is the Shiraz, which is used for dry reds but mostly for "Port". The only other black grapes grown, and in limited quantities only, are Cabernet Sauvignon and Pinot, which are used exclusively for the making of dry red wines. The white-grape varieties grown are the Palomino, Pedro Ximenez and Rhine Riesling for the making of Sherry; Marsanne for both Sherry and sweet white wines; Chasselas, Tokay (Pinot Gris), Rutherglen Pedro, and White Grenache for Sweet White; Rutherglen Brown Muscat for Muscats.

During the summer, the vineyard is given a light irrigation watering from the Murray River whenever necessary.

The chief production of the All Saints vineyard is sweet wine: "Port", Muscat and Sweet White; also Flor Sherries. The quantity of dry red wines is now increasing, but dry white wines are still produced merely experimentally.

In 1960 the Melbourne offices of the All Saints Vineyard, which had been in Selborne Chambers, in the City, for eighty-four years, moved to more commodious premises in Queensberry Street, North Melbourne, in order to ensure that the bottling and distribution of All Saint wines would take place under more modern and suitable conditions.

A healthy crop of grapes ready for picking at a vineyard supplying the Mildara Winery at Merbein, Victoria.

J. Y. TULLOCH AND SONS PTY. LTD.

At Branxton, in the Hunter River Valley, there was a prosperous business man with a number of young children during the last decade of the nineteenth century; he owned the chief general store in the little town, and he also had grazing interests. His name was John Younie Tulloch.

He had money to spare and to give credit to those who needed it, which is how it happened that in 1893 he took possession of Glen Elgin "in satisfaction of an overdue debt". Glen Elgin was the name of a small vineyard and winery at Pokolbin, some twelve miles west of Branxton; its grapes had ceased to be cultivated, and there had been no wine made for a year when John Tulloch became the owner.

There was good wine being made in the Pokolbin area then, as there is now, and John Tulloch must have made up his mind right away to make wine as good as if not better than the best red table wine of the Hunter. He planted none but Shiraz or Black Hermitage vines, on the advice of Professor J. Blunno, of the New South Wales Department of Agriculture, who also supervised the making of the first few hogsheads of dry red wine that were produced at Glen Elgin in 1897.

It so happened that John Tulloch had an uncle, J. A. Russell, who was a wine traveller, and, evidently, a good wine traveller who had no difficulty in selling Glen Elgin dry red to his clientele in Newcastle and Cessnock and to the well-to-do farmers of the district. So John Tulloch planted more vines and made more grapes: he must have fallen in love with the grape as *vignerons* beyond count have done everywhere since Noah came out of the Ark. It must have been so, since John Tulloch decided to leave Branxton, with its cultural amenities and social ties, and to live at Glen Elgin, where conditions must have been distinctly more austere and lonely for his family.

After the initial success of his new venture, John Tulloch had to face an unexpected and serious difficulty. In 1900, the Federation of the six Australian Colonies into the Commonwealth of Australia removed trade barriers throughout Australia: all of a sudden, Sydney and New South Wales were flooded with table wines and fortified wines from South Australia—wines which could be offered, and were offered, for sale at lower prices because of the subsidy given to the growers by the South Australian Government. Quite a number of the small growers of the Hunter River Valley gave up the fight and pulled up their vines. Not so John Tulloch: he made fortified wines for the first time at Glen Elgin to meet the new demand, but continued making and selling dry reds that were better—and dearer—than the South Australian table wines.

In 1919 the Australian Government settled a number of returning soldiers from the First World War in different parts of the country that were suitable for viticulture. Some of these men were given fifty-acre blocks at Fordwich, twenty-five miles from Pokolbin, but some of them, after planting ten acres or so, decided to sell their blocks and find more congenial work elsewhere. This gave John Tulloch the chance to buy six of those fifty-acre blocks and to have presently a second vineyard of 300 acres. But there has never been a winery at Fordwich: the grapes grown there are picked and conveyed by lorry to the Pokolbin Winery to be processed.

In 1939 John Tulloch formed his business into a limited liability company, and when he died in 1940, Hector Tulloch, the eldest son, became manager of the Glen Elgin Winery, with his brother Keith as his assistant; another brother, Jim, took over the management of the Fordwich vineyard, and yet another, Alex, was given the control of the company's cattle properties. John Younie, Hector's son; John and Younie, Jim's sons; and Alex, son of Alex, are already giving to the company the benefit of their intelligence and energy.

Hector Tulloch, who died in 1965, used to say with legitimate pride that the dry red which he sent to the 1956 Sydney Royal Show is the only wine to have won first place in both the Claret and Burgundy classes, as well as the trophy for the best red

Bailey Brothers' vineyard at Glenrowan, in north-eastern Victoria. Glenrowan is noted for its distinctive style of full-bodied red wines. It is also remembered by Australians as the headquarters of Ned Kelly, the most notorious of the bushrangers.

wine in the exhibition. In 1963, in Melbourne, a Gold Medal was given to a Glen Elgin dry red, made exclusively from the Hermitage grapes of the first five acres planted in 1893.

Tulloch's are also makers of very good white wines which, even today, have to be rationed.

Chateau Yaldara, at Lyndoch, South Australia, is one of the newer Australian wine-making enterprises. It was founded after the Second World War by Hermann Thumm, a member of a German family with a tradition of wine-making going back for centuries.

CHATEAU YALDARA PTY. LTD.

Hermann Thumm comes from a German family with a traditional interest in wine. His father's people had been wine-makers in the Rhine Valley for centuries, and there was never much doubt about what occupation Hermann Thumm would follow when he left school. He took a two-year course at a wine college, gaining its diploma, then had practical experience in wine-making with a large company.

In 1930 he and a friend went to Persia, where they became business partners in several ventures, including a wine-making firm. Mr Thumm was still in Persia when the Second World War began, but for two years after the start of the war was able to carry on his business enterprises without interference. Then, however, in 1941, the British and the Russians occupied Persia, and all Germans living there were interned.

For a time it looked as if Mr Thumm might be transported to a Russian labour camp, but he was sent instead to Australia, and spent the remaining years of the war there in internment centres.

After the war he took over the ruins of an old winery and flour-mill at Schlenke's Gully, near Lyndoch, the gateway to the Barossa Valley, where he has since built up one of the most flourishing of South Australia's new-generation wine-making enterprises. It is named Yaldara from an Aboriginal word meaning "sparkling".

Since 1960 Mr Thumm has been carefully remodelling and extending the buildings at Yaldara with the aim of reproducing something of the atmosphere of the vineyard chateaux of Europe.

A. P. BIRKS

The vineyard and winery which now trades under the name of A. P. Birks' Wendouree Cellars was established in bush country two and a half miles south-east of Clare, in South Australia, towards the end of the last century by Alfred Percy Birks. He began wine-making as a hobby, and in 1895 his vintage was 140 gallons, which, by 1913, had grown to 4,000 gallons.

In the early days, the wine was made and stored in semi-underground thatched-roofed cellars close to Wendouree homestead. In 1914, however, new cellars were built; these were extended in 1921 and 1924 and are still in use today, having narrowly escaped destruction in a great bush-fire on 21 February 1965.

The output at Wendouree is now 40,000 gallons a year, almost entirely dry wines. The dry reds are well known in Australia for their quality; the dry whites are sold for making sparkling wine.

Alfred Percy Birks died in 1948, in his eighty-first year. Today the proprietors of the business are Roland Napier Birks (the third son of the founder), who has been wine-maker since 1917, and his wife, Olive Wakefield Birks.

Wendouree has a seventy-acre vineyard, in which the main grape varieties grown are Shiraz, Mataro, Riesling and Pedro.

In 1965, a bushfire threatened A. P. Birks' Wendouree Winery at Clare, in South Australia, with destruction. The fire reached the back of the winery and damaged this old hydraulic press.

WESTERN AUSTRALIA

SANDALFORD. The first vines to be planted in Western Australia were planted in 1840 by Captain John Septimus Roe, who named his vineyard Sandalford, which was the name of an estate owned by his family on the site of a priory built in 1066. Captain Roe had been one of the passengers on board the *Parmelia* who reached the mouth of the Swan River in 1829, and Captain Roe's vineyard is not only the oldest in Western Australia but the only one still in the hands of the family of the original owner.

John Frederick Roe, Captain Roe's grandson, greatly increased the family business and, in 1945, wine was made at Sandalford for the first time on a commercial scale: it had been up to then a hobby and sideline. Part of the 300 acres of Sandalford vineyard is given to the growing of table grapes for export.

HOUGHTON. It was at Houghton, in the Swan Valley, that wine was made for the first time commercially, in 1859, by Dr. Ferguson, and the vineyards, winery and distillery remained in the hands of his descendants until July 1st, 1950, when they were acquired by Valencia Vineyards Pty. Ltd., a subsidiary Company of the Emu Wine Company of Morphett Vale, South Australia.

VALENCIA. The Valencia Vineyards Pty. Ltd., originally known as Santa Rosa, were planted at Caversham, Guildford, in the Swan Valley, in 1890, by Messrs. J. L. Nanson, editor of the Perth *Daily News*, Lindley Cowan, head of the Government Bureau of Agriculture, and Adrian Despeissis, Government Viticulturist at the time. The Emu Wine Company acquired the Valencia Vineyards Pty. Ltd. in 1945, and it has spared neither cash nor effort to provide both Houghton and Valencia with the latest and best wine-making equipment.

QUEENSLAND

Queensland has much the smallest output of wine of any of the five wine-producing States.

Its best-known vineyard is Romavilla, near Roma, 311 miles west of Brisbane. It was planted in 1863 by S. S. Bassett and is still owned by the Bassett family.

The vineyard covers 240 acres, on which no less than ten varieties of grape are grown. Both fortified and table wines are produced.

A family company, Romavilla Vineyards Pty. Ltd. now controls the vineyard and winery.

APPENDIXES

PRESSING

128

THE
SYDNEY GAZETTE,
And New South Wales Advertiſer.

WE HOPE TO PROSPER
THUS

PUBLISHED BY AUTHORITY.

METHOD
OF PREPARING A PIECE OF LAND
For the Purpoſe of forming a Vineyard

[Tranſlated from the French]

The ground is to be turned up, cleared of weeds, and trenched out, to the debth of 18 inches; or, ſhould it not be encumbered with ſtumps or roots of trees, underwood, or brambles, the cuttings of vines may be immediately planted without that precaution.

The mode of planting on hills or mountains, is performed by a pointed iron bar or borer, but care muſt be taken to fill up the extra ſpace in the hole round the ſtalk of the vine, with aſhes or fine mould, to prevent the rain forming a ſlime therein, which on drying chokes the vine, and prevents its ſhooting fibres at the root.

For the purpoſe of planting the young vines already rooted, holes are to be made with a ſtrong hoe, or broad pick-axe, at a diſcretionary diſtance of about 2 and a half or 3 feet open from each vine, and ſome mould or old turf muſt be lain round the foot of each.

For planting vines in Eſpalier, the ground muſt be opened in a line, at the diftance of between five and feven feet, and the trenches left open, which may be performed by plough, being the moft cheap and expeditious way, and equally beneficial.

In order to retrieve a barren vine, and render it fruitful the fame year, holes muft be dug near the main root, and fufficiently broad that the fhoots from the fame vine may be lain in, to replace the old ones, which are after to be removed, to prevent the roots and fibres entangling and choaking each other.

The method of dreffing the vines after the vineyard being formed, is principally to prune them well, and to attend to a minute knowledge of their nature; alfo what influence the change of climate may have operated on them: fome will not produce without being propped, others beft without; and the fituation of the land and temperature of the climate will determine if the branches are to be carried more of lefs in height and confequently how to be fupported; they may be cut off either in a flat or floped manner, but care muft be taken to clear away all dead or defective parts.

The pruning is to be performed in January and February, after having felected the layers and bearing branches, yet the vine may be increafed from fhoots laid under ground, and led to fpring up when any deficiency may happen.

At the commencement of the fpring the ground fhould be opened with a pick-axe, (one end of which muft be fharp and broad) and for ftony ground, one with two prongs, or a ftrong hoe, and care muft be taken in digging, to remove the young fhoots round the root of the vine, as they diminifh the vigour of the main trunk.

The other modes of opening the ground of a vineyard, are with a fpade or implement which only differs from the former ones, by being thinner and broader.

The vines fhould be carefully pruned or thinned about thrice during the feafon, by clearing away all the exuberant fhoots from the body, which deprive thofe detained for production, of their vigour.

On the approach of the vintage, fhould the feafon prove rainy, and caufe apprehenfions of the grapes decaying before brought to maturity, the vines fhould be thined of leaves towards the Weft, but not on the other fides, leaft change of weather might dry up the grapes.

The following procefs is neceffary for making red and white wines:

To prepare wine preffes, butts, large tubs, and barrels.

For Red Wine, viz.

Whenever the clufter of red grapes are perfectly ripe (but not rotten), as great attention muft be paid to exclude every grape either rotten or dried, fome of which will always be met with in the branches, as the decayed ones give a mufty flavor to the wine, and the unripe caufe it to four.

The grapes being gathered, are to be put into a wine-prefs and fqueezed, but fhould they not be fo ripe as wifhed for, the bunche or ftalks fhould be raked out, which will prevent the wine being fo tart as it otherwife would have been; but if the grapes are perfectly ripe, you may put the whole together into butts or vatts, where it is to be ftirred four or five times during the firft twenty-four hours, that the wine may acquire a deeper colour; it muft then be left to ferment and fettle, and when cold and clear, drawn into cafks, previoufly rinced out with wine, the bungs to be left out for fome time, and care taken to keep the cafks filled up; when the fret is over the wine muft be cleared off from the dregs.

For white wines different modes are neceffary, tho' the like may be bruifed as with the red, which gives it a ftronger body but generally a tart flavour, and caufes it to ferment in a greater degree, and confequently more proper for brandy; but to give the white wine a proper and agreeable flavour the grapes (contrary to the red) are to be left until rotten, and conftantly gathered as they become fo, which caufes them to produce the greater quantity of wine, the whole mafs diffolving the better; they are put into the wine-prefs, and all the pulp and liquid particles fqueezed out and poured into the tub, without lees. It muft be conftantly watched for the beginning, which is governed by the weather, but it is generally effected in 48 hours: fhould it be drawn off too late it will turn, which is perceived by its becoming dark or muddy, and when drawn off too foon it ferments in the butts and is greatly injured thereby.

TO MAKE BRANDY

A copper muft be erected over a furnace, the cover to be hermetically fcrewed on, fo that the fteem may be forced to pafs through a pipe fixed near the cover, and joined to a fpiral worm, which paffes through a veffel of cold water, and the liquor drawn from a brafs cock at the extremity thereof; the copper being charged with wine, the veffel through which the worm paffes must be kept continually fupplied with cold water, as otherwife the worm being heated would inftead of producing a liquid, fly off in fmoke. A conftant regular fire should be kept up with billets of wood, as fhould it be too brifk, the worm would drip wine inftead of brandy. The firft liquid produced immediately after the ftill being fet to work, not being perfect brandy, is returned into the copper whenever it may be replenished with frefh wine, for further diftillation; as finally every particle of the wine is diftilled into brandy, and nothing but pure water left, which can be afcertained by a proper hydrometer, which, with pails and clofe casks to prevent evaporation, are alfo neceffary.

[This article is not reproduced in facsimile, but the type in which it is set is as close as practicable in appearance to the original.

The article appeared in the *Sydney Gazette*, the first newspaper published in Australia, in three instalments. The first instalment was in the *Gazette's* first issue (5 March 1803), and the second instalment in the second issue a week later. However, although the editor George Howe (a transported convict) ended the second instalment with the promise, "To be concluded in our next", the third instalment did not appear until the fourth issue (26 March).

Howe did not offer an explanation for the delay in publishing the final instalment, but one may guess that he found that he had run out of space in issue No. 3 after having given up almost half of his paper to telling (in two separate reports) of the appearance in the Criminal Court of a number of convicts who had absconded from Castle Hill, near Sydney, and committed a series of thefts. On the back page (page 4) of issue No. 3, in approximately the position where the first two instalments of the article on the vine had appeared there was the heading:

TRIAL OF INSURGENTS &c.

MARCH 16

The report under the heading began: "This day the court assembled at 10 o'clock, when John Lynch, Thomas Shanks, John Morgan, Laughlan Doyle, Timothy Malahoy, John Brown, James Conroy, and Patrick Ross, stood indicted for feloniously entering the house of Thomas Neal, of Richmond Hill, Settler, on the 22nd of February last, and taking therefrom one bushel and one peck of wheat, his property". It ended: "The evidence being closed, the Court, after some minutes deliberation, returned a verdict—all Guilty—Death!"]

APPENDIX I

2. A VINEYARD IS A
VERY DESIRABLE THING

[From *A Manual of Plain Directions for Planting and Cultivating Vineyards and for Making Wine in New South Wales*, by James Busby. The *Manual*, first published in Sydney in 1830 by the Government Printer, George Howe, was for many years the "Bible" of Australian *vignerons*].

... I will take for granted that two hundred and fifty gallons will be the average produce of an acre of vines, observing, nevertheless, that this will allow the family to consume as many grapes as they please, and, provided they be ripe, they cannot consume too many. It will allow also, of a little loss by depredation; although I hope, that within a very few years, vineyards will be as common as corn fields, and the grapes so abundant, that no one will think it worth while to steal them. Now, then, two hundred and fifty gallons of wine, will be about twelve hundred bottles, and the cost of this is £12 16s. I ought, however, to have added a small sum for the expense of casks to make the wine in, and for keeping it when it is made, for I would not advise any one to go to expense in having vats made expressly for the produce of one acre. By adding, therefore, twenty-four shillings to the above sum, the expense of casks will be covered, for they will last for several years. The whole cost, may accordingly be stated, at fourteen pounds, or something more than two-pence three farthings a bottle. It must not be lost sight of, that this produce of twelve hundred bottles is obtained by treating the vines in the way calculated to procure the very best wine, they are capable of yielding, in a climate much colder than that of New South Wales, and consequently less capable of ripening so large a crop of grapes; and that the vines could with equal ease, be made to yield double that quantity. The wine would, of course, have less body, and it would be inferior in flavour, but it would still be an excellent drink for daily use.

It thus very plainly appears, I think, that an acre of vines would yield a tolerably abundant supply of wine for a family, and a large family too, and, were part of it made of second rate quality, for two or three servants also. Can it then be accounted for, on any other ground, than that of ignorance, that every settler who holds thirty acres of land, does not drink his bottle of wine daily, and seeing that it can be obtained at from three halfpence, to threepence a bottle, who is there that would grudge a bottle every day of the year, to each of his assigned servants and labourers?

The daily consumption of the farmer's own family, being thus easily provided for, the next step with most of them, will be, to try how the produce of their vineyards would meet the market. I have tasted samples of wine made by five different individuals, in different parts of the Colony, and though it would be unfair to say that most of them were such wines as would come into competition, in the markets of Europe, with what is produced in older wine countries, yet I have no hesitation in saying, that they were all very promising wines. A bottle of wine, made about fifteen months ago, from the vineyard which I myself planted, in the year 1825, at the Male Orphan School, at Cabramatta, was lately produced at a dinner party, in Sydney, and was tasted by some of the best judges in the Colony. It was perfectly sound, and was said to resemble a Burgundy wine, which bears a very high price.—And yet this wine grew upon a soil naturally inferior to most soils in the Colony for a vineyard.—One thing I have, however, observed, that all the wines I have tasted of this country's growth, have been entirely free from that peculiarly nauseous and earthy taste, which distinguishes almost all the Cape wines which are brought to this Colony, and consumed in such abundance. When I consider, therefore, that all these samples, with one exception, came from vineyards, which had not been more than five years planted, and that in France, they scarcely reckon upon a wine being fit for the market, till the vines are six years old; and also, that the quality of the wine invariably improves with the age of the vines. When I consider this, I can no more doubt that this Colony is capable of producing wine, and good wine too, than I can doubt of its being capable of producing wheat and maize.

I consider it therefore, as a matter of course, that when the settler has raised wine for the consumption of his own establishment, he will begin to extend his vineyards, in order to supply the wants of the Towns-people, who have no vineyards of their own; and having thus always a marketable commodity, he will become at length, in a great measure, independent of the uncertainty of the climate; for it will rarely, if ever, happen, that the grain crops and the vintage will fail in the same season; the vine being a plant that bears drought better than almost any other.—When, therefore, it becomes necessary to send to Van Diemen's Land for wheat, instead of draining the Colony of money to pay for it, the Sydney merchant can pay for it in the wine, with which the settler pays him his bill. And, I think it likely enough, from the coldness of the climate of the Sister Colony, that they will require as much of our wine as we shall require of their wheat. Last of all, if neither the Sydney people, nor the Van Diemen's Land people, should relish the settler's wines, he is sure of another vent for them; for he has only to dispose of them to the distiller, who will be able to obtain one gallon of brandy from every four or five gallons of wine. And, if we *must* consume ardent spirits, this is the spirit which ought to be consumed, in preference to the brandy which is brought over half the world from France, or the rum from the West Indies, or even the spirit which is made from grain produced in the Colony.

I think I have said enough to satisfy every person, who takes the trouble of reading the foregoing observations, that a vineyard is, in every way, a very desirable thing. . . .

APPENDIX I

3. WHO STOLE
JOHN MACARTHUR'S VINES ?

[Every Australian knows that the turbulent Captain John Macarthur, who arrived in Sydney with the New South Wales Corps in 1790, was the man who first imported merino sheep to Australia—a fact that is commemorated by the two-dollar note in Australia's new decimal currency. It is less well known that he also imported vines and was one of the first settlers to plant a vineyard for wine-making on a commercial scale. John Macarthur's son William was, like his father, an enthusiastic vigneron and in 1844 published a book *On the Culture of the Vine, Fermentation, and the Management of Wine in the Cellar*, from which the following curious extract is taken.]

. . . It may naturally be asked how it happens, if the soil and climate be so favourable for vineyard culture, that we do not see our hills clothed with vines, and their produce the common beverage, of every class in the community? The reply is simple and obvious; it is owing to the almost entire absence of practical acquaintance with its details. Had our Home Government fulfilled its duty, there would have been conveyed to our shores, during the prevalence of the Bounty System of Emigration, two or three hundred families of German, Swiss, or French vine dressers. Had this been done, vineyards would, ere this, have become common amongst us. . . .

The want of foreign vine dressers is, however, not the only reason why the cultivation of vineyards has made such singularly slow progress. The colony has been most unfortunate with respect to the sorts of vines, which, up to a comparatively recent period, were introduced into it, of which I am about to give the reader one or two curious examples. During the earlier years of the colony, the wars of the French Revolution were the means of preventing communication with the Continent of Europe; but in 1815 and 1816, my father made a tour of eighteen months' duration through France and Switzerland, for the express purpose of collecting vines, and of obtaining information respecting their culture, previously to his return to New South Wales. In this tour, which was made chiefly on foot, through the greater part of the best wine districts, to the extent of many hundred miles, he was accompanied by my brother and myself. He returned to England in 1816, with, I think, about thirty of the best varieties of the vine (from six to twelve cuttings or plants of each) which were collected in the vineyards in which they grew, and taken from the vines, in most instances, literally under our eyes. Circumstances preventing his embarkation for this colony until the following year, the whole of these vines, with a great variety of olive and fig trees, the caper, and other valuable plants, were entrusted to the care of a nursery man near London. In April, 1817, this collection, or what was *said to be* this collection, was embarked with us, together with several other sorts of vines, and a number of fruit trees, and other plants from England. At Madeira, where we touched, the season being too far advanced to obtain cuttings at the time, a mercantile correspondent undertook to procure and forward to Sydney, by the first eligible opportunity, several tubs full of the best varieties of wine grapes (which are understood to be seven in number) cultivated in the island.

In October, 1817, a great part of the collection we had with us was landed alive at Sydney, and in the course of time throve. But after several years' careful cultivation, the only sorts which we obtained, were those now known as the Gouais (La Folle), Muscat Noir, Black Hamburgh, little Black Cluster, Miller's Burgundy, and Sweet Water, of which, all but the first three had been before introduced, and probably only the first two had formed part of the original collection from France. We have never been able to account in any manner for the remainder of the French vines, and from the information we now possess, we know that they ought to have consisted, after making a due allowance for deaths, of from twenty to twenty-five of the most valuable varieties in France. The Madeira collection arrived in good order the following year, 1818, but instead of comprising *seven* distinct sorts, consisted of only *one*, and that so worthless, as to be utterly unfit for wine, or, indeed, any other useful purpose. However mortifying it is to discover at the end of a voyage, that one has incurred much trouble and expense to introduce plants of little value, it is infinitely more so, when several years elapse before the fact is ascertained, as in this instance, proved to be the case. We cultivated our vines, and in the course of time planted a vineyard of more than an acre in extent. We fully believed that it contained the best varieties grown in Languedoc, at the Hermitage, Côte Rotie, in the Côte d'or, &c., &c. And were greatly surprised to discover, when they bore fruit, that so little variety existed amongst them; as if one or two sorts only were prevalent over such an immense extent of vineyard country. Our wine, too, did not answer expectation. In short, although the vines flourished, the vineyard seemed to be a failure, and ignorant of the true cause, we were half inclined to give the matter up.

In 1825, the Australian Agricultural Company imported other sorts of vines from the Horticultural Society's Garden at Chiswick. Of the genuineness of these, there could be no doubt; and amongst them was the Verdeilho, one of the best sorts cultivated at Madeira. From this variety, and from two sorts of Muscat, we, in a few years more, began to make good wine, but in very small quantity. Having, however, now ascertained that our earlier failures were attributable rather to the sorts of grapes we had to plant, than to any fault in the soil, we proceeded with greater confidence in our experiments. But, by this time, ten or twelve precious years had been *lost*.

In 1832, Mr. Busby's collection was imported, and the vines began to bear in 1834. The spurious nature of our importation in 1817, was now made very evident. I may here observe, that on two other occasions, within my knowledge, have spurious collections been sent to the colony, one from Xeres, the other from the Constantia Vineyard, but it would little interest the reader, were I to enter into the details.

I have stated the foregoing facts, that the causes of our slow progress in vineyard cultivation may be better comprehended. . . . How different is the field now thrown open to the cultivator! We have varieties, the genuineness of which is unquestionable, suited to almost every variation of our climate . . .

3. THE GRAPES THE EARLY COLONISTS GREW

[From *A Manual of Plain Directions for Planting Vineyards and for Making Wine in New South Wales*, by James Busby, 1830]

. . . I must say a few words about the varieties of grapes that are now to be procured in this colony. Most of the varieties I am about to describe, are, however, still scarce in the Colony, and are not to be procured by every one; for it is not reasonable to expect, that those who have taken the trouble and incurred the expense; and a great deal of trouble and expense it is, to import new sorts from wine countries, should part with any of them till their own wants be supplied.—From what I am about to say of each variety, it will easily be seen which are the most desirable, but I must here repeat, that the changes which the vines undergo, not only in different climates, but in different soils and situations, are so great as to have become quite proverbial, and a grape which may be of little value in one situation, may prove most valuable in another. Besides as I have before said, I do not consider that any sort has yet had a fair trial.

BLACK GRAPES

The Burgundy Grape.—Generally, but improperly, called the *Claret grape*. This variety, and the following one,—namely, the *Miller's Burgundy*, have produced the most of the red wine which has, as yet, been made in the Colony. It is a small grape, and the berries are very closely set on the bunch.—It does not blight, but in some situations is apt to shrivel in very hot weather.—It is rather a free bearer in this Colony, though in Burgundy and Champagne, where it is the grape which yields the first-rate wines, it is remarkable for producing little.

Miller's Burgundy.—This grape resembles the foregoing in many particulars, and is not easily distinguishable from it, the bunches and berries, though rather larger, being very similar in appearance. But, on the same bunch, part of them may be observed to be still green, while others are perfectly ripe. It is rather a sweeter fruit, though not so highly flavoured as the preceding.—It ripens earlier, and is known from it, chiefly by the hoariness of its leaves, which are covered with a thick down, especially when they first break forth.—As this is generally understood to be the variety, originated from seed about a century ago by the celebrated gardener, *Miller;* it cannot be said that it has been proved as a wine grape, in any country, and it is certainly a less valuable one than the *Burgundy*, on account of its ripening so unequally.

These two grapes are the only ones which Mr. Gregory Blaxland, has cultivated for several years, in his vineyard, at Brush Farm, near Parramatta, having rooted out all the other sorts on account of their liability to take the blight.—Cuttings of both these varieties can be obtained, in great abundance, at Mr. Blaxland's at Brush Farm; at Mr. Macarthur's, at Camden; and at the Male Orphan School, at Cabramatta. I have not been able to ascertain by whom the Burgundy grape was first introduced, but I have heard that the Miller's Burgundy, was first brought to the Colony by the Reverend Mr. Marsden—both sorts were also brought out by Mr. Macarthur, in 1817.

The Muscadelle Grape.—There are, I believe, three varieties of the Black Muscadelle grape in the Colony.—One variety has long been cultivated by Mr. Robert Campbell, sen. of Sydney, and this gentleman has very liberally distributed cuttings of it throughout the Colony.—I am not aware by whom it was first imported.—Another variety was introduced by Mr. John Macarthur, in 1817. This is of a much deeper colour than the former one, and has a remarkably rich vinous flavour.—A third variety of the black, and one of the *Red Muscadelle*, were introduced by the Australian Agricultural Company, in 1825.—None of the last three varieties have, as yet, taken the blight at Camden, where they have been cultivated.—The first variety is unfortunately more or less subject to it. Grapes of this species are generally cultivated for sweet wines, in all wine countries, and the late Dr. Townson made a very passable sweet wine from Mr. Campbell's variety, at Bunbury Curran, near Campbell-Town.

The Tinta or Tintilla.—This is a highly valued grape for making wine in hot countries, but is chiefly cultivated, in colder climates, to colour other wines; the juice being of a deep purplish red colour. This variety was imported by the Australian Agricultural Company, in 1825, and has been since cultivated at Camden, where it has not yet blighted.—Mr. Fraser, has also, in the Government Gardens, at Sydney, two plants which he raised from seeds of the same variety, sent him from the Cape of Good Hope.—These seedlings have borne fruit, and are in every respect similar to those brought out by the Company.

Black Portugal, or Oporto Grape.—This variety was introduced by Mr. John Macarthur, in 1817, and has been cultivated at Camden. There are a few plants of it at the Male Orphan School, and, I believe, also at the vineyard, near Campbell Town, which belonged to the late Dr. Townson.—I am not aware whether it is to be found elsewhere in the Colony.—It is the grape from which the Port wine is chiefly made, but Mr. William Macarthur remarks, that it has not yet yielded a wine of agreeable flavour with him, and it has also produced a very weak and insipid wine at the Orphan School, where a small quantity of it was made from it, the last season.—It is, however, well worthy of further attention, being the grape of a warm climate, a prolific bearer, and not subject to blight.

Wantage Grape.—This variety was imported by the Australian Agricultural Company, in 1825, and is also cultivated at Camden.—It has not yet taken the blight.— The berries are very large, of a pale violet colour, very thin skinned, and juicy, and exceedingly well flavoured.—I am not aware, whether or not, this has been cultivated as a wine grape.

Black Hamburgh.—This variety has been cultivated for many years in the Government Gardens, at Sydney, and has never blighted.—Mr. Fraser has distributed a great many cuttings from it throughout the Colony. Though an excellent eating grape, it is not known as a wine grape.

Black Cluster.—This, which is most likely a variety of the *Burgundy*, has also been in the Colony for many years, and has been cultivated in the Government Gardens, at Sydney. It is not a very plentiful bearer, and is late in ripening.—The berries do not ripen regularly.

Besides the above, there is also another black grape in the Colony, which was first, I believe, cultivated in the garden of Mr. Campbell, senior, of Sydney. There are also a few plants at Mr. Johnstone's, at Annandale, and at the late Dr. Townson's.— In all these places it has proved a very poor bearer,—each vine producing at the most only two or three bunches. Some cuttings of it, however, which were lately transferred from the latter place to Bayley Park, by Mr. Jones, appear to have altogether renewed their vigour, and have produced, during the last season, a very abundant crop. The fruit of this variety is of an oblong shape, and of a much larger size than any of the preceding—many of the grapes being as large as pigeons' eggs. It is altogether a most valuable grape, and very suitable for raisins.

WHITE GRAPES

The Sweetwater.—This is the most common variety of the vine in the Colony, and has been for many years cultivated as a table grape. It is generally subject to blight, but is so very prolific a bearer, that even in the most blighting seasons, there will often be a large number of bunches uninjured, especially of those which are well shaded by the leaves.—There are, however, several sub-varieties, and some of them do not blight in all situations. One of these was amongst the number which Mr. John Macarthur imported in 1817.—It has produced with Mr. William Macarthur, a pleasant

139

light wine, and as it does not appear to be liable to injury, either from excessive heat or moderate rains, that gentleman considers it well worth cultivating as a wine grape.

There is also another description of white grape, which was imported at the same time, by the abovenamed gentleman, as a wine grape from France, supposed to be the French *Gouais*, which is a very prolific bearer, and does not blight.—This variety is distinguished by a peculiar flavour, and is not a very good table grape.— It is apt to rot if much rain fall as it approaches to maturity, but in other respects, it is very hardy.—It has hitherto produced only a weak and insipid wine in this Colony.

The Verdelho, or Verdelet.—The Madeira Grape.—This variety, which is principally employed in making Madeira wine, was imported by the Australian Company, in 1825.—It has been cultivated since that time, at Camden, is a plentiful bearer, and appears to be free from every sort of disease.—This variety has, also, I believe, been imported on several other occasions, and is to be found in several gardens in the Colony.—I have understood, that Mr. George Townsend, and Mr. Park, of Williams' River, have imported this and several of the other varieties which are cultivated at Madeira.

White Muscat of Alexandria.—This variety was sent from the Cape, to Sir Thomas Brisbane, by Lord Charles Somerset, in 1824, and it is understood to be one of the varieties from which Constantia wine is made. It was observed, both by Mr. Macarthur and Mr. Fraser, that the plants of this variety blighted, for the first time, last spring.

White Muscadelle.—This variety, which has long been cultivated by Mr. Campbell, sen. was originally brought by that gentleman, from the Cape, in 1805. Mr. Fraser is of opinion, that is the same as the preceding.

Green Grape from the Cape.—This was also sent by Lord Charles Somerset, to Sir Thomas Brisbane.—It has been cultivated at Camden, and in the Government Gardens, at Sydney, and appears to be free from any disease. It ripens very late, and is said to be a delicious table grape.

Besides, what I have above-mentioned, or described, Mr. William Macarthur has lately received from England, the following varieties, which are the surviving plants of a considerable collection for which he sent an order; namely—*the Black Hamburgh; Red ditto; Royal Muscadine; White Frontignac; White Corinth, and Red ditto.* A very valuable importation of vines has lately been made from Lisbon, by Captain Wilson, Director of Public Works—including the *Collares grape*—the *Bucellas—Port— Calcavella—Muscatel,* and the large white, red, and pink eating grapes, which are brought from Portugal to London in jars. Mr. Alexander Riley, of London, has also sent to the Colony, the *Pansé,* a raisin grape, which is cultivated in the South of France.—A variety of *Muscatel,* from Marseilles, and the white and red *Hermitage* grapes.—These were very lately brought out by Mr. Dutton, in the Lady Blackwood.

So, that altogether, by the time these varieties have increased, so as to allow of their being generally distributed, the Colony can hardly to fail to be possessed of some varieties, capable of yielding good wine.—I must not omit to mention, however, in addition to the foregoing foreign varieties, that a number of native varieties have been originated from seed, by Mr. William Macarthur, and as these have no new habits to acquire, I think there is every chance that some of them will prove more suitable to the climate, and more valuable for cultivation than any of the imported varieties, whose habits have been formed in a different climate.

Mr. William Macarthur informs me, that about two hundred and fifty seedling vines, out of a large number which he raised from seed, in 1824, have produced fruit this year, and the year preceding; they were raised from the seeds of the *Burgundy*, the *Miller's Burgundy*, the *Sweetwater*, and another white grape. The greater part, more or less, resemble their parents, but there is a considerable number which assume an appearance and flavour so entirely different, that their origin cannot be detected. He considers a few of them to be very superior to their parents, but the greater part, as will always happen in similar cases, are decidedly inferior. Mr. Macarthur, has also, some young seedlings, of a twelvemonth old, raised from the seed of these last, and from the different varieties of the Muscadelle grape.—It is his intention, not to distribute the cuttings from these seedlings, till he has had a longer experience of their qualities; but, in the meantime, he proposes to increase these, and also the foreign varieties, which have lately been imported, as rapidly as possible. He states, that by this means, he hopes they will become earlier available to the Public, than if they were now distributed in very small quantities. And, I will add, that by his attention to this subject, he has merited the thanks of that Public, to an extent which they will be able more justly to appreciate, when they become better acquainted with the subject. I, for my part, have always been of opinion, that we must look forward to raising new varieties from seed, as the surest means of obtaining grapes, suitable to the climate. . . .

5. AN EMPEROR'S COMPLIMENT

[James King arrived in the Colony of New South Wales in 1827 as a free settler. He obtained a grant of about two thousand acres of land on the Williams River, a tributary of the Hunter. On this property, which he named Irrawang, he grew grain and raised cattle, but for some years his main interest was in establishing himself as a merchant in Sydney. Later, however, he planted a vineyard at Irrawang. In 1857, while on a visit to Europe, he printed in Edinburgh, for private circulation, a booklet titled *Australia May Be an Extensive Wine-Growing Country*, from which the following extract is taken.]

. . . In the year 1854, I was solicited specially, and by circular, to send specimens of my vineyard produce to the Commissioners in Sydney, for the purpose of being transmitted by them to the Paris Exhibition. Before they were sent to France, they with others were tested in Sydney by a special jury, and testimonials, according to their merits, were awarded to some of the growers by the local commission. On account of the approved quality of my samples, I was awarded one of the highest premiums in the power of the Commissioners to bestow.

When the samples reached the Exhibition at Paris, they were reported on very favourably by the special jurors of the Exhibition. The commission, consequently, awarded me a medal.

A few days after the ceremony of closing the Exhibition by the Emperor, I was informed by Sir William Macarthur (who, from the feeling of patriotism alone, was Commissioner from Sydney at Paris, a liberality for which the colony is highly indebted), that the most approved specimens of New South Wales wines at the Exhibition had been requested for the purpose of being placed on the table in front of the Emperor, along with other choice articles, during the ceremony of closing.

Sir William Macarthur's wine and my own were accordingly selected for that purpose, with the view, most assuredly, of paying a compliment to the British crown, it being the production of one of Great Britain's dependencies. Such a compliment from France, the greatest wine-growing country in the world, might well be regarded with satisfaction. Such of my samples as were left at the close of the Exhibition, were at my request sold in Paris. They realised 3 francs 75 cents per bottle, some being only pint bottles. The gentleman who bought them afterwards said that they were well worth 8 francs per bottle. The whole, including some other trifling articles, produced 120 francs, which sum I directed to be paid over to the French Widows' Fund in Paris.

About three years ago, I commenced making sparkling wine; and with that object I had expended at least £500 in wages, apparatus, material, &c., besides having the unfinished wine on hand. I had only completed about 200 dozen, when I became deficient of the proper corks, and an additional supply had to be procured from France. By the time they arrived, I became unwell, and was induced shortly after to undertake a voyage to London, in the hope of recovery; consequently, the further production at Irrawang of the sparkling wine was suspended until I am able to return.

The quality of that made was unexceptionable.

A gentleman about that time returning to England, procured a case to take with him. He reached home, and in writing from Wales in November last, to a friend in London, spoke of what was to be seen at L———, and added: "They one day there broached two bottles of Mr King's champagne at a dinner-party; it was part of the case you gave me on leaving. It was so good that I thought it was French until they told me otherwise; you therefore see that it keeps well."

The samples sent by me to the Paris Exhibition included that of sparkling wine, which I believe was that alluded to by the jurors of the Commission, since the gentleman named in the Report besides myself, did not, I think, send any samples of that sort of wine. The following is an extract from the Report; "In the department of Australia (New South Wales), the evidence of the increasing importance of the vineyards of that colony, in the specimens of the wines exhibited by Messrs Macarthur, King, and Brown, are deserving of special notice.

"The wines include white wines akin to those of the Rhine; red light wines like those of Burgundy; Mousseux varieties, with a bouquet, body, and flavour, equal to the finest champagnes: Muscats and other sweet wines, rivalling the Montignac of the Cape." . . .

6. VICTORIA BEFORE PHYLLOXERA

[On 25 April 1866, the *Illustrated Australian News* published the hopeful account of Victoria's wine industry that appears below. The "large illustration" mentioned in the article as showing the busy and joyous scene of gathering in the vintage appears on this page.]

The vineyard interest in Victoria, should it progress in the future as it has done during the last decade, will be entitled to rank as the fourth great producing interest of the colony.

From comparatively small beginnings, for the early plantations of the vine embraced only in an acre here and there, it has now attained a position which has obtained for it a special recognition at the hands of the Legislature. The odd acres have swelled to thousands; at Sunbury, Tabilk, Yering and in the Albury districts may now be found vineyards, each comprising from fifty to a hundred and thirty acres of land, whilst on every side the traveller cannot fail to meet with plots of the life-giving plant, of dimensions according with the objects of the owner, be they growing wine for sale or simply for family use.

The notable increase of private vineyards is one of the most cheering signs of the times; a few years hence and every country resident will be enabled to entertain his visitors with the produce of his own little vineyard, and that too without stint or measure. Nor will this be without effect upon the health and morals of the people. Already in the western districts, in which vine culture is longest established, many hotels have been closed in consequence solely of the facilities for obtaining native wines from the numerous growers. Thus, instead of frequenting public-houses and ruining his health by the consumption of ardent spirits, the working man of the Western and other vine-bearing districts of Victoria can quaff, equally with the wealthiest in England, his draught of the pure and invigorating juice of the grape.

The price of the lighter descriptions of wine varies from three to five shillings a gallon, at which a well-managed vineyard will yield a very respectable income, and at which, too, the working man of Victoria can well afford to make a liberal use of it.

But we have touched upon only one phase of the question. The southern half of the continent of Australia would appear to be peculiarly adapted for the vine. In other countries, as in Germany and France, the vine will flourish only in certain situations few and far between; but in Victoria more especially, the whole country seems adapted for growing the vine to perfection. Excepting only on the very highest portions of our mountain ranges, the vine thrives and produces wines of the most delicate quality, for which at some future date, when we produce them in excess of our own wants, a demand will doubtless arise in Great Britain.

On several occasions of late years the value of our vines has been emphatically pronounced upon by judges at the English exhibitions, where our wines, young as they were, competed successfully with many of European growth. When our wines shall have attained their ripe age at which they yield the finest qualities of wine, Victoria will have no cause to dread competition with any.

On reference to the map of Australia, it will be seen that a mountain range divides the northern portion of Victoria from the southern; and this division is of very great importance to the vigneron. The climate north of the range resembles that of some portions of Spain; whilst the southern side, in which are included the Upper Yarra ranges, present so great a diversity of climate that emigrants from the Rhine, Switzerland, or any part of France cannot fail to find a site and a climate that will remind them of home. Victoria will be, therefore, enabled to produce not only light wines like those of France, but also others that will equal in strength and surpass in bouquet the highly esteemed wines of the Spanish peninsula.

Some of the best wines produced on the Murray contain naturally as large a percentage of spirit as the strongest of Spain; such are not the wines that can be drunk in quantity as a regular beverage. For general use the lighter products of the southern districts are far better adapted.

Around Melbourne and Geelong the chief grapes employed for wine-making are the Chasselas, Gouais, several varieties of Burgundy and Frontignan, the Hermitage, the Mourastelle or Espart, the Mataro, Carignan, Grenache, Verdeilho, &c. Most of these are also extensively used on the Murray, and in addition the Aucarot, Reisling, Palomino, Muscat of Alexandra, Pedro Ximenes, Carbinet, and others too numerous to mention. In fact, Australian vine growers have ransacked the world for varieties of the grape, so that novices are somewhat puzzled to decide upon the sorts they should grow.

Experience, however, is yearly deciding in favor of certain kinds and against others; the value of the Hermitage, for example, is now generally recognised, and the Aucarot bids fair to become an established favorite around Melbourne as it already is upon the Murray.

The process of making wine from the grape is remarkably simple, for the juice of thoroughly ripened grapes requires no addition of any kind. The juice having been separated by pressure from the husks and stalks, fermentation proceeds and converts the luscious must into the beverage known as wine.

The large illustration of this month gives the busy and joyous scene of gathering in the vintage. The sketch was taken at Yering, the property of Mr Castella, on the Yarra flats. 100 acres are there under vine cultivation, while fresh ground is being occupied yearly. Some of the vines are now of twenty years' standing, and their healthy and luxuriant aspect testify the suitability of the soil for vine culture, as well as admirable management. About one-half of the 100 acres are in bearing, and the yield is about 400 gallons per acre.

The soil is a loamy clay, with a gravelly substratum. The grape varieties are Pineau Hermitage, Burgundy, White Chasselas, Gouais and Tokay.

The group of vignerons which so briskly ply the secateur, and carry the grapes to the cart provided for their conveyance, is composed of all nationalities, German, Swiss and Italian, as also American, Irish and Scotch, while the energetic manager of the wine press is an Englishman.

The group of visitors so courteously chaperoned by the proprietor are a few of the many who enjoy the liberal hospitality of this Australian Arcadia.

The wines of this district are becoming very popular in Melbourne, and other enterprising colonists are fast filling up the valley with similar establishments, three being already in good working order, and ardently competing for superiority.

A wine-tasting at the cellars of A. and R. Caughey, Melbourne, in 1882.
The cellars were on the south bank of the Yarra River, near Princes Bridge.

7. VINTAGE TIME IN SOUTH YARRA

[South Yarra today is a fashionable and rather densely populated suburb of Melbourne less than three miles from the city's centre, but a hundred years ago there were vineyards there. The following extract is from *The Vine and Wine Making in Victoria*, published in 1861 by Wilson and Mackinnon, at that time proprietors of the once influential but now defunct Melbourne newspaper the *Argus*. The book is a compilation of letters to the newspaper signed "V." and "Beberrao". Apparently, however, there was only one author, who used two pseudonyms.]

. . . I have come to the conclusion that the Riesling is the best white wine grape we possess. . . . I have not during the four years I have been in the colony, seen the failure of a vine, or of any amateur in his wine-making with this grape. My own experiment this season afforded me especial pleasure. I obtained about one gallon of wine per 15lb.

of grapes. In making white wine, as colour is no object, I separated the skins, stalks, &c., from the juice, by straining at the time of crushing. Fermentation commenced within 24 hours, and continued for about 7 days. I then re-strained the wine, which had become almost still, and found a fermentation, scarcely perceptible, for some 8 or 10 days more, whenever the day was hot; but within three weeks from the time of crushing I had a perfect wine, light and exhilarating, and as refreshing as tea. Its fitness for immediate use was soon proved. I have tasted numerous samples when equally young, made by other parties this season, and found the same maturity and fitness for immediate consumption in them all.

The largest quantity I have seen of this wine, made in the neighbourhood of Melbourne this season, was in the vineyard of Mr. Wisewould, at South Yarra (about 300 gallons.) The vines are grown on the yellow rock, which may be observed in the cutting of the railway in that neighbourhood. The wine is exceedingly good; and, indeed, the vineyard and the three wines made therefrom, are alike creditable to the young Swiss who has the management.

The day I visited this vineyard, I had drunk some two or three tumblers of Riesling, made by different amateur friends, and wound up with a tumbler of the same, made by the young Swiss, making my consumption in the course of the afternoon more than a bottle, but found myself in good working condition, and went to work. Had I drunk an equal quantity of imported beer, or one-fourth the quantity of imported wine, I would not have risked my repute as an accountant by at once going to work. . . .

8. SOUTH AUSTRALIAN VINEYARDS
IN THE EARLY 1860's

[The following extracts are from *The Vineyards and Orchards of South Australia*, by Ebenezer Ward (Adelaide, 1862), "being a series of articles written expressly for the 'South Australian Advertiser' and 'Weekly Chronicle', and now reprinted from those journals."]

AULDANA
THE RESIDENCE OF MR. PATRICK AULD

. . . Mr. Auld, recognising the importance of enabling the manager of an extensive vineyard always to overlook as far as possible the proceedings of his employes, has

Auldana Vineyard at Magill, near Adelaide, in the 1880s. The vineyard was planted about thirty years earlier by Patrick Auld. It is now owned by Penfold's Wines, but the Auld family still has links with the wine industry. Michael Auld, a great-grandson of Patrick Auld, is a director of H. M. Martin and son, owners of Stonyfell Vineyard.

erected a substantial dwelling-house on the crest of an adjacent hill, which commands a view of the whole of the south vineyard, and en passant we may mention that the prospect obtained from the situation of this residence is magnificent in the extreme. An uninterrupted bird's-eye view of the whole extent of the plains surrounding Adelaide and of the city itself, with the Gulf and its shipping in the background, is afforded to the spectator, and it would be difficult we imagine to discover a more enchanting or more varied scene even in lands of far greater pretensions to scenic advantages than South Australia.

Entering the south vineyard on its northernmost side, the visitor finds himself at the foot of what is known as the Verdeilho Hill, the whole of which was planted in 1860 with vines of that sort. To the right of the hill are planted some Tokay, Muscat of Alexandria, and a few Gouais. This hill and those beyond it to the south are admirably situated for the growth of the vine, inasmuch as they form a perfect natural basin and the slopes on which the vines are planted shelter each other from all winds, especially from the destructive wind which blows periodically from the south-west. An adjoining hill affords an additional protection to the vineyard from the ravages of the north winds. At the very bottom of this natural basin, and where the soil is richest and

148

deepest, an orchard has been planted, comprising a well chosen selection of the most favorite varieties of fruits. The trees are remarkably healthy and bearing well.

Above the orchard, on the southernmost slopes of the vineyard, is a considerable extent of Grenache, Verdeilho, and Donzelinho, planted in 1856. Parallel therewith is an acre of Carignan grafted with Carbonet for the purposes of classification.

Mr. Auld has been taught by experience the necessity of ascertaining by careful study and observation the particular kinds of grapes adapted to produce the best kinds of wine, and the exact proportion in which they must be respectively used for that purpose, and then of classifying his vineyard accordingly. Having acquired a knowledge of this nature upon which he is prepared to rely in the manufacture of his wines, Mr. Auld has for the last year or two devoted considerable attention to classification. To this end a portion of the vineyard has been devoted to the growth of particular sorts of vines in their required proportions, while the yield of other vines has been

An early picture of Auldana Winery. The old cellars at Auldana are still in use.

reduced by grafting upon them the necessary sorts. Thus, for instance, Carbonet have been grafted upon Carignan, and Verdeilho upon Muscat of Alexandria.

The Grenache on the southern side of the vineyard are flourishing in great luxuriance, but Mr. Auld has not thought it necessary either to trellis or stake them. Yet he entirely abjures the theory of thick planting, multiplied centres of vitality, and close pruning. His vines are all planted at 10 feet by 5, except the Verdeilho, which stand at 7 feet by 7. The vineyard is generally hand-weeded as many as four times in each year. . . . Mr. Auld prefers doing this work by hand labor to using the horse-hoe, which he regards as at the best a slovenly and incomplete process.

Amongst the sorts planted in the south vineyard during the years 1857-'8-'9 and '60 are the Mataro, the Malbec, Black Portugal, and Shiraz. In the early part of 1860 Mr. Auld had an additional extent of 30 acres, equally as well situated and as well adapted for the growth of the vine as is the south vineyard, trenched and prepared for planting. He was, however, deterred from carrying out his intentions of putting in the vines by the high price of labor and the uncertainty whether he would be able to procure a sufficient number of laborers to cultivate them. Above the South Auldana Vineyard Mr. Auld has, however, planted five acres, and to the eastward another five acres were planted in 1860 with Donzelinho, Verdeilho, Muscat of Alexandria, and Shiraz.

Besides all these there is the Home Park Vineyard, in which ten acres have been planted with Donzelinho, Shiraz and Verdeilho. The soil is very rich, of unusual depth and particularly well adapted for vine-growing, being throughout a good loam, intermixed with decomposed slate and limestone.

Mr. Auld's cellarage is rather limited, but hitherto it has been his practice to store his wines on his premises in Adelaide. . . . Mr. Auld does not use a press in the manufacture of his wines, but relies solely upon a crushing mill and fermentation.

REYNELLA FARM
THE RESIDENCE OF MR. JOHN REYNELL

The township of Reynella is about 13 miles from Adelaide, on the Great South-road. The section on which the Crown hostelrie, the Reynella mills, stores, etc., now stand was originally taken up by Mr. Reynell in 1838, and he has resided in the locality ever since. His present residence is situated barely a quarter of a mile south-east of the township, on a slight eminence rising from Peel's Creek. He has now about 450 acres of land in his possession, and in its management he aims at a combination of vinegrowing, grazing, and farming. He has 15 acres of vines, 2 of orchard and garden, about 100 under crop, and the remainder of the estate is fenced off for grazing.

Mr. Reynell commenced planting 21 years ago, when a considerable portion of the present orchard was formed. A few vine-cuttings obtained from Tasmania were planted at the same time, and three years afterwards wine was made from them. The vineyard proper dates from 1844, when half an acre was planted with cuttings from Mr. Anstey's. In the following season four and a half acres were planted with cuttings obtained from the Macarthur's, of New South Wales, of the sorts recommended in "Maro's" letters—viz., the Verdeilho, Carbonet, Malbec, Pineau Gris, and Gouais.

The situation, however, was too dry, and the soil too light, for most of these varieties to bear largely there, and a number of them have already been superseded. One acre of Pineau Gris has been grubbed up, the Rousillon varieties having previously been planted alternately with rows of Pineau, and the Rousillon have also been grafted on the Carbonet.

In 1847 and 1848 Mr. Reynell obtained cuttings of the white sorts from the Clarendon Vineyard—viz., Pedro Ximenes, Doradilla, Temprana, Palomino-blanco, etc.; and since then he has planted a considerable extent with the Rousillons. Thus his vineyard on the hilly land is chiefly confined to the Clarendon sorts, the Rousillon, and the Verdeilho.

The Carbonet—a variety which, for the quality of its produce, cannot be too highly valued—Mr. Reynell has planted in another vineyard which he formed in 1848 on the flat bordering the creek, and where the soil is a black alluvial deposit on the surface, with a red loam subsoil, In this vineyard there are also Malbec and Shiraz to mix with the Carbonet, the Rousillon sorts, and (planted in 1861) Frontignac, Verdeilho, and Riesling.

None of Mr. Reynell's vines are either staked or trellised, and the Rousillon sorts appear very well able to support themselves. The Verdeilho have a more straggling growth, but Mr. Reynell thinks the cost of staking is greatly in excess of the advantage to be gained. Throughout the vineyard the rows are 6 feet apart, and the vines stand at from 4 to 5 feet in the rows.

The vineyard has a northern to north-eastern aspect, and is well sheltered on the south and west. The ground between the rows is stirred with horse-hoe or plough two or three times every season, and is flanked with rows of almond-trees planted for shelter. On the highest point of the hill the soil is very sandy; but on the lower slopes it is a good red loam on the surface, with a sprinkling of ironstone intermixed, and the subsoil is chiefly composed of friable limestone. Mr. Reynell has about 40 acres of this kind of land at a sufficient elevation above the creek to be secure from frosts, but he is unwilling to increase his vineyard very largely until there is a prospect of our wines being admitted to the Melbourne markets without an import duty. We certainly hope the day is not far distant when our friends across the border will be wise and magnanimous enough to reduce very much, or altogether remove the present impost....

APPENDIX II

AUSTRALIAN WINE GRAPE VARIETIES

[Compiled by Graham Gregory, B.Sc.Agr., R.D.Oen., Principal Viticultural Officer, Department of Agriculture, New South Wales.]

All commercial wine grapes grown in Australia are varieties of the species *Vitis vinifera*, as are the wine-grape varieties of Europe, California and South Africa. They are commonly referred to as European varieties, but their true origin was Asia Minor, where grape culture began many centuries B.C.

The names given to the grape varieties of Australia have been queried from time to time. Some of the doubters have argued that, since no real record of the importation of vines from Europe in the early days of Australian viniculture exists, many of the names given to today's varieties are the product of guesswork. However, recent importations of new stock from Europe and California have shown that all the main Australian varieties, and most of the varieties of lesser importance, are, in fact, correctly named.

The varieties in common, or fairly common, usage in Australia today are listed below in order of tonnages produced during the 1964 vintage. Much the same order applied for the 1965 and 1966 vintages.

WHITE WINE VARIETIES

MUSCAT GORDO BLANCO (Syn. Muscat of Alexandria). 1964 production: 38,660 tons. This is Australia's leading wine-grape variety, well known as the common white muscat dessert grape. It is grown widely throughout Australia and particularly in the irrigation districts of the Murrumbidgee and Murray Valleys. Its prime use today is in the production of the so-called "Cream" Sherry styles, to which it imparts its mild, fruity, muscat character.

In recent years Gordo has been fermented out dry by some makers to produce white table wines, and this style may yet assume some importance on the commercial market. But the quantity being used in this way is small at present.

Gordo is not a vigorous grower, but if the vines are planted reasonably close to one another, the yields per acre are good.

DORADILLO (Syn. Jaen). 1964 production: 22,392 tons. Australia's main distillation variety, Doradillo is grown in most wine districts, but the main plantings are in the irrigation districts. The variety produces a wine of neutral flavour, and thus is good material for the production of fortifying and brandy spirit. However, some wine-makers regard it very highly as a base wine in the making of premium-quality dry Sherry. The results achieved by these makers certainly justify their high regard for this grape.

Doradillo is a late-maturing variety of moderate vigour producing exceptionally heavy crops in large bunches. Yields of fifteen tons per acre are not uncommon in irrigation districts.

SULTANA (Syn. Thompson's Seedless). 1964 production: 20,476 tons. It is somewhat surprising to find that so much of the Sultana grape—the basis of the Australian dried fruits industry—is used for the making of wine. But it has great advantages for the wine-maker in that it matures early. So it can be used as a distillation wine for the manufacture of fortifying spirit and be available early in vintage, avoiding the need to hold large spirit stocks from year to year. Some wine-makers find they can use Sultana to advantage for Sherry.

It is a vigorous, heavy-yielding variety, but is prone to fungus diseases and berry splitting should rain occur near to its maturity on the vine. For this reason its culture is mostly confined to the hot, dry inland irrigation districts.

PEDRO XIMINES. 1964 production: 16,345 tons. One of the best-known varieties for the making of Sherry in Spain, and put to the same use in Australia. It produces a wine of clean and neutral character, enabling Sherries of excellent flavour and delicacy to be made.

Pedro is a vigorous and exceptionally heavy-cropping vine, producing its fruit in big bunches. Yields of as much as twenty tons to the acre have been produced in irrigation areas. The variety has one serious disadvantage in that the bunches of fruit are very prone to rain damage when nearing ripeness. Pedro is therefore best suited to the dry regions, and even then it is tending to be replaced by the more rain-resistant Palomino variety.

SEMILLON (Syn. Hunter River Riesling). 1964 production: 11,338 tons. Semillon is the major white table-wine variety of Australia and is in abundance in most of the wine-growing districts of New South Wales and South Australia.

It is the famous grape of the Sauternes region of France, but in Australia it is used to produce several types of table wine of a drier style, depending on the district in which it is grown. The South Australian Semillons, for instance, are like Hocks, while those grown in the Hunter Valley of New South Wales could only be classified as White Burgundy or Chablis in style. In the Hunter, Semillon is the district's most important white variety.

The grape produces distinctive, high-quality table wines with a mildly fruity flavour and it is therefore fortunate that it is a heavy cropper with moderate vigour, producing its fruit in medium-sized bunches. It is well suited to irrigation districts, where it produces wines of a surprisingly high standard.

WHITE SHIRAZ (Syn. White Hermitage, Ugni Blanc, Trebbiano, St. Emilion). 1964 production: 9,277 tons. The variety is grown extensively in South Australia, where it is usually called Trebbiano or White Hermitage, and it has also become a very popular variety in the Murrumbidgee Irrigation Area of New South Wales. It can be used for several purposes: in the making of white table wines, as a base wine for Sherries, for white dessert wines and for distillation purposes, the use to which this same variety is put in the Cognac area of France.

The Hunter Valley has appreciable areas under the White Shiraz vine, and the region's makers use it solely for white table wines which tend to be rather neutral in character, with a high acid content. Yet some wine-makers regularly produce table wines of distinction from it.

It is an excellent grower's grape, being vigorous and highly productive of big bunches of fruit.

PALOMINO. 1964 production: 7,703 tons. Another famous Sherry grape from Spain which has become very popular in Australia in recent years, since Australian wine-makers have found it eminently suitable for the production of high-quality dry Sherry. It is extensively grown throughout the South Australian wine-growing areas, in New South Wales and in Victoria.

It is a vigorous variety with a high yield, the bunches being large and much more resistant to rain damage than the Pedro Ximenes variety, which it is gradually replacing.

RHINE RIESLING (Syn. White Riesling). 1964 production: 2,336 tons. The famous grape of the Rhine Valley of Germany. Its sole use in Australia is for the production of quality white table wines. It produces wines of strong, distinctive fruitiness which are fresh and grapey when young and which become luscious—with an almost oily characteristic—when aged.

There are extensive plantings of Rhine Riesling in the Barossa Valley of South Australia and in the southern districts of that State. It is a highly prized grape type, but unfortunately it is a very poor bearer, and this has inhibited more widespread plantings by growers. It is characterized by its small bunches.

MADEIRA. 1964 production: 1,717 tons. It is not clear which of the grape types of the island of Madeira this variety is. The traditional Madeira varieties are Boal, Sercial, Verdelho and Malmsey or Malvasia. There are plantings of both Verdelho and Sercial in Australia, but it is not certain whether the Australian variety known as

Madeira is either Boal or Malvasia. This type is grown almost exclusively in the unirrigated districts of South Australia, where it is mostly used for the production of dessert wines of some merit. It is a good cropping variety.

TOKAY. 1964 production: 1,397 tons. Of all the grape types used for dessert-wine production in Australia, Tokay is perhaps the most highly prized for the extreme lusciousness of flavour it imparts to its wine. Most plantings of the variety are in the unirrigated districts of South Australia, but the variety is most famous in the Rutherglen district of Victoria, where production is small but the wines second to none in style, character and flavour.

Tokay is a weak-growing, poor-yielding variety in Australia, but it is believed that the reason for these drawbacks lies in the fact that the variety is almost totally infected with a severe strain of leaf-roll virus.

ALBILLO (Syn. Sherry). 1964 production: 1,142 tons. This variety is confined to South Australian areas, chiefly the districts of the Barossa Valley and Reynella–McLaren Vale areas south of Adelaide. It is used mainly in the production of Sherry, and for this purpose has a great deal of merit. Albillo is a good cropper, but it is not a popular variety and it is unlikely that new plantings of any great extent will be made.

SERCIAL. 1964 production: 816 tons. The occurrence of this variety is confined to the unirrigated districts of South Australia, mainly the Barossa Valley. It is the Sercial of the Madeira Islands, and is used in Australia to produce dessert wines of the Madeira type, although it has been used in the production of blended table wines. The variety is not being replanted by growers and seems certain to decline in significance.

VERDELHO. 1964 production: 496 tons. One of the four main grape types of the island of Madeira. This variety is often given the name of Madeira in Australia—incorrectly. It is most commonly used for white table-wine production and in these wines it develops a full, distinctive character, particularly with age. It is a very useful grape in blends of the white Burgundy type.

Most plantings of Verdelho are located in the unirrigated districts of South Australia, but the variety is also of some importance in the Hunter Valley of New South Wales and in the Swan Valley of Western Australia.

It is a moderately vigorous variety, a good cropper showing medium-sized·bunches that are unfortunately susceptible to the fungus disease oidium because of their compactness.

MARSANNE. 1964 production: 190 tons. Plantings of Marsanne are confined to the unirrigated areas of north and north-eastern Victoria, where it is used for white table wines of a definite varietal character.

CHASSELAS. 1964 production: 149 tons. This variety belongs almost entirely to the north and north-eastern districts of Victoria, although there are very limited plantings in all States. It produces a very delicate white table wine which many wine-makers find eminently suitable as a base wine for Champagne.

Chasselas is a low cropper, of poor vigour, but this again may be the result of leaf-roll virus infection. The fruit shows in small bunches.

WHITE PINOT (Syn. Pinot Chardonnay). White Pinot—under the name of Chardonnay—is the grape of the Burgundy region of France, the grape responsible for that district's famous white wines.

In Australia the White Pinot produces wines of clean, delicate character, particularly favoured as a base for high-quality Champagne. There are small plantings in most of the more important districts, but probably the most famous are those at Great Western, in Victoria, where it has been suggested that these vines are incorrectly named and should be called Irvine's White. This name is undoubtedly only a local name, since the founder of the Great Western vineyard was named Hans Irvine.

The grape is one of the earliest to mature and is moderately productive.

CLARE RIESLING. This variety is grown mostly in the Clare Valley and Watervale districts of South Australia. Considerable confusion has surrounded the naming of this variety, and until recently many Semillon plantings have been called Clare Riesling. But the Clare Riesling is a distinct variety producing high-quality, delicate wines of the Hock type. The variety is a good cropper of moderate vigour.

TRAMINER. The only Traminer plantings of any consequence in Australia are at Minchinbury, near Sydney, and in the Hunter Valley of New South Wales. The variety has the most pronounced varietal characteristic of any white grape, producing a wine with a very aromatic, pungent aroma and flavour.

The variety is extensively grown in the Alsace district of France, where it gained its famous reputation. There is some argument as to whether Traminer and the Gewurztraminer are different varieties, but importations of both named varieties to Australia recently have shown the two to be identical in all respects.

In recent years Traminer wines made in Australia have been found to possess the same classical characteristics as the Alsatian wines and the two main plantings in New South Wales have, in consequence, become even more highly prized. The variety yields good crops of small, tight bunches, but the vine lacks vigour.

BLANQUETTE. This variety is not widely grown in Australia. The largest plantings are in the Hunter Valley of New South Wales, where the grape produces table wines with a marked varietal flavour. It is considered to be a variant of the Doradillo variety, and it resembles this more common type very closely in growth characteristics. However, the berries of the Blanquette in the Hunter Valley are more oval and pointed than those of Doradillo, and there is no resemblance between the wines of the two varieties. Blanquette is a vigorous and productive variety, and its flavour could give it a big future as a blending wine in table wine production.

MONTILS. The variety is grown commercially only in the Hunter Valley of New South Wales, where it has merit in blends with White Shiraz for white table wines. It is thought to be the same grape as Folle Blanche, a widely grown variety of Europe.

Montils produces good crops of medium- to large-sized bunches and possesses moderate vigour, but at present growers show little interest in increasing the Australian acreage of the variety.

AUCEROT RIESLING. There is a very small planting—almost experimental in size—of this variety in the Hunter Valley of New South Wales, and wines from the grape are well known for their distinctive character. But the Hunter plantings are old and no new plantings have taken place, indicating that the variety is likely to go out of existence in the commercial sense.

RED WINE VARIETIES

GRENACHE. 1964 production: 33,299 tons. In terms of quantity of production, Grenache is the most important red-wine variety in Australia, but the variety is declining in popularity. Its wines tend to lack colour and tannin, particularly in the hot irrigation districts, where deficiencies of this kind are accentuated.

Grenache is widely grown in South Australia and to a lesser extent in New South Wales and Victoria, where it is used for both table wines and ports. Its low tannin content causes its wines to age quickly, and for this reason the variety has been in favour in the past for the production of commercial-grade tawny ports, but in recent years increasing quantities of Grenache have been used for table wines. It can produce Rosé wines of merit, but when used for the Claret and Burgundy styles, the wines often lack character.

It is a moderately vigorous and heavy-yielding grape, showing its fruit in medium-sized, tight bunches.

BLACK SHIRAZ (Syn. Red Hermitage, Syrah). 1964 production: 18,941 tons. Shiraz is Australia's most useful red-wine variety. It can be used for either dry red table wines or ports and is grown in all districts. It is the basis of most of the better-quality red table wines, often blended with other varieties. It is the same variety that is planted extensively in the Rhone Valley of France, where it is the basis of the Hermitage wines.

In the southern districts of South Australia and in Victoria it produces wines of the Claret type, with relatively high acid and tannin content. In the warmer districts of

New South Wales and Victoria its wines have a softer finish and are more akin to the wines of Burgundy.

The Shiraz grape is also extensively used for the making of Ports—tawny, vintage and ruby. It is a vigorous variety with good yields in medium-sized to large bunches.

MATARO. 1964 production: 5,371 tons. Most plantings of this variety occur in South Australia, principally in the Barossa Valley and adjoining unirrigated districts. It is used for all types of red wines, but in the red table wines tends to produce a rather harsh character, and the strong tannin finish of many Barossa Valley red wines could be due, in part at least, to the use of this variety. However, some excellent red table wines are now being made from blends of Mataro and Black Shiraz.

It is a heavy-yielding variety, of good vigour.

FRONTIGNAC. 1964 production: 2,252 tons. This is the premium Muscat grape of Australia and is grown throughout South Australia, New South Wales and, to a limited extent, in northern Victoria. It produces dessert wines with a strong, luscious, Muscat character.

It is a good-yielding and moderately vigorous variety, displaying its fruit in medium sized, tight bunches.

ULLIADE (Syn. Oeillade, Cinsaut, Blue Imperial). 1964 production: 1,058 tons. The variety has shown a decline in popularity in recent years, although plantings remain in most States, with the exception of Western Australia. It is used for red table wines and Ports, but is not highly regarded as table-wine material, although some makers have found it useful in blended dry reds.

It is a vigorous variety and produces large crops of meaty grapes.

CABERNET SAUVIGNON. 1964 production: 496 tons. This variety is used exclusively for the production of premium-quality red table wines, particularly of the Claret type. It is the famous grape of the Bordeaux district of France, and is much sought after in Australia. Most plantings are in the unirrigated areas of South Australia, particularly in the districts south of Adelaide, at Reynella-McLaren Vale, and at Coonawarra. There has been a great deal of interest shown in the variety recently in the Hunter Valley and the Murrumbidgee Irrigation Area of New South Wales.

Cabernet Sauvignon produces wines of distinct varietal character and is mostly blended with Black Shiraz in Australia. Its wines are highly coloured and high in tannin and take a longer time to mature than red wines of other grape types. It holds its colour and tannin well even in irrigation districts, where other grape types produce wines deficient in these respects.

The vine itself is vigorous, but the crop is poor, in small, scattered bunches which are difficult to pick. For these reasons it is not popular with growers and explains why it has not so far been more extensively planted in Australia.

CARIGNANE. 1964 production: 684 tons. The variety is of Spanish origin and plantings in Australia are confined mainly to the Barossa Valley of South Australia. It is a heavy-yielding, vigorous grape, but its wines do not have great quality and possess little varietal character.

PINOT NOIR. 1964 production: 319 tons. The highly regarded grape of the Burgundy district of France and the premium grape for the production of French Champagne. It is put to similar good use in Australia in at least one district—the Great Western area of Victoria, where it forms the base wine of some of Australia's premium Champagne. There are also small plantings of the variety in northern Victoria and in the Hunter Valley of New South Wales, and in these regions it is used for the making of dry red table wines. It is usually blended with Black Shiraz for this purpose, its own softness and varietal flavour complementing the colour and body of the Shiraz. Wines made solely from Pinot tend to be deficient in colour and tannin, and only in a very big year can they exist on their own.

Pinot Noir is not a good-yielding variety, and this again may be due to almost total infection of leaf-roll virus—an infection which could have something to do with the lack of colour in the grapes. They appear on the vine in small bunches.

MALBEC. 1964 production: 147 tons. The variety is grown mainly in the Swan Valley of Western Australia, but there are some plantings in northern Victoria and vines have been set in a new development at Wybong, at the northern end of the Hunter Valley of New South Wales. It is used for dry red table wines and is often blended with Black Shiraz.

It crops well when young, but the yield becomes very erratic as the vine ages—due to poor berry setting. This factor seems certain to inhibit further plantings of the variety.

TOURIGA. 1964 production: 78 tons. Touriga is well suited for the making of Tawny Ports of premium quality, and is one of the top grapes of the Douro Valley of Portugal. It is not widely grown in Australia because of its extreme susceptibility to rain damage as the fruit approaches maturity.

The variety may be wrongly named in Australia. There are strong suggestions that most of the so-called Touriga plantings in Australian areas are really Bastardo, another leading port variety.

MORASTEL. 1964 production: 70 tons. Morastel is very similar to, though not identical with, the Carignane variety. It is grown almost exclusively in the Barossa Valley of South Australia, but no new plantings have been made and it would appear that the variety will not enjoy any great importance in the future of Australian wine-making.

APPENDIX II

GENERAL

In addition to the varieties named above, there are many other wine-grape types being grown on a minor commercial scale in Australia. In the white-wine types, these lesser varieties include Folle Blanche, Gouais, Mont Baden, Sauvignon Blanc. In the red-wine types, they include Alicante Bouschet, Aramon, Bastardo, Caniolo, Mammalo, Merlot, Verdot and many others.

In recent years wine-makers and grape-growers alike have shown great interest in the introduction into Australia of new varieties and strains, particularly those which will impart a distinct varietal flavour to their wines. This interest has prompted research organizations, such as the State Departments of Agriculture and the Commonwealth Scientific and Industrial Research Organization, to become very active in the fields of variety introduction and improvement. Numerous introductions of new types have been made from California and Europe in recent years, and some of the more interesting varieties now being tested include Sylvaner, Muellar-Thurgau, Traminer, Grey Riesling, Sauvignon Vert, Chenin Blanc, Rubired, Gamay Beaujolais, Royalty, Trousseau and Tinta Cao.

There are also good prospects of obtaining higher-yielding strains of the quality-grape varieties now being grown in Australia, either by clonal selection or heat therapy to free the vines of virus diseases. Much work is being done in these fields in Australia and in other parts of the world, and it could be that in a few years Australian wine-makers can be supplied with much better-yielding strains of such premium varieties as Pinot Noir, Tokay, Cabernet Sauvignon and Rhine Riesling. The benefits that would accrue to the Australian wine industry from such an advance are immense.

APPENDIX III

CHARACTERISTICS TO LOOK FOR

IN AUSTRALIAN WINES

[For the 1965 Wine Show of the Royal Agricultural and Horticultural Society of South Australia the Society's Wine Committee for the first time drew up a series of precise specifications for the various types of wines that were to be exhibited.
Members of the committee were Messrs. M. Auld (chairman), C. R. Gramp (vice-chairman), K. T. Hardy, I. H. Seppelt, J. R. W. Robertson, C. P. Haselgrove, T. W. C. Angove and R. Tolley.
The specifications provide a useful guide for Wine and Food Societies, Beefsteak and Burgundy Clubs and similar organizations, as well as for anyone wishing to build up a stock of good Australian wines.
The committee's statement setting out the specifications appears below.]

The following specifications are for the assistance of exhibitors and judges in Wine Shows conducted by the Society. Where analytical standards are mentioned, it is in general left to the exhibitor to see that his entries conform, but in case of doubt the judges may submit samples for analysis to the Australian Wine Research Institute.

AUSTRALIAN HOCK. Should be in brilliant condition, pale to light straw in colour, preferably with a slight greenish tinge, light to medium bodied, medium to high acidity and yet soft with a fresh and flowery bouquet and a clean aftertaste free of bitterness or lingering sweetness. It should not contain more than 0·50 per cent reducing sugar and alcoholic strength should be between 17 per cent and 24 per cent proof spirit.

AUSTRALIAN MEDIUM DRY WHITE TABLE WINE. Specification similar to Hock, but with some sweetness not exceeding 1 degree baume.

AUSTRALIAN WHITE BURGUNDY. Should be in brilliant condition, light to medium straw in colour. Medium to full bodied and yet delicate, with medium acidity and a fresh bouquet. Its aftertaste may be a little more pronounced than in Hock even with a very slight bitterness, but no lingering sweetness. It should not contain more than 0·50 per cent reducing sugar and alcoholic strength should be between 17 per cent and 24 per cent proof spirit.

AUSTRALIAN SAUTERNES. A white table wine of straw to light golden colour. It should be in brilliant condition, medium to full bodied with, a bouquet which is aromatic rather than flowery and distinctly sweet in flavour. Its alcoholic strength should not exceed 24 per cent proof spirit and it should not show excessive SO2. Baumé should not be less than 1·5 degrees.

AUSTRALIAN CLARET. A dry red table wine which may vary from fairly dark to light red in colour according to the age of the wine and from light to medium body. The acidity and body should be well balanced and the wine, whilst soft and rounded on the middle palate should finish firm and astringent and showing, as well as grape tannin flavour, some but not excessive flavour of oak tannin from the maturation wood. The bouquet should be fruity and in harmony with the body and flavour of the wine. An amber colour is objectionable. The alcoholic strength should be between 17 per cent and 25 per cent proof spirit.

AUSTRALIAN BURGUNDY. A dry red table wine of colour and body similar to Claret but a softer wine which may be of somewhat lower acidity and which must be soft and round on the middle palate and lack the characteristic astringency of Claret on the finish. The alcoholic strength should be between 17 per cent and 25 per cent proof spirit.

SWEET WHITE NOT EXCEEDING 27 deg. Should be straw to light golden colour. Usually with some Muscat character. Bouquet must be fruity and attractive without objectionably excessive SO2. Flavour should be soft, round and well balanced. Strength not to exceed 27 per cent proof spirit and sweetness not to exceed 7 degrees baumé.

SWEET WHITE DESSERT. Golden to amber in colour, depending on age. Must not show Muscat character but have fruity and aromatic bouquet. It must be full bodied, soft and round and yet with an acidity sufficient to prevent mawkishness. Strength not to exceed 36 per cent proof spirit and baume not to exceed 6 degrees in the commercial class or 10 degrees in the open class.

SWEET WHITE MUSCAT. Colour light golden to deep amber. Distinct Muscat bouquet and palate. Full bodied, soft and round and yet firm enough not to be maw- exceed 36 per cent proof spirit and baumé not to exceed 6 degrees in the commercial in the commercial class or 10 degrees in the open class.

SWEET RED NOT EXCEEDING 27 deg. Colour medium to dark red. May show some amber tinge. Bouquet to be characteristic of red dessert wine without excessive SO2. Palate to be full flavoured with some astringency on the finish but without excess acidity. Strength not to exceed 27 per cent proof spirit and baume not to exceed 7 degrees.

SWEET RED, RUBY PORT STYLE. Colour medium to dark red. May only show slight amber tinge: excessive amber colour is objectionable. Bouquet and palate full and fruity. Finish firm and astringent leaving no lingering sweetness. Strength not exceeding 36 per cent proof spirit and baume not exceeding 6 degrees.

SWEET RED, TAWNY PORT STYLE. Colour pale red with distinct amber tinge to deep amber with reddish tinge. Bouquet fruity and aromatic, palate full and soft with distinct dryness on the finish. Some flavour of oak tannin from the maturing wood is desirable. A lingering sweetness on the after palate is undesirable. Strength not to exceed 36 per cent proof spirit and baume not to exceed 6 degrees.

AUSTRALIAN VINTAGE PORT. Colour deep ruby to light ruby, possibly with slight amber tint, depending on age. Bouquet fruity and characteristic of bottle-aged Vintage Port. Should not show wood character. Flavour full and soft with firm, astringent finish and no lingering sweetness. Strength not to exceed 36 per cent proof spirit nor baume 6 degrees.

AUSTRALIAN SHERRY, PALE DRY FINO STYLE. Colour straw to pale golden. Bouquet characteristic of Flor Sherry. Flavour light and dry without excessive acidity or astringency but some oak character. Finish dry, aromatic with distinct "nutty" after-taste of Flor Sherry. Strength not to exceed 36 per cent proof spirit and specific gravity not to exceed 0·990.

AUSTRALIAN SHERRY, AMONTILLADO STYLE. Colour golden to light amber. Bouquet similar to pale dry Sherry but more aromatic. Palate fuller and softer than pale dry with some oak astringency showing through. Finish dry and aromatic with characteristic "nutty" aftertaste of Sherry. Strength not to exceed 36 per cent proof spirit nor specific gravity 1·000.

AUSTRALIAN SHERRY, BROWN OLOROSO STYLE. Colour amber to deep amber. Bouquet fruity and aromatic and showing both oak wood and Sherry character. Palate soft and round but with firm oak-tannin finish. Strength not to exceed 36 per cent proof spirit nor baume 3 degrees.

AUSTRALIAN CHAMPAGNE. Colour should be pale to light straw. Should have good acidity and not be too light in body. Bouquet should be fresh, fruity but without particular varietal character, and should indicate some years in bottle. The wine should be fairly dry but show no astringent finish. Bone-dry or excessively sweet wines should be penalized. Bubbles should be fine and persistent. (Make sure tasting glasses are not washed in detergent.)

AUSTRALIAN SPARKLING BURGUNDY. Colour should be light to medium ruby. In older wines may show a trace of amber, but not more than a trace. Bouquet fruity but should show bottle age. Fairly pronounced acidity. Full flavour and body, some sweetness but with dry finish. May show slight oak character. Bubbles should be fine and persistent. (Make sure tasting glasses are not washed in detergent.)

AUSTRALIAN VERMOUTHS. These should approximate European counterparts. Colour of Dry Vermouth should be light straw and Sweet Vermouth from golden to deep amber.

TWO-YEARS-OLD BRANDY. Entries in this class should be representative of popular commercial Brandies but should avoid fruitiness. The Brandy should be a well-balanced distillate of wine made from neutral grape varieties. It should avoid excessive heads or tails and should not show varietal character (e.g. Muscat). It should be smooth but not too sweet (1·5 degrees obscuration is suggested as maximum). A clean, balanced bouquet is essential. Colour not too dark.

OLD BRANDY. Colour may be somewhat darker than in young Brandy class. Well-matured oak should be distinguishable on both bouquet and flavour. Bouquet should be clean and somewhat ethereal but well balanced, showing no particular constituent to excess. Flavour should be full, smooth and aromatic. Finish aromatic without trace of fusil oil. No varietal character or fruitiness should be evident. Some slight sweetness is acceptable.

APPENDIX IV
A WINE-LOVER NAMES HIS FAVOURITES

[This list has been compiled by Victor Gibson, Counsellor and Past President of the Wine and Food Society of Victoria. Victor Gibson writes: "In listing my favourite wines I have excluded treasures that can no longer be obtained commercially. All of the listed wines may be bought in Australia from the larger wine and spirit merchants; one store in Melbourne had almost all of them in stock at the time of writing. Many of these wines are also available at the better restaurants, and some at the Australian Wine Centre in London".

There are, of course, many fine-quality Australian wines apart from those Victor Gibson has mentioned. The list represents his personal choice; other Australian wine-lovers would, no doubt, have included some wines that are not in his list.]

	Year	Approx. Price ($. Aust.)	
SHERRY			
Yalumba Chiquita Very Dry Show Sherry.*		1.75	All of these sherries are very dry, have good flor and wood character. The Chiquita Show Sherry may be difficult to obtain, but the standard Chiquita at $1.10 is very close. Hardy's say that their Florfino is their actual Show wine.
Hardy's Florfino Sherry.*		1.05	
Stonyfell Extra Dry Sherry.*		0.90	
Penfold's Dry Fino Sherry.*		1.20	
Reynella Bone Dry Sherry.		1.50	
Stonyfell Amorita Sherry.		0.80	Here is an intriguing wine, especially for those whose taste is not so dry. It could be taken for a full-bodied Amontillado or a dry Oloroso. Wonderful with the soup.
SPARKLING			
Seppelt's Great Western Imperial Reserve. Brut.*		3.40	Few people dispute that Great Western is without peer. It is Seppelt's masterpiece. The "Extra Dry" is of the same high standard as the Brut.
WHITES			
Lindeman's Reserve White Burgundy. Bin 2250.	1963	1.35	From Hunter and Clare districts. Two gold medals in export class.
Lindeman's Sunshine Reserve Chablis. Bin 2755.	1965	1.65	From Sunshine vineyard in Hunter Valley. Delightful with seafoods. 1966 Sydney gold medal winner in Open Chablis class.

* Indicates that the wine named is available at Australian Wine Centre, 25 Frith Street, Soho, London, W.1.

Lindeman's Reserve Riesling. Bin 2464.	1965	1.65	*Riesling and Traminer from Ben Ean and Sunshine Hunter Valley vineyards.*
Gramp's Orlando Barossa Riesling.*	1962	1.40	*Rhine Riesling. Barossa Valley. Gold medals Sydney 1964 and 1966.*
Gramp's Orlando Barossa Riesling.*	1963	1.40	*Gold Medal Sydney 1965.*
Gramp's Orlando White Burgundy.	1962	—	*Gold medals Adelaide 1965, Sydney 1966. To be released commercially late in 1966. Made from Trebbiano (Ugni Blanc) and Madeira.*
Milawa White Frontignac.	1965	0.85	*One of John Brown's fine distinctive wines.*
Stonyfell Rhine Riesling.	1965	0.90	*Grown in Eden Valley.*
Penfold's Traminer Riesling. Bin 202.	1964	1.30	*A rare wine and a distinctive one because of the character and nose from the Traminer grape. Double gold-medal winner.*
Penfold's Pinot Riesling. Bin 539.	1964	1.30	*Fine Hunter White made from Pinot Blanc and Semillon.*
Hamilton Springton Riesling.*	1965	0.95	*A very fruity type.*
Mildara Golden Bower Riesling.	1958	1.25	*Superb examples of Hunter whites.*
Mildara Golden Bower Riesling.	1961	1.00	
Yalumba Carte D'Or Riesling.*	1964	0.85	*A fine wine each year. Eden Valley. All Rhine Riesling. Chosen by Wine and Food Society, London, for its welcome-home banquet to André Simon after his visit to Australia.*
Yalumba Carte D'Or Riesling.*	1965	0.85	
Houghton's Verdell.	1964	1.25	*Swan River. Verdelho grape.*
Yalumba Pewsey Vale Riesling.	1965	—	*This is the first vintage from the new Pewsey Vale vineyards in S.A. All Rhine Riesling planted 1700 ft. above sea-level. Real German style. Watch for this beauty in future years.*
Henschke Ugni Blanc.	1965	1.00	*Distinctive character from Keyneton, S.A. area.*
Mt. Pleasant Anne Riesling.	1963	1.25	*From a selected part of McWilliam's Mt. Pleasant vineyards in the Hunter Valley.*

REDS

Stonyfell Metala Cabernet Shiraz.	1961	1.10	*Won coveted J. Watson Award in Melbourne.*
Saltram Specially Selected Claret. Bin 33.	1961	0.90	*Good example of fine South Australian Shiraz.*
Mildara Cabernet Shiraz.	1958	1.35	*Hunter River and Coonawarra Blend.*
Mildara Coonawarra Cabernet Sauvignon.	1963	1.85	*First vintage of this beautiful wine. Makers declare it is all Cabernet. Matured in 65-gallon Limousin new wood for two years. Won Dr Phillips Award for best red in Show, Sydney, 1966. Wonderful already, but a pity to drink it yet as it will improve with age.*
Mildara Coonawarra Cabernet Shiraz.	1963	1.85	*The Cabernet–Shiraz version of the above. One third Cabernet. Excellent and more forward than the straight Cabernet.*
Seppelt's Chalambar Burgundy.*	1962	0.95	*Light, delicate style of Burgundy.*
Seppelt's Chalambar Burgundy.*	1963	0.95	
Seppelt's Moyston Claret.*	1963	0.95	*Excellent example of a Great Western Claret.*
McWilliam's Mt. Pleasant Pinot Hermitage.	1962	1.25	*Has pronounced bouquet and soft finish of Pinot Noir from Hunter Valley.*
Galway Vintage Claret.	1959	0.95	*This was Yalumba's standard commercial wine for the year, yet it has won four principal prizes, including a gold medal at Adelaide in 1965.*
Galway Vintage Claret.	1961	0.85	*This wine contains some Cabernet Sauvignon, grown under irrigation at Waikerie.*
Hardy's Cabernet Sauvignon.	1957	1.50	*Straight Cabernet from McLaren Vale.*
Hardy's Cabernet Sauvignon.	1958	1.50	
Orlando Barossa Cabernet.	1963	0.95	*Gold Medal in Sydney 1964; also a principal prize at Montpellier, France.*
Rouge Homme Claret.	1962	1.35	*Both fine Coonawarra wines with some new wood character.*
Rouge Homme Cabernet.	1961	1.65	
Wynn's Coonawarra Estate Cabernet.*	1959	1.50	*A superb example of what The House of Wynn can do at Coonawarra.*

Chateau Reynella Claret.	1963	1.10	*Fine examples from a vineyard which*
Chateau Reynella Burgundy.	1961	1.10	*has produced some memorable wines.*
Tulloch's Pokolbin. Private Bin Dry Red.	1963	—	*Hermitage grape. Hunter River. Distinctive bouquet.*
Penfold's Grange Hermitage.	1960	1.75	*Penfold's led the movement towards adopting the wood maturation used by the great growths of the Médoc. The wine is held in new oak hogsheads for up to two years. This imparts the new-wood character sometimes likened to fresh black currants. Grange '53 was the first. The 1955 is a renowned prize-winner. In the 1959 and 1960 the wood character is not so assertive, a change which is approved by many.*
St. Henri Claret.	1961	1.75	*Made by Penfold's at Auldana next to*
St. Henri Claret.	1962	1.75	*Grange Vineyards. A cousin to Grange Hermitage. The stalks are left in during the fermentation and the wood character is not as pronounced as in Grange.*

DESSERT WINES

Stonyfell Old Lodge Port (Tawny).	1.05	*100 per cent. Grenache from Burnside, S.A. Multiple prize-winner.*
Stonyfell Old Liqueur Muscat.	0.80	*Made from non-irrigated Muscat and Frontignac. Youngest wine in this blend is twelve years old.*
Yalumba Galway Pipe Tawny Port.*	1.45	*Justly famous.*
Hardy's Tawny Port.	1.25	*Made in 1943. Battles out the rounds of the shows with Stonyfell.*
Morris's Liqueur Muscat.	1.00	*A famous prize-winner from north-eastern Victoria.*

APPENDIX V
THE CARE
AND SERVICE OF WINE

If a wine is to live through the distemper of early fermentation, resist and beat the attacks of wild yeast and hostile microbes, be sound and wholesome until it reaches a ripe and mellow old age, whenever allowed to do so, it must be given, from the start, the care which it needs, deserves and repays. Wine does receive the intelligent and loving care of the wine-maker, who not only possesses the necessary technical knowledge, but costly, up-to-date equipment, air-conditioned cellars, and all that he must have to see his wine through press to cask or tank, and in bottles, safely corked, packaged and delivered through retailers to the public: that is to say, to men and women who have other things to think about and know little, if anything, about wine, except that they like it.

They are the people who, we hope, may appreciate a few words of advice on how best to handle, keep, serve and partner the wines which wine-merchants sell to them.

Wine demands and repays a greater amount of interest and care than the milk and groceries that are delivered to our door daily or weekly. There are so many different types of wine, young and old, dry and sweet, light and heavy, with many shades of differences in colour, alcoholic strength, sweetness and acidity, that we can and we should make sure to have at hand, at home, a selection—however small it may be—of different wines to suit different occasions, the taste of our guests, and the mood of the moment. This means, of course, having a little stock of wine of your own, which is so much better than sending to the shop round the corner for a bottle or two when an old friend happens to drop in and stay for a meal.

A cellar is the proper place for a stock of bottled wine, but it is out of the question for most city dwellers who live in flats or apartments. The bed which they must give to each one of their bottles of wine has to be a bin under the stairs or in a cupboard, or some odd corner—whatever happens to be available. What one must bear in mind, however, is that wine loves peace above all things! It will put up with a cold bed or bin, but will not mind a warm one: what wine dislikes intensely is changes from cold, which contracts, to heat, which expands. This is, of course, why deep cellars are best, where the temperature is practically the same in summer and winter. Wine also hates draughts as well as stuffiness, just as most of us do. Wine dislikes sunshine and any bright light, which we love. This is because the ruby and gold of wine are not chemical

Johnston's Vineyard at Sunbury, Victoria, in 1875. Sunbury was once a notable vine-yard area, but no wine is made there today.

dyes, but natural colours which fade in sunlight. Obviously, even if the home found for wine cannot be as dark, cool, quiet and airy as the wine would like it to be, it can always be, and it must be, spotlessly clean. So long as corks of cork-bark are used, they are porous and perishable, liable to get musty and they will then taint the wine which will become undrinkable.

When the day dawns for which every bottle of wine has been waiting—that is, the moment when a corkscrew will remove the cork that has been holding the wine prisoner for weeks, months or years—the first question which the host has to ask himself is, "Decant or not?"

The decanting of old red wines and more particularly old vintage Ports, used to be quite a ritual in England for many years, but it has almost died out since old wines with loose sediment in the bottle no longer exist. With new or fairly young wines, there is so little sediment, and generally speaking, none at all, that decanting is no longer necessary. Whether it be still desirable or not is entirely a matter of personal taste. There are people, and I am one of them, who would rather see a wine on the table in a fine decanter of pure white crystal than in a bottle: the decanter is an ornament, but a wine-bottle is not; a decanter also shows off the colour of the wine much better than a wine-bottle.

Glasses are, of course, indispensable, and of greater importance than decanters, since they can and should give the ruby and gold of red and white wines a better chance to be admired at close quarters: this is why coloured glasses must not be used when good wine is to be served. Whatever their shape, wine-glasses must be of a fair size to give a chance to a fair measure of wine being in them without being filled to the top. A wine-glass that holds four fluid ounces is a sensible all-purpose size, although personally, I prefer a five-ounce glass, not out of greed for more wine, but for more room for my nose to look for the wine's bouquet. The miserable miniature glasses which so many hotels and restaurants ought to be ashamed to use for Port and Sherry, ought to be prohibited by law: a three-ounce glass is the smallest that should be used for wine, be it still or sparkling, fortified or not.

A vineyard planted at Sunbury in 1864 by J. G. Francis. The picture appeared in the Illustrated Australian News of 10 June, 1879. Francis was a member of the Victorian Legislative Assembly.

The temperature at which wine should be served is an important question, but there is no chance and little need to deal with it in any dictatorial manner. A great deal depends upon the wines to be served in the first place, and also in what happens to be the temperature indoors and out of doors at the time. There is a generally accepted rule that all still and sparkling white wines are better when served chilled, but chilled within reason. A slightly chilled white wine is cool and refreshing, whereas a deep-freeze type of wine burns rather than cools: it does not refresh, but leaves us with an unholy thirst instead.

It is customary to say—and to read—that red wines should be served at the temperature of the room, but this is not very helpful, since room temperature varies a great deal. What should be avoided at all costs is to serve red wines warm or at the temperature of the blood. Wine should always be below blood temperature so as to have a fresh impact on the tongue. Should we find it too fresh, we can easily raise the temperature of the wine, gently and nicely, by the warmth of our two hands, whereas a red wine that is too warm cannot be cooled ever.

If one is to enjoy wine as wine should be enjoyed, so that it be really worth all the money that it costs to buy, one has to bear in mind the fact that wine, unlike hard liquor and soft drinks, owes its appeal to a *bouquet* or fragrance, and to a flavour or taste which are discreet, subtle, delicate, and not obvious and brutal. This is why the housewife who loves good wine as she loves her husband will not have any flowers on the dining-room table with strong scents, but choose those with little or no scent at all: they will not compete unfairly with the *bouquet* of any of the wines to be served. And she will, of course, exercise the same care in the choosing of the fare to be served when wine-conscious friends are to be entertained and given some of the best wines in the home larder or store: no curried kangaroo!

APPENDIX VI

WINE IN THE KITCHEN

"Wine for drinking, water for cooking" is quite a good rule, and, like many other good rules, it has its exceptions. There are people who use water for drinking and they do not appear to be any the worse for it: there are also people who use wine for cooking, and they are all the better for it! They claim that food cooked in wine is more easily digested than when cooked in water: this may possibly be due to the fat-splitting action of the acids in wine, and it is obvious that wine—that is, the right wine—used in cooking is likely to impart to the food a distinctive flavour, which is entirely lacking in water, and it not only may but should add to the gustatory appeal of the food.

It is unlikely that anybody will be so extravagant as to use fine, rare and expensive wines in the kitchen, but it is by no means uncommon to meet people who believe that "cooking wine" is good enough. It is not! There is no such wine as a "cooking wine", but there is cooked wine—maybe some propped-up, sick, dying or even dead wine, which is unfit for human consumption. Common sense does not whisper but shouts at us that any wine which is not good enough to drink cannot possibly be good enough to use in cooking: it cannot be good for the food in the pot any more than for us. One might as well say that rancid butter is good enough for cooking as to imagine that a corky wine will do.

Which wines are best with different foods is chiefly a question of tradition, but it is imperative that every cook, amateur or professional, novice or not, should use his or her own imagination, instinct, and intelligence, thus enjoying making experiments likely to lead to pleasant surprises.

The few receipes selected and given here are some of the better known and classical recipes of food cooked or prepared with wine: they give a good idea of quantities to be used and of the manner which the experts have found best to use wine in the kitchen.

RECIPES

SOLE AU CHABLIS

For four persons, take 4 sole weighing about 7 oz. each; wash them and trim them, and break the backbone of each in the middle so that they will be flat. Butter a large fire-proof dish and put into it 4 thin rounds of onion. On this, put the sole, placing them so that they will not touch each other. Cover with some Chablis, if possible, or else with the best dry white Burgundy you can get or spare. Add the liquid from a handful of mussels, cover with greased paper and cook for about 15 minutes in the oven.

Strain the liquid from the sole, placing them somewhere where they will be kept hot, and reduce the liquid to half its original quantity. Thicken with a little flour and some butter. Take the sauce off the fire after it has cooked for 8 minutes and add the yolks of 2 eggs diluted with a few drops of water. Beat well till thoroughly mixed. Put the sauce back upon a strong flame, and let it come just to the boil, stirring all the time. Add the juice of half a lemon and 3 oz. of butter, a little at a time. Stir vigorously, without letting the mixture come to the boil, until it has thickened.

Pour this sauce over the sole in the fireproof dish. Put the dish in another containing hot water, and brown in a very hot oven. Serve piping hot.—CH. BERGERAND, Hotel de l'Etoile, Chablis.

SOLE AUX CREVETTES

1 Large sole	*Thick white sauce*
Some good dry white wine	*Breadcrumbs*
½ lb. large brown shrimps	*Lemon juice*
Sifted flour	*Salt and pepper*
Fresh butter	

Remove head and skin of the sole; cook gently in the wine with heads and shells of the shrimps, which should previously be pounded; let it simmer gently for about 20 minutes; strain the liquid through a fine sieve, and use it to moisten the flour and butter to make a white sauce. Cover the fish in the dish with this sauce; sprinkle with shrimp tails, breadcrumbs, and season with salt, pepper and lemon juice. Bake for 25 to 30 minutes, according to size of the sole, and serve in the dish.

SOLE VOISIN

1 Large sole filleted	*Tomato sauce*
White dry wine	*Pepper and salt*

Have the sole filleted. Stew gently for about 20 minutes head and bones, with pepper and salt. Make a "short", i.e. much reduced, sauce of fresh tomatoes. Lay the fillets of sole longways in a baking dish, cover with the white wine and the strained liquid from the bones; bake for about 5 minutes and serve with the tomato sauce piping hot.

FILLETS OF SOLE "CARMEN SYLVA"

Fillets of sole	*Thick cream*
Dry white wine	*Tomatoes*
Flour	*Salt and cayenne pepper*
Cucumber	

Peel and slice a firm cucumber. Peel and cut up 1 lb. ripe, firm tomatoes. Put the white wine, the cucumber and tomatoes in a saucepan. Season to taste with salt and cayenne pepper. Cook until cucumber and tomatoes are soft enough to be sieved. Heat the butter, add the flour and moisten the mixture, stirring all the wine with the cucumber and tomato purée. Poach the fillets of sole in this sauce, and, just before serving, add the cream, bring it to the boil and serve immediately.

DARNE DE SAUMON CHAMBORD

Poach a *darne* (middle cut) of salmon on a slow fire in an open pan, without any water but a sound, young red wine, which should just cover the fish; also put in the pan an onion and a carrot, duly cut up, a bayleaf and some parsley; season with salt and whole peppercorns.

When the fish is cooked—time depends on its weight—stand it in an oval serving dish with its classical *garniture* round it, if you wish and can do so; if not, with creamed mushrooms and a white wine sauce *Genevoise*, forgetting the *ecrevisses*, the truffles and *quenelles* demanded in the classical recipe.

TROUT WITH WINE

Clean some fine trout. Put in the belly of each one of them a piece of butter which has been pounded with savoury herbs and seasoned with pepper and salt. Place the trout in a fish kettle and pour over them enough white wine to cover them a thumb-breadth above their heads. Season with pepper, salt and nutmeg, 2 onions and 2 crusts of bread with 2 cloves stuck in them. Cook the fish upon so fierce a flame that it will set fire to the wine. When they are cooked and the sauce reduced, add a piece of butter and stir it well in. When ready and when you are content with the seasoning, place the trout in a serving dish and pour the sauce over them.—*Les Gons de Comus*, Paris, 1793.

MERLANS DIEPPOISE

Split 4 whiting along the backbone and cook them in the oven with just plain, young, wholesome dry white wine, some mussels and mushrooms. Serve with a garnish of mussels and mushrooms and a well seasoned white wine sauce.—ESCOFFIER'S, *Ma Cuisine*.

LOBSTER BEAUGENCY

1 Boiled lobster	*Cream and cream sauce*
Sherry	*2 Egg yolks*
Butter	*Pepper and salt*

Having boiled the lobster of your choice, let it get cold, then split it in two and dice the meat. Heat about a couple of tablespoons of butter and fry the pieces of lobster lightly in it for a few minutes, when you will refresh the lobster with some *vino de pasto* or any such undistinguished but honest and not too sweet sherry. Then back goes the pan on the fire and you add gradually 2 tablespoons of fresh cream, plus about half a pint of cream sauce for good measure. After about 10 minutes over the fire, the pan should be removed for the diced lobster to be mixed with a rich sauce made of 2 beaten egg yolks, fresh cream and melted butter. The shells of the lobster are then filled with a thoroughly well mixed diced lobster and sauce. Back again into the oven until it starts bubbling and is slightly browned.

HOMARD NEWBURG AND HOMARD THERMIDOR

One of the differences between the recipes of these two traditional very popular lobster dishes is that sherry must be used in the cooking of the *Homard Newburg*, whereas light white wine, not only lighter in colour but in alcoholic strength, must be used in the cooking of the *Homard Thermidor*.

ENTRECOTE BERCY

Heat a sufficiency of butter in a pan; when sizzling hot, put in it a fairly thick piece of steak and brown it quickly; then take it out and keep it warm; put in the pan about half a pint of either red or white wine, as you prefer, and add some chopped shallots; salt and pepper. Simmer gently until greatly reduced; skim any excess of fat, add some meat glaze and meat marrow cut up in very small pieces; cook the lot for another 5 minutes or so; check and make sure that the seasoning is right; add a squeeze of lemon and some chopped parsley before pouring it all over the steak. Give it all a chance to be really hot and serve at once.

BOEUF A LA BOURGUIGNONNE

2 lb. tender cut of lean beef	*3 or 4 onions*
2 oz. fat salt pork	*Flour and butter*
½ bottle good red Burgundy	*Pepper and salt*

Cut the beef into 2-inch cubes. Put the cut-up salt pork in a heavy iron stewpan, and cook until all fat has run out; then remove any small pieces of pork left in the pan and brown the cubes of beef in the hot pork fat, together with the sliced onions. When all has been duly browned, sprinkle in the flour and stir for a moment; then pour in the wine and season to taste with pepper and salt. Cover closely and cook very gently for 3 hours, or longer should the meat not be quite tender. Just before serving, add a glass of brandy, set it alight, and simmer for another minute or two before dishing up.

FILLET DE BOEUF MADERE

Middle piece of beef fillet	*Butter*
Larding bacon	*Pepper and salt*

Lard the meat with the bacon fat with a larding needle; trim, shape and tie the fillet: put it in a very hot oven so that the surface is quickly seared and allow from 15 to 20 minutes per pound for cooking, basting frequently while cooking. Serve with some Madeira sauce over it, and with Madeira sauce as well in a sauce boat.

Madeira sauce is made with butter, a little flour, onions, mushrooms, and of course, Madeira wine, but when Madeira wine is not available, its place can be taken by a cream sherry or any good, rather rich sherry.

VEAL KIDNEYS AND WHITE WINE

Parboil the kidneys for a few minutes. Remove skin. Soak in cold water for half an hour. Slice and season with salt and pepper. Cook some mushrooms in a little water for three quarters of an hour. Cook some onions in very hot butter for 3 or 4 minutes. Add the kidneys to the onions as they are cooking in the hot butter, and let them cook together for 5 minutes. Then add the white wine—a dry white wine, young and sharp is best. Let most of the water in the wine depart in steam, and serve.

SHEEP'S KIDNEYS "BERRICHONNE"

Skin and cut in halves as many kidneys as you require. Toss the kidneys in hot butter and then place each half upon a small piece of thick toast, and keep them covered and warm. Pour a glassful or two, according to number of kidneys, of a stout red wine into the pan in which they were cooked; season to taste and cook quickly until half the original volume of wine has left (steamed away); then add some butter and, when available, some meat glaze, making a fine wine sauce that is poured over the kidneys.

COQ AU VIN

Take a young chicken and cut it into 6 pieces. Fry the pieces quickly and lightly in butter, together with some diced lean bacon and the same quantity of fresh mushrooms. When the lot has turned to a good colour, add a bunch of mixed herbs, and a chopped clove of garlic. Sprinkle with brandy and set it alight; then add a pint of the best red wine you can spare. Cover the saucepan and let the chicken cook for 20 minutes. Thicken the sauce.

POULET CHASSEUR

Cut up the chicken and brown the pieces in a blend of olive oil and butter which you will have heated together in a pan together with a minced clove of garlic and some cut-up shallots. When the meat has been nicely browned, sprinkle in a tablespoon of flour and moisten with either a dry sherry or a dry white wine; add a teaspoonful, or maybe two, of tomato purée, some chopped chives, chervil and parsley; season to taste with pepper and salt. Cover the pan and cook rather quickly for about half an hour, or until the chicken is tender. Strain the gravy over the chicken and serve with mushrooms tossed in butter as well as some buttered *croutons* of fried bread.

HARE SOUP SCOTS STYLE OR BAWD BREE

1 Hare, fresh killed   Oatmeal and Port wine
Onion, turnip and carrot, herbs, salt and pepper, peppercorns

Skin hare and clean thoroughly, holding it over large basin to collect all the blood. Joint the hare and put into pot with water, carrot, onion, turnip, peppercorns, herbs, salt and pepper, and simmer for 3 hours. Strain soup. Cut the meat into small pieces and return to pot with stock; add a handful of oatmeal. Strain the blood and gradually add to the soup, stirring all the time, and bring to boil. Then add the port wine and serve. A boiled potato should be served at the same time to each person.—*Scottish Women Rural Institutes' Farmhouse recipes.*

BRAISED HARE EN CASSEROLE

Skin, draw and bone a good hare; stuff it with chopped fat bacon and seasoning; roll into a ball, dust with flour and tie in shape.

Put 2 oz. of butter in a casserole, heat up, and brown the beast nicely. Take out and put a layer of fat bacon at the bottom of the pan; then replace the hare and place round it the bones, etc., which you have broken in a mortar; a calf's foot cut in chunks, carrots and onions cut in rings; add a selection of seasonings and spices. Add a glass of white wine, a squeeze of lemon, and enough good stock, and above all a dessertspoonful of brown sugar. Put a disc of buttered paper to fit between the lid and the pot, or lute it down with paste. Let it cook on the side of the stove, simmering slowly for 4 hours at least. Strain before serving. This dish can be eaten hot or cold, which is the reason for the calf's foot. If hot, subtract a good cupful of the gravy and reduce to half, adding red-currant jelly and wine to make a sauce. If cold, strain it all out into a large pudding basin, when the gravy will set in a jelly, and the excess fat can easily be removed.—MAJOR HUGH POLLARD'S *The Sportsman's Cookery Book.* (This recipe can easily be adapted for cooking kangaroo.)

TIPSY CAKE

Procure a sponge-cake three or four days stale, as stale cake is more suitable for the purpose. Cut the bottom of the cake level so that it may stand up firm in the dish: make a small hole in the centre and pour into it, as well as over the cake, either some sweet white wine or a medium-sweet sherry, laced with as much brandy as you believe will be good for you and your friends. When the cake is thoroughly well soaked and may rightly be called "tipsy", blanch and cut 2 oz. sweet almonds into strips and stick them all over the cake. Finally pour round the cake a nice custard.

POIRES BOURGUIGNONNE

Peel, halve and core as many ripe pears as may be required; stew them gently in plenty of Burgundy or any good and strong red wine that may be available, adding sugar, either much or not so much according to taste: when the pears have absorbed nearly all the wine, all will be well as soon as they have had time to get quite cold.

CUMBERLAND SAUCE

Cumberland sauce is the one and only truly English wine sauce and it cannot be better than when made with Australian wine. Ingredients:

1 Orange	2 Tablespoonfuls vinegar
1 Lemon	½ Teaspoonful made Mustard
1 Gill Port wine	Cayenne pepper and salt
2 Tablespoonfuls red-currant jelly	Chopped glace cherries

Peel the orange and lemon very thinly without taking off any of the white pith. Cut this peel into very fine shreds. Cook in 1 gill port wine for 5 minutes, strain and put back into the saucepan. Add red-currant jelly, mustard, cayenne, salt, the juice of the orange and lemon, and the vinegar. Boil this for a few minutes and wait for the sauce to be quite cold before adding the chopped glace cherries.—Adapted from the recipe of Mrs Hyne, for many years cook to the late Dowager Lady Swaythling, one of the founders of the Wine and Food Society. (Mrs Hyne used half a gill water and half a gill port wine.)

SAUCE DIABLE

This is a sauce which strict teetotallers regard as responsible for causing an unholy thirst that may lead to the fall of too-earnest imbibers. Its basis is a blend of sharp white wine and wine vinegar, with chopped shallots, cayenne pepper, salt and various flavoursome herbs. It is all boiled together until "reduced" to half its original volume, when it is strained and some *demi-glace* is added to it.

A scientist at work in one of the laboratories of the Australian Wine Research Institute at Glen Osmond, a suburb of Adelaide. The Institute, founded in 1955, carries out basic research that is recognized as being of world importance.

APPENDIX VII

THE WORK OF THE AUSTRALIAN WINE
RESEARCH INSTITUTE

[The Australian Wine Research Institute is the most important organization investigating the scientific problems of the wine industry in Australia. Under the guidance of its director, Mr J. C. M. Fornachon, M.Sc., B.Agr.Sc., its work has gained world-wide recognition. The 1965 annual report of the Institute, extracts from which are published below, surveys the Institute's activities during its first ten years.]

The year under review marks the completion of ten years' activity, for on the 1 July 1955, the institute first began to assume responsibility for the research which had up till then been carried out by the Oenological Research Committee of the C.S.I.R.O. [Commonwealth Scientific and Industrial Research Organization.]

During its early years the Institute continued the programme of research which had been undertaken by the Oenological Research Committee, but the greater resources of the Institute soon made possible the provision of improved research facilities, including new laboratories, additional equipment, and a pilot winery. These facilities, together with an increased staff, have allowed the research programme to be extended and have also made possible the provision by the institute of further technical services, including consultation and advice on day-to-day technical problems of individual winemakers, lectures to groups of wine-makers, and the supply of cultures of selected yeasts to wine-makers. Every effort has been made to maintain a balance between these different activities of the Institute.

In broad terms the research programme of the Institute has been concerned with a study of the factors which influence the quality of wine, with the objective of so controlling these factors as to improve quality. The work includes both the investigation of specific problems of the wine industry, and also rather more basic research aimed at extending our knowledge of the chemistry of grapes and wines and of the biochemistry of the various events which occur during the ripening of grapes, as well as during the making and maturation of wines.

Wine-making quality of grapes. Notwithstanding modern advances in methods of making and maturing wine, the quality of the final product is still very largely determined by the quality of the grapes from which it is made. It is known that grapes differ in their wine-making quality and that they differ in composition as regards both major and minor constituents. It is widely believed that such differences are very largely determined by soil and climatic factors, but reliable data on this are scarce and are almost completely lacking for Australian conditions.

This subject has been under investigation by the Institute in co-operation with the State Departments of Agriculture, C.S.I.R.O., and the Commonwealth Bureau of Meteorology. The work has involved the making of experimental wines from plots of several varieties of grapes grown on different soils and in different districts and subsequent evaluation of these experimental wines by chemical analyses and by tasting. The first phase of this work is being wound up but the problem is highly complex and further investigation is needed before conclusions can be drawn.

The Organic Acids in Grapes. The concentrations and amounts of tartaric and malic acids in grapes have been found to vary in different districts and different varieties. The acids are important factors in the wine-making quality of grapes. The factors which influence their accumulation at different stages of ripening and in different districts are the subject of present investigations.

Sampling Grapes in the Vineyard. An investigation of various methods of collecting grapes in order to obtain a representative sample from a vineyard was carried out in collaboration with officers of the South Australian Department of Agriculture and the C.S.I.R.O. Division of Mathematical Statistics. This work involved a study of the variation in the sugar and acid content of grapes from different parts of a vine and from different vines. The results of this work are of value in indicating the most appropriate method of sampling grapes in the vineyard for either research or commercial purposes.

Yeasts. In the field of microbiology, much attention has been devoted to the study of yeasts for, of course, these represent the most important group of micro-organisms to the wine-maker. In order to select suitable yeasts for use by wine-makers, a large number of strains has been tested for their fermentation characteristics in the laboratory following the earlier investigations carried out by the Oenological Research Committee.

An important recent finding in this field has been the fact that some strains of yeast reduce sulphur dioxide to hydrogen sulphide during fermentation. Consequently the spasmodic occurrence of hydrogen sulphide odour which has plagued generations of wine-makers is largely a result of undesirable yeasts. Other "off odours" have also been shown to be due to unwanted yeasts. On the other hand, the ability of some yeasts to decompose portion of the malic acid during wine fermentation may be useful in certain circumstances.

Working in collaboration with a commercial manufacturer of compressed yeast, the Institute carried out some experimental fermentations with specially prepared compressed wine yeast. The results indicated that this product may have a place in the Australian wine industry, but its use is likely to depend on convenience and on economic rather technical considerations.

Bacteria. Earlier work carried out by the Oenological Research Committee was concerned with bacterial spoilage of wine. However, under certain conditions some bacteria play a useful role in the maturation of wine by decomposing malic acid.

This malo-lactic fermentation, as it is called, has been studied at the Institute. The bacteria responsible have been isolated and described and the influence of various factors on their growth in wine has been determined. It has been shown how their growth in wine can be prevented when the malo-lactic fermentation is undesirable. On the other hand, when the malo-lactic fermentation is considered desirable, it can be promoted by means of cultures of selected bacteria. Investigations have indicated how suitable strains of bacteria can be selected and how they can be used. The ability of some of these bacteria to form diacetyl and acetoin from citric acid and from pyruvic acid in wine has recently been established. The significance of these products and the conditions favouring their formation are being further studied.

Stabilization. Work commenced by the Oenological Research Committee had shown how the use of ion exchange resins could best be adapted to Australian conditions in order to prevent the deposition of potassium bitartrate in our wines after bottling. Subsequently it was found that some wines after treatment with ion-exchange resins could not be clarified with bentonite in the normal way. This failure to clarify with bentonite was shown to be due to removal by the resin of the bi-valent cations which are necessary for flocculation of bentonite. Consequently bentonite treatment should usually precede rather than follow ion-exchange treatment.

Sulphur Dioxide and Other Antiseptics. The role of sulphur dioxide in preventing the growth of lactic acid bacteria in wine has been studied and it has been shown that, in contrast to yeasts, these bacteria are influenced to some extent by combined as well as by free sulphur dioxide.

The compounds diethyl pyrocarbonate and sorbic acid are known to be capable of fulfilling some of the functions of sulphur dioxide under certain conditions, although they cannot replace this substance entirely. Tests carried out at the Institute have indicated the doses which might be useful in Australian wines and also some of the uses and limitations of these compounds.

Chemistry of Grapes and Wines. In their efforts to develop more effective control over the processes of making and maturing wine, both the wine-maker and the wine researcher have been handicapped by lack of basic knowledge of the chemistry of grapes and wines. This lack of knowledge has been particularly evident with red wines, where the nature of the phenolic compounds responsible for colour and astringency has been imperfectly understood and even less has been known about the changes which these compounds undergo during maturation of the wine.

In order to throw more light on the subject, an investigation of the phenolic compounds in the variety Shiraz has been undertaken. The phase of the work comprising the isolation and identification of the various components of Shiraz pigment and the study of the chemistry of these components has been completed. Current work is concerned with other phenolic compounds (tannins) and the nature of the extraction process during red-wine fermentation.

Methods of Analysis. From time to time improved methods of analysis have been **developed** at the Institute, usually by modification or adapatation of a method for some special purpose.

In this way methods suitable for use in the winery have been developed for determination of sulphur dioxide, for detection of malo-lactic fermentation and for identification of the causes of turbidity and deposits in wine. Methods for the determination of lactic acid, malic acid, pyruvic acid, diacetyl and acetoin suitable for research purposes have also been developed.

Technical Services. An important function of the Institute has always been the provision of technical advice on oenological problems to members of the Australian wine industry, and wine-makers have made increasing use of this service.

The problems on which advice has been sought have usually been associated with the growth of unwanted organisms during the making and maturation of wine or with difficulties encountered in clarifying and stabilizing wines. From about thirty to forty samples of wine and various winery materials have been submitted to the Institute each year for examination, diagnosis of faults and advice. Many other requests for advice concerning methods of analysis, treatment of wines and other problems have also been dealt with each year.

The Institute also supplies, for a fee, pure cultures of tested and selected yeasts, and the demand for these cultures by wine-makers has grown to between fifty and sixty cultures each year. A number of cultures has also been supplied free of charge to various teaching and research organizations.

It is pleasing to note that wine-makers in all the wine-producing States of the Commonwealth have continually made use of the technical services provided by the Institute.

A GLOSSARY
OF WINE-TASTING TERMS

Wine is the child of an ardent father, the Sun, and of a cold mother, the Earth. Weak, restless and ungracious at birth, wine grows under proper care and becomes strong, stable and gracious for a while; it may be a short time or three score years and ten, or even longer. The life of every wine, however, whether it be short or not, just like our own, is subject to illness and doomed in the end to death. It is therefore quite understandable that a number of words have been given a special meaning when used in connection with wine, young or old, sound or sick, good, bad or indifferent. Here is a list of some of the more commonly used terms used in wine tasting:

ACETIC. A vinegary smell and pricking of the tongue which are a warning that a wine is on its way to the vinegar tub; it is a disease which the weaker wines are more likely to suffer, when ethyl alcohol turns to acetic acid and a wine becomes vinegar.

AFTER-TASTE or FAREWELL. The final, and pleasurable sensation which a good wine gives to our senses of taste and smell as it leaves our taste-buds and slips away "down the hatch"!

AROMA. The fragrance that a good wine relays to the brain through the senses of taste and smell when approved of by expectant taste-buds.

AROMATIC. An unusually pronounced scent which some wines possess when made from Muscat grapes or other varieties of grapes with highly scented grape-juice.

ASTRINGENT. A hard, dry, unpleasant taste chiefly due to an excess of tannin. There is always hope that a very young wine which is hard may mellow with age, but a mature wine which is hard had better be used in the kitchen.

BLEACHED. There never was and never can be a "paper-white" grape or wine, and all white wines vary in colour from pale or "straw" gold to deep or "old" gold in colour, the gold turning to dark gold and brown as the wines gets older. Fickle fashion now demands that all white wines be as colourless as possible, which is why so many of them are bleached and smell of sulphur instead of wine.

BODY. A wine is said to have "body", "full body", or a "big body", when it gives us the impression of combined firmness and fullness, a right balance of richness (sweetness) and liveliness (acidity), also the stability of a fairly high alcoholic strength.

BOUQUET. The gentle scent which has to be looked for and discovered in a good wine: the bouquet of a good wine is never brutal and aggressive. The bouquet varies according to vineyard, vine and vintage, and it is through their bouquet that an expert can identify different wines.

CLEAN. There may be dirt on ripe grapes, but there is none in wine; it is all discarded in the course of fermentation. When tasting wine, however, the first thing one must do is to smell the empty glass first of all, and make sure that it has no smell of detergent or anything else; then smell with great care the wine that is poured in the glass and make sure that there is no trace whatever of either musty stink, vinegary sharpness, sulphur dioxide or anything of the kind.

CORKED. A wine awaiting a corkscrew to get out!

CORKY. A wine that is unfit to drink, to cook with or to make vinegar with. It has been tainted by a mouldy, musty or otherwise defective cork and it is past salvation.

DRY. No wine can help being wet, but most of those which are called "dry" are by no means "bone dry". Champagne with the label "dry" or "sec" is sweet, but not as sweet as the "demi-sec". "Extra dry" or "extra sec" champagne is drier than the "dry" but not so dry as the "brut" or "nature". There are sherries which are dry in name and in taste, but most of them are dry in name only.

FATTY. An incurable disease of a wine which has acquired a greasy, oily consistency through some malevolent yeast or microbes!

FLAT. A wine which has grown up unloved and unlovely; stale and dull on the tongue, without any bouquet and appeal.

FLESHY. A badly balanced wine, with insufficient acidity to match its richness. It is a drinkable wine, but it never will be the friendly wine that one is glad to meet again.

FRESH. A rare compliment for a mature wine at the top of its form and not showing age; also either the only or the best quality of an immature, undistinguished wine.

FRUITY. The quality of a fine wine with the attractive fullness of sun-ripe peach without any trace of flabbiness.

HEAVY. A heavy wine is a bad wine, coarse, spirity: either badly made or made from common grapes.

LIGHT. A wine of usually but not necessarily low alcoholic strength with more to lose than to gain by being kept. A light wine may be a modest but pleasing wine or a young wine with great charm and appeal.

MADERISÉ. A white wine which has been kept rather longer than was good for it and has become oxidized; it has acquired a darker colour and a distinctly "off" bouquet, reminiscent of one of the old Madeiras.

MELLOW. A mellow wine is a good wine which has aged gracefully and acquired a particularly attractive silky softness which taste-buds love above all.

O'ER THE TOP. It describes the fine wine which has been kept too long: a dead or dying wine.

PEEPING. It is used for a wine which is asking to be drunk; it is just looking up for a corkscrew before it is o'er the top!

PIQUÉ. The French for a pricked wine, a victim to acetic acid.

RACE. French for a wine which possesses that most elusive of all good qualities called "breed"—unmistakable and yet so difficult to describe.

RICH. This applies to what is called in French *La Robe* and *Le Corps* of a wine, that is its colour—a "rich" ruby or gold—or its body—rich in strength, fullness and general excellence.

ROUND. A wine is said to be "round" when well balanced, without any sharp points and really good company.

SCANTY. A wine that is too thin, not acid but lacking in appeal.

SHORT. A wine lacking in character: it is quite acceptable; it has no vice; but it slips away down the hatch leaving no regret.

SOFT. A wine which is short of tannin; it is pleasant enough to drink, but it would be unwise to keep it too long.

WOODY. A smell or taste, or both, of oak, which is not objectionable in itself, but is not in its right place in wine; it occurs when a young wine is lodged for too long a period in an oak cask of unseasoned wood.

BIBLIOGRAPHY

Australian Wine Board: *Wine, 1788–1939; Compiled in the Interests of the Australian Wine Industry*: Adelaide: Australian Wine Board: 1939: 21 pp.

Bear, J. W.: *The Viticultural Resources of Victoria*: Melbourne: Melville, Mullen and Slade: 1893: 30 pp.

Beck, E. J. *editor*: *The Aesthetics of Wine, the History of Wine in Australia, the Story of the Making of Outstanding Wines, together with a Complete Dictionary of Wine Terms in Common Usage*: Sydney: Rhinecastle Wines: 1946: 58 pp.

Benwell, W. S.: *Journey to Wine in Victoria*: Melbourne: Sir Isaac Pitman and Sons: 1960: 120 pp.

Boake, W. B.: *The Production of Wine in Australia*: London: A. Boake, Roberts and Co.: 1889: 13 pp.

Bleasdale, *Rev.* J. I.: *Essay on the Wines Sent to the Late Intercolonial Exhibition by the Colonies of Victoria, New South Wales and South Australia, with Critical Remarks on the Present Condition and Prospects of the Wine Industry in Australia*: Melbourne: F. F. Baillière: 1876: 35 pp.

Bleasdale, *Rev.* J. I.: *On Colonial Wines*: Melbourne: Stillwell and Knight: 1873: 24 pp.

Bleasdale, *Rev.* J. I.: *Two Essays Drawn Up for the Official Record of the Exhibition Held in Melbourne in 1872–3*: appended, two reports and a paper read before the Royal Society: Melbourne: Mason Firth: 1873.

Buring, H. P. L.: *Australian Wines: 150th Anniversary of the Wine Industry of Australia*: Sydney: Federal Viticultural Council of Australia: 1938: 15 pp.

Busby, J.: *Journal of a Recent Visit to the Principal Vineyards of Spain and France, Together with Observations Relative to the Introduction of the Vine into New South Wales*: London: Smith Elder: 1834: 177 pp.

Busby, J.: *A Manual of Plain Directions for Planting and Cultivating Vineyards, and for Making Wine in New South Wales*: G. Howe: 1830: 96 pp.

Busby, J.: *Treatise on the Culture of the Vine, and the Art of Making Wine; Compiled from the Works of Chaptal and Other French Writers, and from the Notes of the Compiler, during a Residence in Some of the Vine Provinces of France*: Sydney: Govt. Printer (G. Howe): 1825: 270 pp.

Castella, H. de: *John Bull's Vineyard; Australian sketches*: Melbourne: Sands and McDougall: 1886: 263 pp.

Castella, H. de: *Notes d'un Vigneron Australien*: Melbourne: George Robertson: 1882: 87 pp.

BIBLIOGRAPHY

Fallon, J. T.: *Murray Valley Vineyard, and Australian Vines and Wines, Being Extracts from the Press, with a Paper on Australian Vines and Wines by J. T. Fallon*: Melbourne: 1874: 49 pp.

Fornachon, J. C. M.: *Bacterial Spoilage of Fortified Wines*: Adelaide: Australian Wine Board: 1943: 126 pp.

Geelong and Western District Agricultural and Horticultural Society: *The Vine and How to Make Wine from Victorian Grapes*: 1859.

Gramp, G. and Sons Ltd.: *100 Years of Wine Making, 1847–1947*: Rowland Flat, S.A.: 1947: 45 pp.

Guyot, J.: *Culture of the Vine and Wine Making*; translated from the French by L. Marie: Melbourne: Walker May: 1865: 108 pp.

Guyot, J.: *Growth of the Vine and Principles of Wine Making;* translated from the French by L. Marie: Melbourne: *Leader*: 28 pp.

Hardy, Thomas, and Sons Ltd.: *The Hardy Tradition*: Adelaide: 1953: 50 pp.

Heddle, Enid M.: *Story of a Vineyard—Chateau Tahbilk*: Melbourne: F. W. Cheshire: 1960: 56 pp.

James, W.: *Barrel and Book; a Winemaker's Diary:* Melbourne: Georgian House: 1949: 109 pp.

James, W.: *The Gadding Vine*: Melbourne: Georgian House: 1955: 118 pp.

James, W.: *Nuts on Wine*: Melbourne: Georgian House: 1950: 85 pp.

James, W.: *Nuts on Wine*; revised edition: Melbourne: Georgian House: 1955.

James, W.: *Wine in Australia; a Handbook*: Melbourne: Georgian House: 1952: 166 pp.

James, W.: *Wine in Australia; a Handbook*: revised edition: Melbourne: Georgian House: 1955.

James, W.: *What's What about Wine; an Australian Wine Primer*: Melbourne: Georgian House: 1953: 45 pp.

Johnson, G.: *Practical Studies for the Winemaker, Brewer and Distiller*: Perth: 1939.

Keane, E.: *The Penfold Story*: Sydney: O. L. Ziegler: 1950: 77 pp.

Kelly, A. C.: *The Vine in Australia*: Melbourne: Sands Kenny: 1861: 215 pp.

Kelly, A. C.: *Wine Growing in Australia*: Adelaide: E. S. Wigg: 1867: 234 pp.

King, J.: *Australia May be an Extensive Wine-Growing Country*: Edinburgh: 1857: 16 pp.

Laffer, H. E.: *The Wine Industry of Australia*: Adelaide: Australian Wine Board: 1949: 136 pp.

Lamb, D. L.: *A Guide to Bordeaux Wines and Cognac*: Sydney: Sands: 1948: 34 pp.

Lamb, D. L.: *Notes on Hocks and Moselles*: Sydney: Sands: 1950: 16 pp.

Lamshed, M. R. A.: *The House of Seppelt, 1851–1951*: Adelaide: 1951: 51 pp.

Macarthur, Sir W. ("Maro"): *Letters on the Culture of the Vine, Fermentation and the Management of Wine in the Cellar*: Sydney: Statham and Foster: 1844: 153 pp.

Malet, W. E.: *The Australian Wine-Grower's Manual*: London: Boldero and Foster: 1876: 255 pp.

Martin, H. M. and Son Ltd.: *Stonyfell, 1858-1958*: Adelaide: 1958: 25 pp.

Mendelsohn, O. A.: *The Earnest Drinker's Digest; a Short and Simple Account of Alcoholic Beverages*: Sydney: Consolidated Press: 1946: 229 pp.

Moonen, L.: *Australian Wines*: Melbourne: Victorian Chamber of Manufacturers: 1883: 20 pp.

New South Wales Committee for Bordeaux Wine Exhibition: *Official Catalogue of the Wines of New South Wales*: 1882.

Pellicot, A.: *The Vine and Wine Making in Southern France*; translated by E. B. Heyne and A. Murray: Melbourne: Walter May: 1868: 76 pp.

Richards, T.: *Australie; La Nouvelle-Galles du Sud en 1881; Suivi d'une Notice sur la Viticulture Australienne a L'Exposition de Bordeaux*: Bordeaux: 1882: 84 pp.

Royal Commission on Vegetable Products: *Handbook on Viticulture for Victoria*: Melbourne: Government Printer: 1891: 184 pp.

Salter, W. and Son Ltd.: *The Saltram Vineyard, 1859-1959*: Adelaide: 1959.

Smith, S. and Son Ltd.: *100 Years in the Good Earth, 1849–1949*: Angaston, S.A.: 1949: 41 pp.

Seppelt, B. and Sons: *At Home with Wine*: Adelaide: 1949: 16 pp.

"V." and "Beberrao" (pseud.): *The Vine and Wine Making in Victoria*: Melbourne: Wilson and Mackinnon: 1861: 64 pp.

The Vine; Treatment of the Soil, and How to Make Wine from Victorian Grapes (two essays): Geelong: Heath and Cordell: 1859: 97 pp.

Walch, G.: *A Glass of Champagne*: Melbourne: McCarron Bird: 1885: 47 pp.

Ward, E.: *The Vineyards and Orchards of South Australia*: Adelaide: *Advertiser*: 1862: 78 pp.

Whitington, E.: *The South Australian Vintage, 1903*: Adelaide: *Register*: 1903: 74 pp.

Wilkinson, W. P.: *An Examination of the Wines Retailed in Victoria*: Melbourne: Australasian Association for the Advancement of Science: 1901: 9 pp. (a paper read before the Association).

INDEX

Adelaide, 5, 22, 55, 62, 64, 74.
Adelaide Winemaking and Distillation Co., 55.
Albillo, 155.
Albury, 12, 144.
Alcholic strength, 41, 43, 44, 46, 47, 48, 161, 162, 163, 164.
All Saints Vineyard, 18, 117, 118, 120.
Amery Winery, 100.
Angas, George Fife, 26, 72.
Angaston, 26, 28, 68, 71, 72, 88.
Anglo-Portuguese Treaty (1916), 57.
Angove's Pty. Ltd., 48, 52, 98.
Angove, Thomas Carlyon, 98.
Angove, Thomas William Carlyon, 98, 161.
Angove, *Dr* W. T., 23, 98.
Ashman's Vineyard, 114, 115.
Aucerot Riesling, 157.
Auldana Vineyard, 22, 34, 69, 85, 103, 147–150.
Auld, Burton and Co., 102.
Auld, Michael, 87, 148, 161.
Auld, Patrick, 22, 34, 69, 87, 102, 147, 149, 150.
Australian Agricultural Co., 5, 136, 138, 139, 140.
Australian Wine Board, 34, 57, 58, 59, 76, 80, 107.
Australian Wine Centre (London), 59, 165.
Australian Wine Co., 103.
Australian Wine Research Institute, 39, 58, 80, 161, 181–184.
Australian Wines Pty. Ltd., 103, 104.

Badger, Magnus, 96.
Bagenel, Walter, 60.
Bailey. Alan, 19.
Bailey Bros., 19, 123.
Bailey, Roley, 19.
Barossa Co-operative Winery Ltd., 27, 104.
Barossa Valley, 22, 24, 26, 29, 58, 68, 70, 72, 76, 88, 90, 93, 124, 154, 155.
Basedow, Alfred, 96.
Basedow, O., Ltd., 26.
Bassett, S. S., 126.
Bastardo, 159, 160.
Bear, J. P., 18.
Bellevue Vineyard, 11, 54.

Ben Ean Vineyard, 11, 66.
Bendigo, 16, 72, 76.
Berri, 22, 32, 105, 106.
Berri Co-operative Winery and Distillery Ltd., 32, 105, 106.
Best, Henry, 21, 112.
Best, Joseph, 21.
Best's Wines Pty. Ltd., 112.
Binder, R. H., 26.
Birks, Alfred Percy, 125.
Birks, Olive Wakefield, 125.
Birks, Roland Napier, 29, 125.
Blanquette, 156, 157.
Blaxland, Gregory, 8, 138.
Bleasdale, *Rev* J. I., 95.
Bleasdale Vineyard, 22, 32, 56, 93–95.
Booth, Clifford, 19.
Booth, Ezra, 19.
Booth, Geoffrey, 19.
Bramhall, Eliza, 65.
Brandy, xi, 21, 43, 45, 153, 164.
Brown Bros., 19.
Brown, John Francis (John Brown I), 19.
Brown, John, II, 19.
Brown, John, III, 19.
Brown, Lindsay, 18.
Bundarra, 19.
Burgundy, 46, 47, 51, 52, 56, 161.
Butler, Denys, 32.
Buring, A. W. R., 92.
Buring and Sobels, H., Ltd., 29, 52, 91, 92, 93.
Buring, Leo, 66, 93.
Buring, Leo, Pty. Ltd., 52, 93.
Buring, T. G. Hermann, 92.
Busby, James, 5, 6, 10, 22, 66, 133, 137.

Cabernet Sauvignon, 3, 5, 6, 11, 13, 19, 47, 48, 51, 52, 57, 73, 74, 92, 102, 108, 113, 114, 120, 158, 160.
Camden, *Lord*, 5.
Camden (N.S.W.), 5.
Carignan, 159.
Carmichael, Henry, 65.
Cawarra Vineyard, 65.
Chablis, 48, 51, 52.
Chaffey, Ben, 84.
Chaffey Bros., 21.
Chaffey, George, 105, 113.
Chaffey, W. B., 105, 113.
Chaffey, W. H., 113.

Champagne, xi, 36, 156, 159, 163.
Chardonnay, 156.
Chasselas, 6, 156.
Chateau Leonay, 26, 93.
Chateau Reynella, 49, 52.
Chateau Tahbilk, 20, 52, 82, 109, 110, 111.
Chateau Tanunda, 76.
Chateau Yaldara, 124, 125.
Chateau Yering, 16.
Christison, John, 96.
Clarendon Vineyard, 24.
Clare, 22, 29, 83, 96, 104, 125.
Clare Riesling, 156.
Claret, xi, 46, 47, 52, 161.
Clarevale Co-operative Winery Ltd., 29, 104, 105.
Clark, Algernon, 85.
Clark, Francis, 85.
Clark, H. C., 22.
Clark, Henry Septimus, 85, 86.
Commonwealth Bureau of Meteorology, 58.
Commonwealth Scientific and Industrial Research Organization, 58, 160, 181, 182.
Concongella Vineyard, 21.
Coolalta Vineyard, 66.
Coonawarra, 2, 22, 31, 32, 34, 37, 39, 47, 101, 102, 108, 113, 114.
Coonawarra Fruit Colony, 31, 101.
Corowa, 11, 12, 65.
Cowan, Lindley, 126.
Cox, James, 102.
Craig, Skene, 13.
Craven, Walter H., 83.
Crompton, Joseph, 85, 86.
Curren, H. R., 106.

Dalwood Estate, 69.
Dalwood Vineyard, 8, 11, 69.
Darveniza, George, 18.
Darveniza, Trojano, 18.
Davis, A. H., 22.
de Castella, Hubert, 15, 16.
de Castella, Paul, 15, 16.
de Pury, *Baron*, 15, 16.
Deschamps, Clément, 15.
Despeissis, Adrian, 126.
Distillers' Co., 100.
Doradillo, 6, 24, 48, 56, 109, 152, 156, 157.
Drayton family, 54.
Du Rieu, D. T., 32.

191

East Torrens Winemaking and Distillation Co. Ltd., 55, 98.
Eden Valley, 22, 28.
Edwards and Chaffey Ltd., 30, 82, 83.
Emu Wine Co. Ltd., 30, 52, 101, 102, 103.
Ermington, 8.
Everton, 19.
Ewell Vineyard, 23.
Excelsior Vineyard, 18.
Eyre, Edwin John, 92.

Falkenberg, P. T., Ltd., 26.
Fallon, J. T., 12.
Federal Viticultural Council, 34, 58, 91.
Federal Wine and Brandy Producers' Council, 76.
Felton Vineyard, 11.
Fermentation, 37, 38, 41, 43, 70, 182, 183, 184.
Fornachon, J. C. M., 39, 58, 181.
Fortified wines, 41, 43, 44, 45, 48, 56, 57, 67.
Fowler, D. and J., Ltd., 69.
Frontignac, 5, 6, 44, 96, 158.
Fulton, *Lt.-Col.* David, 84.

Gawler, 24.
Geelong, 16, 145.
Gibson, Victor, 165.
Gilbert, Joseph, 73, 74.
Gilbey, W. and A., Ltd., 101.
Gillard, Joseph, 67.
Gillard, W., 106.
Gilles, Lewis W., 84.
Gilles, O. H., 84.
Gilles, Osmond, 23, 83, 84.
Glass, Hugh, 16.
Glendore, 11.
Glenelg, 23, 63, 64.
Glen Elgin Vineyard, 121, 122, 123.
Glenloth Wines Pty. Ltd., 23, 107.
Glen Osmond, 51, 58, 83, 180.
Glenrowan, 123.
Gordo, 6, 152.
Goulburn River, xii, 16, 18, 110.
Goulburn Vineyard Co., 16.
Graham, John, 18.
Gramp, Colin, 70, 161.
Gramp, Fred, 70.
Gramp, G. and Sons Ltd., 18, 26, 49, 51, 52, 69, 70.
Gramp, Gustav, 70.
Gramp, Hugo, 70, 73.
Gramp, Johann, 70.
Gramp, Keith, 70.
Gramp, Sidney, 70.

Great Western, 20, 21, 36, 77, 112.
Gregory, Graham, 152.
Grenache, 5, 6, 48, 157.
Griffith, 12, 68, 115.

Hack, J. B., 22.
Haffner's Vineyard, 65.
Hamilton, Eric, 64.
Hamilton, Frank, 64.
Hamilton, Henry, 64.
Hamilton, Richard, 60, 63, 64.
Hamilton, Robert, 64.
Hamilton's Ewell Vineyards Pty. Ltd., 23, 28, 60, 63, 64.
Hardy, David, 80.
Hardy, Jim, 80.
Hardy, Joanna, 78, 79.
Hardy, Kenneth T., 80, 161.
Hardy, Mary Anna, 78.
Hardy, Robert, 80.
Hardy, Thomas, 30, 78, 79, 80, 81.
Hardy, Thomas and Sons, Pty. Ltd., 52, 77–81, 90.
Hardy, T. M., 80.
Hardy, Tom, 80.
Haselgrove, Colin, 63, 161.
Haselgrove, H. R., 113.
Hawkesbury, 8.
Hawker, *Capt.* C. E., 84.
Henschke, C. A. and Co., 95, 96.
Henschke, Cyril, 28, 29, 95, 96.
Henschke, Paul Alfred, 29, 96.
Henschke, Paul Gotthardt, 29, 95, 96.
Henty, Edward, 15.
Hermitage (see also *Shiraz*), 6, 47, 48, 52, 115, 123, 145.
Hermitage, white (see also *Ugni Blanc*), 6, 19.
Hill, *Sir* Rowland, 64, 85.
Hock, xi, 48, 49, 52, 161.
Hoffmann, Bruce, 82.
Hoffmann, Chris, 81.
Hoffmann, Christian I, 82.
Hoffmann, Christian II, 82.
Hoffmann, Erwin, 26, 82.
Hoffmann, Laurel, 26.
Hoffmann, Samuel, 81, 82.
Holbrook, John, 78.
Horndale Distillery, 45.
Horne, R. H. ("Orion"), 16, 18, 110.
Horrocks, *Capt.* John Ainsworth, 92.
Houghton Vineyard, 103, 126.
Hughes, *Sir* Walter, 92.
Hunter River, xii, 5, 8, 9, 10, 11, 13, 19, 47, 48, 54, 65, 66, 68, 69, 114, 115, 117, 121, 122, 154, 155.

Hunter River Riesling, 115, 153.
Hyland, Thomas Francis, 67, 68.

Illustrated Australian News, 143.
Ingoldby, Jim, 91.
Ingoldby, Jim, *Jun.*, 91.
Irrigation, 3, 56, 57.
Irvine, Hans, 21, 156.

Johannisberg, 48.
Johnston, A. C., Ltd., 101.
Johnston, Alex, 101.
Johnston, Digby, 101.
Johnston, Ian, 101.
Johnston, Lex, 101.

Kaiser Stuhl, 104.
Kalimna Estate, 66, 68, 69.
Kavel, *Pastor* Augustus, 74.
Kay Bros., 30, 100, 101.
Kay, Frederick Walter, 100.
Kay, G. W., 83.
Kay, Herbert, 100.
Kelly, *Dr* A. C., 5, 30, 38, 79, 80.
Kelman, James, 66.
Keyneton, 22, 28, 29, 95.
Kidd, R. H., 66.
Kilmore Examiner, 18.
King, Charles, 116.
King, James, 141, 143.
King River, 19.
Kirkton Vineyard, 5, 10, 66.
Knappstein, J. H., 96.
Kook, Hermann, 76.
Kronberger, Rudolph, 73.

Laffer, H. E., 57.
Lake, Max, 11, 13.
Lang, Andrew, 9.
Lang, *Dr* John, 9.
Langhorne Creek, 22, 32, 56, 95.
Lankester, J. D., 12.
Latrobe, C. J., 13, 15.
Lindeman, Charles Frederick, 65.
Lindeman, *Dr* Henry John, 10, 64, 65.
Lindeman's Wines Pty. Ltd., 10, 12, 31, 39, 47, 48, 49, 52, 64, 93, 102.
Loxton, 22, 32, 105.
Loxton Co-operative Winery and Distillery Pty. Ltd., 34, 105.
Lucas, Mary, 62.
Lyndoch, 23, 124.

Macarthur, James, 6.
Macarthur, *Capt.* John, 4, 5, 6, 135, 138, 139.
Macarthur, William, 5, 135, 139, 140, 141, 142.
McCrae, Georgina, 13.

McDonald, J., 66.
McLaren Vale, 30, 31, 68, 79, 80, 82, 91, 92, 100, 101.
McMahon, John B., 30.
McWilliam, J. J., 115.
McWilliam's Wines Pty. Ltd., 15, 49, 51, 52, 115–117.
Madeira, 43, 44, 57, 154.
Magill, 22, 23, 67, 68, 69, 108.
Malbec, 6, 159.
Manning, George Pitches, 30, 79, 82.
Manning, W., 30.
Marie, Ludovic, 16, 18.
Marsanne, 120, 155.
Martin, Henry Maydwell, 86, 87.
Martin, Henry M. II, 87.
Martin, H. M. and Son, Pty. Ltd., 22, 28, 32, 85–87, 91, 148.
Martin, Ronald H., 86, 87, 91.
Mataro, 5, 6, 125, 158.
Matthews, C. D., 6, 60.
Mayr, Valentine, 29.
Mazure, L. E., 104.
Melbourne, 13, 15, 55, 145.
Melbourne Club, xii.
Menzies, Sir Robert, 111.
Merlot, 48, 160.
Metala Vineyard, 32.
Mia Mia Vineyard, 18, 113.
Milawa, 19.
Mildara Wines Ltd., 21, 32, 47, 52, 78, 113, 114, 121.
Mildura, 21, 113, 114.
Miller, Elliot, 106.
Minchin, Capt. William, 68.
Michinbury Vineyard, 8.
Modbury, 23, 69, 108.
Mondeuse, 19.
Montils, 157.
Montrachet, 48.
Mooney, J. and M., 21.
Morastel, 159.
Morphett Vale, 30, 103.
Morris, Charles, 113.
Morris Charles Henry, 113.
Morris, C. H. and Sons, Pty. Ltd., 113.
Morris, Frederick, 113.
Morris, Frederick John, 113.
Morris, George Francis, 18, 113.
Morris, Gerald, 113.
Moselle, xi, 48, 49.
Mount Pleasant, 11, 12, 47, 49, 115, 116, 117.
Murray River, xii, 12, 16, 18, 32, 34, 69, 70, 105, 112, 113, 115, 118, 145, 152.
Murrumbidgee River, 12, 69, 115, 152.

Murrumbidgee Irrigation Area, 15, 115, 154.
Muscat, 6, 43, 152, 158, 161.
Muswellbrook, 8.

Nagambie, 18.
Nanson, J. L., 126.
National Trust of Australia, 111.
Nildottie Vineyard, 64.
Nomenclature, 51.
North Para Vineyard, 26.
Nuriootpa, 25, 27, 28, 68, 76, 99, 100, 104.

Oakvale Vineyard, 11.
Oeillade, 66, 158.
Oenological Research Committee, 58, 181, 182, 183.
O'Halloran Hill, 23, 107.
Orlando Winery, 26, 70.
O'Shea, John Augustus, 116.
O'Shea, Maurice, 116, 117.
Ovens River, 19, 109.

Palomino, 6, 24, 36, 48, 106, 108, 109, 120, 154.
Para River, 24.
Paradale Vineyard, 26.
Parramatta, xii, 8, 68.
Parsons, G. Angas, 74.
Paterson River, 5, 65.
Pedro Ximinez, 6, 24, 48, 92, 108, 109, 120, 125, 153.
Pelet, Rose, 15.
Penfold, Dr Christopher Rawson, 22, 65, 66, 67.
Penfold, Georgina Ann, 67.
Penfold Hyland, Frank Astor, 68.
Penfold Hyland, Francis William, 69.
Penfold Hyland, Gladys, 69.
Penfold Hyland, Herbert Leslie, 68, 69.
Penfold Hyland, Jeffery, 69.
Penfold, Mary, 67.
Penfold Vale Vineyard, 69.
Penfold's Wines Pty. Ltd., 8, 22, 26, 32, 34, 49, 52, 66, 148.
Pewsey Vale Vineyard, 73, 74.
Phillip, Capt. Arthur, 6.
Phoenix Distilling Co., 98, 99.
Phylloxera, 4, 12, 16, 18, 19, 20, 22, 55, 111, 112, 120, 143.
Pinot, 6, 120, 156, 159, 160.
Pirrimimma Vineyard, 101.
Pokolbin, 8, 11, 66, 116, 121, 122.
Porphyry Vineyard, 65.
Port, xi, 41, 43, 44, 45, 57, 163.
Potts, Frank, 32, 93, 95.
Potts, Robert, 56.

Pownall, A. W., 103.
Pridmore, H. V., 84.
Purbrick, Eric, 111.
Purbrick, John, 111.
Purcell, John, 16.

Quelltaler Vineyard, 29, 91, 92, 93.
Quirke, P. H., 105.

Redman, Don, 102.
Redman, Owen, 102.
Redman, William Leonard, 31, 102.
Redman, W. L. and O. D., 101, 102.
Refrigeration, xii, 38.
Renmark, 22, 32, 41, 98, 105.
Renmark Growers' Distillery Ltd., 32, 41, 105.
Reynell, Carew, 63.
Reynell, John, 30, 60, 62, 79, 150, 151.
Reynell, Richard, 63.
Reynell, Walter, 62.
Reynell, Walter and Sons Ltd., 30, 52, 62, 63.
Reynella, 30, 52, 60, 62, 63, 82, 150, 151.
Richman, James, 92.
Riddoch, John, 31, 32, 101, 102.
Riesling, 3, 5, 6, 19, 48, 51, 52, 57, 69, 73, 74, 96, 106, 108, 120, 125, 146, 154, 156, 160.
Robertson, J. Harper, 107.
Robertson, J. R. W., 107, 161.
Robinvale, 117.
Roe, John Frederick, 126.
Roe, Capt. John Septimus, 126.
Romalo, 104.
Romavilla Vineyards Pty. Ltd., 126.
Rooty Hill, 8, 68.
Rosevale Vineyard, 26.
Roseworthy Agricultural College, 39, 60.
Rouge Homme Wines Pty. Ltd., 39, 101, 102.
Rum, xi, 10.
Rutherglen, 18, 19, 47, 76, 113, 118, 155.
Ryecroft Vineyards Pty. Ltd., 30, 91, 92.
Ryrie, William, 15.

St Hubert Vineyard, 16.
Salter, Edward, 88, 90, 91.
Salter, Leslie, 91.
Salter, W. and Son Pty. Ltd., 88–91.

Salter, William, 88, 90.
Saltram Vineyard, 28, 88–91.
Sandalford Vineyard, 126.
Sauterne, 48, 49, 65, 161.
Schomburk, *Dr* R. M., 24.
Scott, Thomas, 98, 99.
Seager, Evans and Co. Ltd., 23, 107.
Seaview Vineyard, 30, 52, 67, 82, 83.
Semillon, 3, 6, 48, 73, 115, 153.
Seppelt, B. and Sons Pty. Ltd., 21, 26, 74–77, 78.
Seppelt, Benno, 76.
Seppelt, Ian, 76, 161.
Seppelt, Bill, 77.
Seppelt, John, 76.
Seppelt, Joseph Ernst, 74, 76, 77.
Seppelt, Karl, 77.
Seppelt, Leo, 76, 77.
Seppelt, Oscar, 76.
Seppelt, Robert, 76.
Seppelt, Waldemar, 76.
Sercial, 154, 155.
Sevenhill College Vineyard, 29, 49.
Sherry, 19, 39, 40, 41, 43, 44, 45, 51, 57, 58, 152, 153, 154, 155, 163.
Shiraz, 3, 6, 19, 47, 52, 92, 96, 102, 106, 108, 113, 115, 120, 121, 125, 157, 158, 184.
Slape, Robert, 85.
Smith, David Sutherland, 118.
Smith, George Sutherland, 18, 117, 118, 120.
Smith, G. Sutherland and Sons, 118–120.
Smith, John Hill, 73.
Smith, Mark Hill, 73.
Smith, *Dr* O. W., 96.
Smith, Percy, 72.
Smith, Samuel, 28, 71, 72.
Smith, S. and Son Pty. Ltd., 49, 52, 71, 72, 73, 74, 99.
Smith, Sydney, 72.
Smith, Sidney Hill, 72.
Smith, Walter, 72.
Smith, Wyndham Hill, 72, 73.
Sobels, Carl, 92.
Sobels, E. E., 92.
South Australian Grape-growers' Co-operative Ltd., 104.
South Australian Wine-Makers' Association, 91.
Southern Cross Vineyard, 12.
Southern Vales, 22, 29, 30.
Southern Vales Co-operative Winery Ltd., 30.
Sparkling Vale Vineyard, 69.

Sparrow, J. C. and Co. Ltd., 30.
Springton, 22, 28.
Stanley Wine Co. Pty. Ltd., 29, 83, 96, 97, 98.
Stawell Vineyard Co., 21.
Steingarten Vineyard, 18, 69.
Stevenson, George, 22.
Stonyfell Vineyard, 22, 32, 85–87.
Sultana, 6, 24, 153.
Sunbury, 128, 144, 170, 171.
Sunshine Vineyard, 11, 65.
Swan Hill, 112.
Sydney Gazette, 6, 129–132.

Tabilk, 16, 110, 144.
Tahbilk Vineyard (*see also* Chateau Tahbilk).
Tanunda, 23, 24, 26, 27, 68, 76, 82.
Tarac Industries Pty. Ltd., 27.
Temprana, 24.
Thomas, Ian, 63.
Thomson, Eric F. H., 112.
Thomson, E. V. H., 112.
Thomson, W. H., 112.
Thumm, Hermann, 124, 125.
Timbrell, Ellen, 67.
Tintara Vineyard Co., 30, 80.
Tokay, 43, 44, 155, 160.
Tolley, Albion Everard, 99.
Tolley, Albion James, 99.
Tolley, David, 100.
Tolley, Douglas A., 23, 98, 99.
Tolley, Douglas A., Pty. Ltd., 100.
Tolley, Ernest, 98, 99.
Tolley, Fred Osborne, 99.
Tolley, Len, 99, 100.
Tolley, Peter, 100.
Tolley, Reg, 100, 161.
Tolley, Sam, 99.
Tolley, Scott and Tolley Ltd., 26, 27, 98–100.
Torrens, Robert, 64.
Touriga, 159.
Traminer, 6, 156, 160.
Treloar, Francis, 92.
Tulloch, Alex, 122.
Tulloch, Hector, 122.
Tulloch, Jim, 122.
Tulloch, John Younie, 121, 122.
Tulloch, J. Y. and Sons, Pty. Ltd., 11, 121–123.
Tulloch, Keith, 122.
Tyrrell, Dan, 114.
Tyrrell, Edward, 114.
Tyrrell, Murray, 114, 115.
Ugni Blanc, 6, 154.
Ulliade, 66, 158.
University of Adelaide, 58.

Valencia Vineyards Pty. Ltd., 126.
Valencia Wine Co., 103.
Verdelho, 5, 6, 140, 154, 155.
Victoria, 4, 5, 13–21.
Viticultural Research Station, Griffith, 36, 114.

Wahgunyah, 18, 19, 117, 118.
Waikerie, 22, 32, 106, 107.
Waikerie Co-operative Distillery Ltd., 34, 106, 107, 115.
Waite Agricultural Research Institute, 58.
Walker, H. F., 104.
Walker, Norman, 104.
Walker, R. C. H., 30, 103.
Wangaratta, 19.
Ward, John, 29.
Wark, Alfred A., 73.
Watervale, 22, 29.
Weidenbach, Benno, 84.
Wendouree Vineyard, 40, 125.
Weste, Peter, 97.
Western Australia, 4.
White Burgundy, 48, 161.
White Shiraz, 154.
Whitington, Ernest, 84.
Wilsford Winery, 23.
Wine Export Bounty Act, 57.
Wine Board (*see also* Australian Wine Board).
Wine Export Encouragement Trust Account, 57, 58.
Wine Industry Assistance Trust Account, 58.
Wine Overseas Marketing Board, Act, 57.
Woodley Wines Pty. Ltd., 23, 32, 83–85.
Wybong Park Vineyard, 70.
Wyndham, George, 8.
Wynn, David, 108.
Wynn, Samuel, 108.
Wynn, S. and Co. Pty. Ltd., 2, 31, 32, 34, 52, 104, 107–109.

Yalumba Vineyard, 28, 49, 71, 72, 73.
Yarra River, 15, 18.
Yates, Harold, 73.
Yeasts, 15, 38, 43, 181, 182, 183, 184.
Yering, 15, 16, 144, 145.
Yquem, 48.